Learning ROS for R Programming

Second Edition

Your one-stop guide to the Robot Operating System

Enrique Fernández

Luis Sánchez Crespo

Anil Mahtani

Aaron Martinez

[PACKT] open source*
PUBLISHING   community experience distilled

BIRMINGHAM - MUMBAI

Learning ROS for Robotics Programming
Second Edition

Copyright © 2015 Packt Publishing

All rights reserved. No part of this book may be reproduced, stored in a retrieval system, or transmitted in any form or by any means, without the prior written permission of the publisher, except in the case of brief quotations embedded in critical articles or reviews.

Every effort has been made in the preparation of this book to ensure the accuracy of the information presented. However, the information contained in this book is sold without warranty, either express or implied. Neither the authors, nor Packt Publishing, and its dealers and distributors will be held liable for any damages caused or alleged to be caused directly or indirectly by this book.

Packt Publishing has endeavored to provide trademark information about all of the companies and products mentioned in this book by the appropriate use of capitals. However, Packt Publishing cannot guarantee the accuracy of this information.

First published: September 2013

Second edition: August 2015

Production reference: 1120815

Published by Packt Publishing Ltd.
Livery Place
35 Livery Street
Birmingham B3 2PB, UK.

ISBN 978-1-78398-758-0

www.packtpub.com

Credits

Authors
Enrique Fernández
Luis Sánchez Crespo
Anil Mahtani
Aaron Martinez

Reviewers
Piotr Gródek
Akihiko HONDA
Matthieu Keller
Aridane J. Sarrionandia de León

Commissioning Editor
Usha Iyer

Acquisition Editor
Richard Brookes-Bland

Content Development Editor
Adrian Raposo

Technical Editor
Parag Topre

Copy Editors
Sarang Chari
Sonia Mathur

Project Coordinator
Sanchita Mandal

Proofreader
Safis Editing

Indexer
Mariammal Chettiyar

Graphics
Sheetal Aute
Jason Monteiro
Abhinash Sahu

Production Coordinator
Arvindkumar Gupta

Cover Work
Arvindkumar Gupta

About the Author

Enrique Fernández has a PhD in computer engineering from the University of Las Palmas de Gran Canaria and is a senior robotics engineer currently working at Clearpath Robotics, Inc. He did his MSc master's thesis in 2009 on SLAM. Enrique addresses the problem of path planning for autonomous underwater gliders (AUGs) in his PhD thesis, which was presented in 2013. During that period, he also worked on Computer Vision, AI, and other robotics topics, such as inertial navigation systems and Visual SLAM at the CIRS/ViCOROB Research Lab of the University of Girona for AUVs. He also participated in the Student Autonomous Underwater Challenge, Europe (SAUC-E) in 2012 and collaborated in the 2013 edition; in the 2012 edition, he was awarded a prize.

After his PhD, Enrique joined PAL Robotics in June 2013 as a senior robotics engineer in the Autonomous Navigation department. There, he developed software for REEM, REEM-C, and mobile-based robots and also for corresponding projects, such as Stockbot, using the ROS framework intensively. He worked on motion planning (path planning and control for mobile robots), robot localization, and SLAM. Recently, in 2015, he joined Clearpath Robotics, Inc. to work as a senior autonomy developer on SLAM, within the Autonomy department.

From an academic perspective, Enrique has published several conference papers and publications, two of them on the International Conference of Robotics and Automation (ICRA), in 2011. He is also an author of chapters of a few books and a previous book about ROS, *Learning ROS for Robotics Programming* by Packt Publishing. His MSc master's thesis was about the FastSLAM algorithm for indoor robots using a SICK laser scanner and the wheel odometry of a Pioneer differential platform. His PhD thesis contributed path planning algorithms and tools for AUGs. He also has experience with electronics and embedded systems such as PC104 and Arduino. His background covers SLAM, Computer Vision, path planning, optimization, and robotics and artificial intelligence in general.

Acknowledgments

I would like to thank the coauthors of this book for the effort put into writing and developing the code for the countless examples provided. I also want to say thanks to the members of the research groups where I did my PhD thesis: the University Institute of Intelligent Systems and Computational Engineering (SIANI) and the Center of Underwater Robotics Research (CIRS/ViCOROB). Also, a big thanks goes to my ex-colleagues at PAL Robotics, where I learned a lot about ROS, robotics for mobile, and humanoid biped robots—not only software, but also electronics and hardware design. Finally, I would like to thank my family and friends for their help and support.

About the Author

Luis Sánchez Crespo completed his dual master's degree in electronics and telecommunication engineering from the University of Las Palmas de Gran Canaria. He has collaborated with different research groups at the Institute for Technological Development and Innovation (IDETIC), the Oceanic Platform of Canary Islands (PLOCAN), and the Institute of Applied Microelectronics (IUMA), where he actually researches the imaging of super-resolution algorithms.

His professional interests lie in computer vision, signal processing, and electronic design applied to robotics systems. For this reason, he joined the AVORA team, a group of young engineers and students working on the development of underwater autonomous vehicles (AUVs) from scratch. In this project, Luis has started developing acoustic and computer vision systems, extracting information from different sensors, such as hydrophones, sonar, and cameras.

With a strong background gained in marine technology, Luis cofounded Subsea Mechatronics, a young start-up, where he works on developing remotely operated and autonomous vehicles for underwater environments.

Here's what Dario Sosa Cabrera, a marine technologies engineer and entrepreneur (and the cofounder and maker of LPA Fabrika: Gran Canaria Maker Space) has to say about Luis:

"He is very enthusiastic and an engineer in multiple disciplines. He is responsible for his work. He can manage himself and can take up responsibilities as a team leader, as was demonstrated at the SAUC-E competition, where he directed the AVORA team. His background in electronics and telecommunications allows him to cover a wide range of expertise from signal processing and software, to electronic design and fabrication."

Luis has participated as a technical reviewer for the previous version of *Learning ROS for Robotics Programming* by Packt Publishing.

Acknowledgments

First, I have to acknowledge Aaron, Anil, and Enrique for inviting me to participate in this book. It has been a pleasure to return to work with them. Also, I want to thank the Subsea Mechatronics team for the great experience working with heavy, underwater robots; we have grown together during these years. I have to mention LPA Fabrika: Gran Canaria Maker Space for their enthusiasm in preparing and teaching educational robotics and technological projects; sharing a workspace with kids can be really motivating.

Finally, I have to thank my family and my girlfriend for their big support and encouragement in every project I'm involved in. I want to dedicate my contribution in this book to them.

About the Author

Anil Mahtani is a computer scientist who has been working for the past 5 years on underwater robotics. He first started working in the field with his master's thesis, where he developed a software architecture for a low-cost ROV. During the development of his thesis, he also became the team leader and lead developer of AVORA, a team of university students that designed and developed an autonomous underwater vehicle for the Students Autonomous Underwater Challenge – Europe (SAUC-E) in 2012. That same year, he completed his thesis and his MSc in computer science at the University of Las Palmas de Gran Canaria, and shortly thereafter, he became a software engineer at SeeByte Ltd, a world leader in smart software solutions for underwater systems.

During his tenure at SeeByte Ltd, Anil was key to the development of several semi-autonomous and autonomous underwater systems for the military and the oil and gas industries. In those projects, he was heavily involved in the development of autonomous systems, the design of distributed software architectures, and low-level software development and has also contributed to providing computer vision solutions for front-looking sonar imagery. At SeeByte Ltd., he has also achieved the position of project manager, managing a team of engineers developing and maintaining the internal core C++ libraries.

His professional interests lie mainly in software engineering, algorithms, distributed systems, networks, and operating systems. Anil's main role in robotics is to provide efficient and robust software solutions, addressing not only the current problems at hand but also foreseeing future problems or possible enhancements. Given his experience, he is also an asset when dealing with computer vision, machine learning, and control problems. Anil is interested in DIY and electronics, and he has developed several Arduino libraries that he has contributed back to the community.

Acknowledgments

First of all, I would like to thank my family and friends for their support and for always being there when I've needed them. I would also like to thank David Rubio Vidal, Emilio Migueláñez Martín, and John Brydon for being the most supportive colleagues and friends, who have taught me so much personally and professionally. I would also like to thank my colleagues at SeeByte and the AVORA team from whom I've learned and experienced so much over the years. Finally, a special thank you to Jorge Cabrera Gámez, whose guidance and advice shaped my career in a way I could have never imagined.

About the Author

Aaron Martinez is a computer engineer, entrepreneur, and expert in digital fabrication. He did his master's thesis in 2010 at Instituto Universitario de Ciencias y Tecnologias Ciberneticas (IUCTC) from the University of Las Palmas de Gran Canaria. He prepared his master's thesis in the field of telepresence using immersive devices and robotic platforms. After completing his academic career, he attended an internship program at The Institute for Robotics at the Johannes Kepler University in Linz, Austria. During his internship program, he worked as part of a development team of a mobile platform using ROS and the navigation stack. After that, he was involved in projects related to robotics; one of them is the AVORA project at the University of Las Palmas de Gran Canaria. In this project, he worked on the creation of an autonomous underwater vehicle (AUV) to participate in the Student Autonomous Underwater Challenge-Europe (SAUC-E) in Italy. In 2012, he was responsible for manufacturing this project; in 2013, he helped adapt the navigation stack and other algorithms from ROS to the robotic platform.

Recently, Aaron cofounded a company called SubSeaMechatronics, SL. This company works on projects related to underwater robotics and telecontrol systems; it also designs and manufactures subsea sensors. The main purpose of the company is to develop custom solutions for R&D prototypes and heavy-duty robots.

Aaron has experience in many fields, such as programming, robotics, mechatronics, and digital fabrication, and devices such as Arduino, BeagleBone, servers, and LIDAR. Nowadays, he is designing robotics platforms for underwater and aerial environments at SubSeaMechatronics SL.

Acknowledgments

I would like to thank my girlfriend, who supported me while writing this book and gave me the motivation to continue growing professionally. I also want to thank Donato Monopoli, head of the Biomedical Engineering department at the Canary Islands Institute of Technology (ITC), and all the staff there. Thanks for teaching me all that I know about digital fabrication, machinery, and tissue engineering. I spent the best years of my life in your workshop.

Thanks to my colleagues from the university, especially Alexis Quesada, who gave me the opportunity to create my first robot in my master's thesis. I have learned a lot about robotics working with them.

Finally, thanks to my family and friends for their help and support.

About the Reviewer

Piotr Gródek is a C++ programmer interested in computer vision and image processing. He has worked as an embedded programmer and now works in banking. He is a developer of open source gaming and a self-driving car. In his free time, he enjoys running, playing squash, and reading.

About the Reviewer

Akihiko HONDA is an engineer of space robotics. He did his master's thesis in 2012 at the Tokyo Institute of Technology (Tokyo Tech). He is currently a PhD course student at Tokyo Tech.

His research interests include the teleoperation and automation of space robots that interact with flexible or deformable materials. He has a goal to improve the performance and stability of spacecraft in space by developing a much better operation and automation system. In his previous research, he worked for an earth observation satellite with a large solar array paddle and a space robotic arm used to capture the ISS supplier. Currently, he is planning to apply his research results to Space Solar Power System, planetary exploration rovers, and so on. He got an award for the best entry and an award from the Astronomical Society of Japan in JSF's Satellite Design Contest by proposing a new exploration spacecraft using his research.

Through his research at university, he has also participated in several projects conducted by Japan Aerospace Exploration Agency (JAXA). In the Robot Experiment on JEM (REX-J) project, he played a role in supporting operations for the experiment facility in orbit and got inspiration for his research. He also joined a project to develop a wearable manipulator for astronauts and developed systems for human control. He is currently working on two exploration robot projects. In one of them, a transformable rover named "KENAGE" is being developed to overcome the extra-rough terrain on the moon and Mars. The rover is now being examined for the possibility of using a GAZEBO simulator prepared by him. In another other project, he is developing an environment recognition system for Jumping Scouter.

In 2013, he participated in the SMART rover project at the University of Surrey and contributed to develop an environment protection and recognition system. Also, he played a role in a field test to check the practical utility of the rover in a real environment.

Acknowledgments

I would like to thank Hiroki KATO from JAXA for opening the door to ROS for me and giving precious suggestions for my research. I would also like to thank Professor Mitsushige ODA, Professor Hiroki NAKANISHI, and my colleagues in the Space Robotics Lab at Tokyo Tech. They share wonderful future visions about cool robots working in space with me, give suggestions, and support my research to realize them using ROS. I would also like to thank my professors and colleagues at STAR Lab at the University of Surrey for providing me with important advice about how to use ROS in a real environment. I would especially like to thank my friends from Gran Canaria who introduced me to this exciting work.

Finally, big thanks go to my family, Yoshihiko, Nobuko, and Ayaka, who have supported my life and my dream, and my girlfriend, who understands me.

About the Reviewers

Matthieu Keller is a French engineer who loves technology and computer science. His education walked him through computing and robotics, which have now become a hobby. He has reviewed the first version of this book.

Aridane J. Sarrionandia de León studied computer sciences and has always had a great interest in robotics and autonomous vehicles. His degree project is about underwater mapping using sonar, for which he has worked with an autonomous underwater vehicle with ROS. He has experience with autonomous systems and ROS. He is familiar with OpenCV and PCL and is currently working on the development of the control system of an autonomous surface vehicle.

> I would like to thank Luis and Aaron for giving me the opportunity to review this book. Also, I would like to thank the AVORA team from the University of Las Palmas de Gran Canaria, especially Aaron, Luis, and Enrique, for introducing me to the wonders of ROS and helping me discover the world of autonomous vehicles, and my tutor, Jorge Cabrera Gámez, who gave me the opportunity to be a part of the AVORA team.
>
> Finally, I would like to thank my family and friends, who supported me through the bugs in my life. Special thanks to Eva for dealing with all my gibberish.

www.PacktPub.com

Support files, eBooks, discount offers, and more

For support files and downloads related to your book, please visit www.PacktPub.com.

Did you know that Packt offers eBook versions of every book published, with PDF and ePub files available? You can upgrade to the eBook version at www.PacktPub.com and as a print book customer, you are entitled to a discount on the eBook copy. Get in touch with us at service@packtpub.com for more details.

At www.PacktPub.com, you can also read a collection of free technical articles, sign up for a range of free newsletters and receive exclusive discounts and offers on Packt books and eBooks.

![PacktLib]

https://www2.packtpub.com/books/subscription/packtlib

Do you need instant solutions to your IT questions? PacktLib is Packt's online digital book library. Here, you can search, access, and read Packt's entire library of books.

Why subscribe?

- Fully searchable across every book published by Packt
- Copy and paste, print, and bookmark content
- On demand and accessible via a web browser

Free access for Packt account holders

If you have an account with Packt at www.PacktPub.com, you can use this to access PacktLib today and view 9 entirely free books. Simply use your login credentials for immediate access.

Table of Contents

Preface	**ix**
Chapter 1: Getting Started with ROS Hydro	**1**
PC installation	**4**
Installing ROS Hydro – using repositories	**4**
Configuring your Ubuntu repositories	5
Setting up your source.list file	6
Setting up your keys	7
Installing ROS	7
Initializing rosdep	8
Setting up the environment	9
Getting rosinstall	10
How to install VirtualBox and Ubuntu	**11**
Downloading VirtualBox	11
Creating the virtual machine	12
Installing ROS Hydro in BeagleBone Black (BBB)	**15**
Prerequisites	16
Setting up the local machine and source.list file	18
Setting up your keys	19
Installing the ROS packages	19
Initializing rosdep for ROS	20
Setting up the environment in BeagleBone Black	20
Getting rosinstall for BeagleBone Black	21
Summary	**21**
Chapter 2: ROS Architecture and Concepts	**23**
Understanding the ROS Filesystem level	**24**
The workspace	25
Packages	27
Metapackages	29

[i]

Messages	31
Services	32
Understanding the ROS Computation Graph level	**33**
Nodes and nodelets	35
Topics	36
Services	37
Messages	38
Bags	38
The ROS master	39
Parameter Server	39
Understanding the ROS Community level	**40**
Tutorials to practice with ROS	**41**
Navigating by ROS Filesystem	41
Creating our own workspace	42
Creating a ROS package and metapackage	43
Building an ROS package	44
Playing with ROS nodes	45
Learning how to interact with topics	48
Learning how to use services	52
Using Parameter Server	55
Creating nodes	56
Building the node	59
Creating msg and srv files	61
Using the new srv and msg files	64
The launch file	68
Dynamic parameters	71
Summary	**77**
Chapter 3: Visualization and Debug Tools	**79**
Debugging ROS nodes	**83**
Using the GDB debugger with ROS nodes	83
Attaching a node to GDB while launching ROS	85
Profiling a node with valgrind while launching ROS	85
Enabling core dumps for ROS nodes	86
Logging messages	**86**
Outputting a logging message	86
Setting the debug message level	87
Configuring the debugging level of a particular node	88
Giving names to messages	90
Conditional and filtered messages	90

Showing messages in the once, throttle, and other combinations	91
Using rqt_console and rqt_logger_level to modify the debugging level on the fly	92
Inspecting what is going on	**96**
Listing nodes, topics, services, and parameters	96
Inspecting the node's graph online with rqt_graph	100
Setting dynamic parameters	**103**
When something weird happens	**105**
Visualizing node diagnostics	**106**
Plotting scalar data	**108**
Creating a time series plot with rqt_plot	108
Image visualization	**111**
Visualizing a single image	112
3D visualization	**113**
Visualizing data in a 3D world using rqt_rviz	114
The relationship between topics and frames	117
Visualizing frame transformations	118
Saving and playing back data	**120**
What is a bag file?	120
Recording data in a bag file with rosbag	121
Playing back a bag file	122
Inspecting all the topics and messages in a bag file	123
Using the rqt_gui and rqt plugins	**126**
Summary	**127**
Chapter 4: Using Sensors and Actuators with ROS	**129**
Using a joystick or a gamepad	**130**
How does joy_node send joystick movements?	131
Using joystick data to move a turtle in turtlesim	132
Using a laser rangefinder – Hokuyo URG-04lx	**136**
Understanding how the laser sends data in ROS	138
Accessing the laser data and modifying it	140
Creating a launch file	142
Using the Kinect sensor to view objects in 3D	**143**
How does Kinect send data from the sensors, and how do we see it?	144
Creating an example to use Kinect	146
Using servomotors – Dynamixel	**149**
How does Dynamixel send and receive commands for the movements?	150
Creating an example to use the servomotor	151
Using Arduino to add more sensors and actuators	**153**
Creating an example program to use Arduino	154

Table of Contents

Using an ultrasound range sensor with Arduino	**157**
How distance sensors send messages	**160**
Creating an example to use the ultrasound range	161
Using the IMU – Xsens MTi	163
How does Xsens send data in ROS?	164
Creating an example to use Xsens	165
Using a low-cost IMU – 10 degrees of freedom	**167**
Downloading the library for the accelerometer	169
Programming Arduino Nano and the 10 DOF sensor	169
Creating an ROS node to use data from the 10 DOF sensor	172
Using a GPS system	**174**
How GPS sends messages	176
Creating an example project to use GPS	177
Summary	**179**
Chapter 5: Computer Vision	**181**
Connecting and running the camera	**182**
FireWire IEEE1394 cameras	182
USB cameras	187
Writing your own USB camera driver with OpenCV	**189**
Using OpenCV and ROS images with cv_bridge	195
Publishing images with image transport	195
Using OpenCV in ROS	196
Visualizing the camera input images	197
Calibrating the camera	**197**
Stereo calibration	202
The ROS image pipeline	**207**
The image pipeline for stereo cameras	210
ROS packages useful for Computer Vision tasks	**214**
Using visual odometry with viso2	**216**
Camera pose calibration	216
Running the viso2 online demo	220
Running viso2 with our low-cost stereo camera	223
Performing visual odometry with an RGBD camera	**224**
Installing fovis	225
Using fovis with the Kinect RGBD camera	225
Computing the homography of two images	**228**
Summary	**229**
Chapter 6: Point Clouds	**231**
Understanding the point cloud library	**232**
Different point cloud types	233

[iv]

Table of Contents

Algorithms in PCL	234
The PCL interface for ROS	234
My first PCL program	**236**
Creating point clouds	237
Loading and saving point clouds to the disk	241
Visualizing point clouds	245
Filtering and downsampling	249
Registration and matching	255
Partitioning point clouds	259
Segmentation	**264**
Summary	**269**
Chapter 7: 3D Modeling and Simulation	**271**
A 3D model of our robot in ROS	**271**
Creating our first URDF file	**271**
Explaining the file format	274
Watching the 3D model on rviz	275
Loading meshes to our models	277
Making our robot model movable	278
Physical and collision properties	279
Xacro – a better way to write our robot models	**280**
Using constants	281
Using math	281
Using macros	281
Moving the robot with code	282
3D modeling with SketchUp	286
Simulation in ROS	**288**
Using our URDF 3D model in Gazebo	289
Adding sensors to Gazebo	293
Loading and using a map in Gazebo	296
Moving the robot in Gazebo	298
Summary	**301**
Chapter 8: The Navigation Stack – Robot Setups	**303**
The navigation stack in ROS	**304**
Creating transforms	**305**
Creating a broadcaster	306
Creating a listener	307
Watching the transformation tree	310
Publishing sensor information	**310**
Creating the laser node	312

[v]

Table of Contents

Publishing odometry information	**314**
How Gazebo creates the odometry	316
Creating our own odometry	319
Creating a base controller	**324**
Using Gazebo to create the odometry	326
Creating our base controller	327
Creating a map with ROS	**330**
Saving the map using map_server	332
Loading the map using map_server	333
Summary	**334**

Chapter 9: The Navigation Stack – Beyond Setups — 335

Creating a package	**336**
Creating a robot configuration	**336**
Configuring the costmaps – global_costmap and local_costmap	**339**
Configuring the common parameters	340
Configuring the global costmap	341
Configuring the local costmap	341
Base local planner configuration	342
Creating a launch file for the navigation stack	**343**
Setting up rviz for the navigation stack	**345**
The 2D pose estimate	345
The 2D nav goal	347
The static map	348
The particle cloud	349
The robot's footprint	350
The local costmap	351
The global costmap	352
The global plan	353
The local plan	354
The planner plan	355
The current goal	356
Adaptive Monte Carlo Localization	**357**
Modifying parameters with rqt_reconfigure	**359**
Avoiding obstacles	**360**
Sending goals	**362**
Summary	**365**

Chapter 10: Manipulation with MoveIt! — 367

The MoveIt! architecture	**368**
Motion planning	370
The planning scene	371

[vi]

Table of Contents

Kinematics	372
Collision checking	372
Integrating an arm in MoveIt!	**372**
What's in the box?	373
Generating a MoveIt! package with the setup assistant	374
Integration into RViz	382
Integration into Gazebo or a real robotic arm	386
Simple motion planning	**387**
Planning a single goal	388
Planning a random target	389
Planning a predefined group state	390
Displaying the target motion	391
Motion planning with collisions	**391**
Adding objects to the planning scene	392
Removing objects from the planning scene	394
Motion planning with point clouds	394
The pick and place task	**396**
The planning scene	397
The target object to grasp	398
The support surface	399
Perception	401
Grasping	402
The pickup action	405
The place action	408
The demo mode	411
Simulation in Gazebo	412
Summary	**413**
Index	**415**

[vii]

Preface

Learning ROS for Robotics Programming, Second Edition gives you a comprehensive review of ROS tools. ROS is the Robot Operating System framework, which is used nowadays by hundreds of research groups and companies in the robotics industry. But it is also the painless entry point to robotics for nonprofessional people. You will see how to install ROS, you will start playing with its basic tools, and you will end up working with state-of-the-art computer vision and navigation tools.

The content of the book can be followed without any special devices, and each chapter comes with a series of source code examples and tutorials that you can run on your own computer. This is the only thing you need to follow in the book.

However, we also show you how to work with hardware so that you can connect your algorithms with the real world. Special care has been taken in choosing devices that are affordable for amateur users, but at the same time, the most typical sensors or actuators in robotics research are covered.

Finally, the potential of ROS is illustrated with the ability to work with whole robots in a simulated environment. You will learn how to create your own robot and integrate it with the powerful navigation stack. Moreover, you will be able to run everything in simulation by using the Gazebo simulator. We will end the book by providing an example of how to use the Move it! package to perform manipulation tasks with robotic arms. At the end of the book, you will see that you can work directly with a ROS robot and understand what is going on under the hood.

What this book covers

Chapter 1, Getting Started with ROS Hydro, shows the easiest way you must follow in order to have a working installation of ROS. You will see how to install ROS on different platforms, and you will use ROS Hydro throughout the rest of the book. This chapter describes how to make an installation from Debian packages, compile the sources and make installations in virtual machines and ARM CPU.

Chapter 2, *ROS Architecture and Concepts*, is concerned with the concepts and tools provided by the ROS framework. We will introduce you to nodes, topics, and services, and you will also learn how to use them. Through a series of examples, we will illustrate how to debug a node and visualize the messages published through a topic.

Chapter 3, *Visualization and Debug Tools*, goes a step further in order to show you powerful tools to debug your nodes and visualize the information that goes through the node's graph along with the topics. ROS provides a logging API that allows you to diagnose node problems easily. In fact, we will see some powerful graphical tools, such as rqt_console and rqt_graph, as well as visualization interfaces, such as rqt_plot and rviz. Finally, this chapter explains how to record and play back messages using rosbag and rqt_bag.

Chapter 4, *Using Sensors and Actuators with ROS*, literally connects ROS with the real world. This chapter goes through a number of common sensors and actuators that are supported in ROS, such as range lasers, servo motors, cameras, RGB-D sensors, GPS, and much more. Moreover, we explain how to use embedded systems with microcontrollers, similar to the widely known Arduino boards.

Chapter 5, *Computer Vision*, shows the support for cameras and computer vision tasks in ROS. This chapter starts with drivers available for FireWire and USB cameras so that you can connect them to your computer and capture images. You will then be able to calibrate your camera using the ROS calibration tools. Later, you will be able to use the image pipeline, which is explained in detail. Then, you will see how to use several APIs for vision and integrate OpenCV. Finally, the installation and usage of a visual odometry software is described.

Chapter 6, *Point Clouds*, in this chapter, we show how to use Point Cloud Library in your ROS nodes. This chapter starts with the basics utilities, such as read or write a PCL snippet and the conversions needed to publish or subscribe to these messages. Then, you will create a pipeline with different nodes to process 3D data, and you will downsample, filter, and search for features using PCL.

Chapter 7, *3D Modeling and Simulation*, constitutes one of the first steps in order to implement your own robot in ROS. It shows you how to model a robot from scratch and run it in simulation by using the Gazebo simulator. You will simulate sensors, such as cameras and laser range sensors. This will later allow you to use the whole navigation stack provided by ROS and other tools.

Chapter 8, *The Navigation Stack – Robot Setups*, is the first of two chapters concerned with the ROS navigation stack. This chapter describes how to configure your robot so that it can be used with the navigation stack. In the same way, the stack is explained, along with several examples.

Chapter 9, *The Navigation Stack – Beyond Setups*, continues the discussion of the previous chapter by showing how we can effectively make our robot navigate autonomously. It will use the navigation stack intensively for that. This chapter shows the great potential of ROS by using the Gazebo simulator and rviz to create a virtual environment in which we can build a map, localize our robot, and do path planning with obstacle avoidance.

Chapter 10, *Manipulation with MoveIt!*, is a set of tools for mobile manipulation in ROS. This chapter contains the documentation that you need to install this package. The chapter also contains example demonstrations with robotic arms that use MoveIt! for manipulation tasks, such as grasping, pick and place, or simple motion planning with inverse kinematics.

What you need for this book

This book was written with the intention that almost everybody can follow it and run the source code examples provided with it. Basically, you need a computer with a Linux distribution. Although any Linux distribution should be fine, it is recommended that you use a version of Ubuntu 12.04 LTS. Then, you will use ROS Hydro, which is installed according to the instructions given in *Chapter 1*, *Getting Started with ROS Hydro*.

For this distribution of ROS, you will need a version of Ubuntu prior to 14.04 because, since this version, Hydro is no longer supported.

As regards the hardware requirements of your computer, in general, any computer or laptop is enough. However, it is advisable to use a dedicated graphics card in order to run the Gazebo simulator. Also, it will be good to have a good number of peripherals so that you can connect several sensors and actuators, including cameras and Arduino boards.

You will also need Git (the git-core Debian package) in order to clone the repository with the source code provided with this book. Similarly, you are expected to have a basic knowledge of the Bash command line, GNU/Linux tools, and some C/C++ programming skills.

Who this book is for

This book is targeted at all robotics developers, from amateurs to professionals. It covers all the aspects involved in a whole robotic system and shows how ROS helps with the task of making a robot really autonomous. Anyone who is learning robotics and has heard about ROS but has never tried it will benefit from this book. Also, ROS beginners will learn advanced concepts and tools of this framework. Indeed, even regular users may learn something new from some particular chapters. Certainly, only the first three chapters are intended for new users; so those who already use ROS can skip these ones and go directly to the rest.

Conventions

In this book, you will find a number of text styles that distinguish between different kinds of information. Here are some examples of these styles and an explanation of their meaning.

Code words in text, database table names, folder names, filenames, file extensions, pathnames, dummy URLs, user input, and Twitter handles are shown as follows: "The `rosdep` command-line tool must be installed and initialized before you can use ROS."

A block of code is set as follows:

```
#include <ros/ros.h>
#include <dynamic_reconfigure/server.h>
#include <chapter2_tutorials/chapter2Config.h>
```

When we wish to draw your attention to a particular part of a code block, the relevant lines or items are set in bold:

```
dynamic_reconfigure::Server<chapter2_tutorials::chapter2Config>::Call
backType f;

  f = boost::bind(&callback, _1, _2);
```

Any command-line input or output is written as follows:

```
$ sudo apt-get install python-rosdep
$ sudo rosdep init
$ rosdep update
```

New terms and **important words** are shown in bold. Words that you see on the screen, for example, in menus or dialog boxes, appear in the text like this: "When it finishes, you can start your virtual machine by clicking on the **Start** button."

> Warnings or important notes appear in a box like this.

> Tips and tricks appear like this.

Reader feedback

Feedback from our readers is always welcome. Let us know what you think about this book—what you liked or disliked. Reader feedback is important for us as it helps us develop titles that you will really get the most out of.

To send us general feedback, simply e-mail `feedback@packtpub.com`, and mention the book's title in the subject of your message.

If there is a topic that you have expertise in and you are interested in either writing or contributing to a book, see our author guide at `www.packtpub.com/authors`.

Customer support

Now that you are the proud owner of a Packt book, we have a number of things to help you to get the most from your purchase.

Downloading the example code

You can download the example code files from your account at `http://www.packtpub.com` for all the Packt Publishing books you have purchased. If you purchased this book elsewhere, you can visit `http://www.packtpub.com/support` and register to have the files e-mailed directly to you. You can also download these code files from `https://github.com/AaronMR/ROS_Book_Hydro`.

Downloading the color images of this book

We also provide you with a PDF file that has color images of the screenshots/diagrams used in this book. The color images will help you better understand the changes in the output. You can download this file from `http://www.packtpub.com/sites/default/files/downloads/7580OS_ColorImages.pdf`.

Errata

Although we have taken every care to ensure the accuracy of our content, mistakes do happen. If you find a mistake in one of our books—maybe a mistake in the text or the code—we would be grateful if you could report this to us. By doing so, you can save other readers from frustration and help us improve subsequent versions of this book. If you find any errata, please report them by visiting `http://www.packtpub.com/submit-errata`, selecting your book, clicking on the **Errata Submission Form** link, and entering the details of your errata. Once your errata are verified, your submission will be accepted and the errata will be uploaded to our website or added to any list of existing errata under the Errata section of that title.

To view the previously submitted errata, go to `https://www.packtpub.com/books/content/support` and enter the name of the book in the search field. The required information will appear under the **Errata** section.

Piracy

Piracy of copyrighted material on the Internet is an ongoing problem across all media. At Packt, we take the protection of our copyright and licenses very seriously. If you come across any illegal copies of our works in any form on the Internet, please provide us with the location address or website name immediately so that we can pursue a remedy.

Please contact us at `copyright@packtpub.com` with a link to the suspected pirated material.

We appreciate your help in protecting our authors and our ability to bring you valuable content.

Questions

If you have a problem with any aspect of this book, you can contact us at `questions@packtpub.com`, and we will do our best to address the problem.

Getting Started with ROS Hydro

Welcome to the first chapter of this book where you will learn how to install ROS, the new standard software framework in robotics. This book is an update on *Learning ROS for Robotics Programming*, based in ROS Fuerte. With ROS you will learn how to program and control your robots the easy way, using tons of examples and source code that will show you how to use sensors, devices, or add new functionalities such as autonomous navigation, visual perception, and so on to your robot. Thanks to the open source motto and a community that is developing state-of-the-art algorithms and providing new functionalities, ROS is growing every day.

Throughout this book, you will learn the following:

- Installing ROS Hydro framework on a version of Ubuntu
- The basic operation of ROS
- Debugging and visualizing data
- Programming your robot using this framework
- Connecting sensors, actuators, and devices to create your robot
- Creating a 3D model to use in the simulator
- Using the navigation stack to make your robot autonomous

In this chapter, we are going to install a full version of ROS Hydro in Ubuntu. ROS is fully supported and recommended for Ubuntu, and it is experimental for other operative systems. The version used in this book is the 12.04 (Precise Pangolin) and you can download it for free from `http://releases.ubuntu.com/12.04/`.

Before starting with the installation, we are going to learn about the origin of the ROS and its history.

The **Robot Operating System (ROS)** is a framework that is widely used in Robotics. The philosophy is to make a piece of software that could work in other robots with only little changes to the code. What we get with this idea is the ability to create functionalities that can be shared and used in other robots without effort, so we do not need to reinvent the wheel.

ROS was originally developed in 2007 by the **Stanford Artificial Intelligence Laboratory (SAIL)** in support of the Stanford AI Robot project. As of 2008, development continues primarily at Willow Garage, a Robotics Research Institute, with more than twenty institutions collaborating within a federated development model.

A lot of research institutions have started to develop in ROS, adding hardware and sharing their code. Also, the companies have started to adapt their products to be used in ROS. In the following set of images, you can see some of the platforms which are fully supported. Normally, these platforms are published with a lot of code, examples, and simulators to permit the developers to start work easily. The first three robots are examples of robots with published code and they are humanoids. The last one is an AUV developed by the University of Las Palmas de Gran Canaria and the code has not been published yet. You can find a lot of such examples at http://wiki.ros.org/Robots.

The sensors and actuators used in robotics have also been adapted for use in ROS. Everyday, more devices are being supported by this framework. Furthermore, thanks to ROS and open hardware, companies are creating cheaper and more powerful sensors. The Arduino board is a good example of this, because using a cheap electronic board you can add a lot of sensors like encoders, light and temperature sensors, and so on.

ROS provides standard operating system facilities such as hardware abstraction, low-level device control, implementation of commonly used functionalities, message passing between processes, and package management.

It is based on graph architecture with a centralized topology, where processing takes place in nodes that may receive, post the multiplex sensor, control, state, planning, actuator, and so on. The library is geared towards a Unix-like system.

The *-ros-pkg is a community repository for developing high-level libraries easily. Many of the capabilities frequently associated with ROS, such as the navigation library and the rviz visualizer, are developed in this repository. These libraries give a powerful set of tools for working with ROS easily, knowing what is happening every time. Visualization, simulators, and debugging tools are the most important. In the next image you can see two of these tools, the rviz and rqt_plot. The screenshot in the center is rqt_plot where you can see the plotted data from some sensors. The other two screenshots are rviz; in the screenshot you can see a 3D representation of a real robot.

ROS is released under the terms of the **BSD (Berkeley Software Distribution)** license and is an open source software. It is free for commercial and research use. The ros-pkg contributed packages are licensed under a variety of open source licenses.

With ROS you can do this and more. You can take a code from the repositories, improve it, and share it again. This philosophy is the underlying principle of open source software.

ROS has numerous versions, the last one being Indigo. In this book, we are going to use Hydro because it is a stable version while Indigo is still experimental and may contain bugs.

Now we are going to show you how to install ROS Hydro. Although in this book we use Hydro, you may need to install older versions to use some code that works only with these versions.

As we said before, the operating system used in the book is Ubuntu, and we are going to use it throughout this book and with all the tutorials. If you use another operating system and you want to follow the book, the best option is to install a virtual machine with a copy of Ubuntu. At the end of this chapter, we will explain how to install a virtual machine to use the ROS inside it or download a virtual machine with ROS installed.

Anyway, if you want to try installing it in an operating system other than Ubuntu, you can find instructions to do so in many other operating systems at `http://wiki.ros.org/hydro/Installation`.

PC installation

We assume that you have a PC with a copy of Ubuntu 12.04. We are using Ubuntu because it comes with a **Long-Term Support** (**LTS**). That means the community will maintain this version for five years.

Furthermore, it is necessary to have a basic knowledge of Linux and command tools such as the terminal, vim, creating folders, and so on. If you need to learn these tools, you can find a lot of relevant resources on the Internet, or you can find books on these topics instead.

Installing ROS Hydro – using repositories

Last year, the ROS webpage was updated with a new design and a new organization of contents. You can see a screenshot of the webpage that follows:

Chapter 1

In the menu, you can find information about ROS and whether ROS is a good choice for your system, blogs, news, and so on.

Instructions for the ROS installation can be found under the **Install** tab in the **Getting Started** section.

ROS recommends that you install the system using the repository instead of the source code, unless you are an advanced user and you want to make a customized installation; in that case, you may prefer installing ROS using the source code.

So to install ROS using the repositories, we will start by configuring the Ubuntu repository in our system.

Configuring your Ubuntu repositories

In this section, you will learn the steps for installing ROS Hydro in your computer. This process has been based on the official installation page, which can be found at http://wiki.ros.org/hydro/Installation/Ubuntu.

We assume that you know what an Ubuntu repository is, and how to manage it. If you have any doubts about it, refer to https://help.ubuntu.com/community/Repositories/Ubuntu.

Before we start the installation, we need to configure our repositories. To do that, the repositories need to allow **restricted**, **universe**, and **multiverse**. To check if your Ubuntu accepts these repositories, click on the **Ubuntu Software Center** in the menu on the left-hand side of your desktop, as shown in the following screenshot:

Click on **Edit | Software Sources** and you will see the next window. Make sure that all the listed options are checked as shown in the following screenshot:

Normally these options are marked, so you should not have any problem with this step.

Setting up your source.list file

In this step, you have to select your Ubuntu version. It is possible to install ROS Hydro in various versions of the operating system. You can use any of them, but we recommend version 12.04 to follow the chapters of this book. Keep in mind that Hydro works in the Precise Pangolin (12.04), Quantal Quetzal (12.10), and the Raring Ringtail(13.04) versions of Ubuntu.

- If you're going follow the book with Ubuntu 12.04 (Precise Pangolin), type the following command to add the repositories:

    ```
    sudo sh -c 'echo "deb http://packages.ros.org/ros/ubuntu precise main" > /etc/apt/sources.list.d/ros-latest.list'
    ```

- If you're going to follow the book with Ubuntu 12.10 (Quantal Quetzal), type the following command to add the repositories:

    ```
    sudo sh -c 'echo "deb http://packages.ros.org/ros/ubuntu quantal main" > /etc/apt/sources.list.d/ros-latest.list'
    ```

- To follow the book with Ubuntu 13.04 (Raring Ringtail), type the following command to add the repositories:

    ```
    sudo sh -c 'echo "deb http://packages.ros.org/ros/ubuntu raring main" > /etc/apt/sources.list.d/ros-latest.list'
    ```

> **Downloading the example code**
>
> You can download the example code files from your account at http://www.packtpub.com for all the Packt Publishing books you have purchased. If you purchased this book elsewhere, you can visit http://www.packtpub.com/support and register to have the files e-mailed directly to you. You can also download these code files from https://github.com/AaronMR/ROS_Book_Hydro.

Once you've added the correct repository, your operating system will know where to download programs to install them into your system.

Setting up your keys

This step is to confirm that the origin of the code is correct and that no-one has modified the code or programs without the knowledge of the owner. Normally, when you add a new repository you have to add the keys of that repository, so it is added to your system's trusted list.

```
$ wget http://packages.ros.org/ros.key -O - | sudo apt-key add -
```

Now we can be sure that the code came from an authorized site and has not been modified.

Installing ROS

We are ready to start the installation now, but before we do that it's better to make an update to avoid problems with the libraries and software with a version other than what ROS needs. This is done with the following command:

```
$ sudo apt-get update
```

ROS is huge; sometimes you will install libraries and programs that you will never use. Normally it has four different installations, but this depends on the final use. For example, if you are an advanced user, maybe you only need the basic installation for a robot without much space on the hard disc. For this book, we recommend you use the full installation because it will install everything necessary to practice the examples and tutorials.

Getting Started with ROS Hydro

It doesn't matter if you don't know what are you installing right now — rviz, simulators, navigation, and so on. You will learn everything in the upcoming chapters:

- The easiest (and recommended if you have enough hard disk space) installation is known as desktop-full. It comes with ROS, the rqt tools, the rviz visualizer (for 3D), many generic robot libraries, simulator in 2D (like stage) and 3D (usually gazebo), the navigation stack (to move, localize, do mapping, and control arms), and also perception libraries using vision, lasers or RGBD cameras:

    ```
    $ sudo apt-get install ros-hydro-desktop-full
    ```

- If you do not have enough disk space or you prefer to install only a few packages, install only the desktop install initially, which comes with only ROS, the rqt tools, rviz, and generic robot libraries. You can install the rest of the packages as and when you need them. For example, using aptitude and looking for ros-hydro-* packages with the following command:.

    ```
    $ sudo apt-get install ros-hydro-desktop
    ```

- If you only want the bare bones, install ROS-base, which is usually recommended for the robot itself, or for computers without a screen or just a tty. It will install the ROS package with the build and communication libraries and no GUI tools at all. With **BeagleBone Black (BBB)**, we will install the system with the following option:

    ```
    $ sudo apt-get install ros-hydro-ros-base
    ```

- Finally, whichever of the previous options you choose, you can also install individual/specific ROS packages (for a given package name):

    ```
    $ sudo apt-get install ros-hydro-PACKAGE
    ```

Initializing rosdep

Before you can use ROS, you will need to initialize rosdep. The rosdep command line too enables you to easily install system dependencies for the source you want to compile and is required to run some core components in ROS. In ROS Fuerte you had to install rosdep after installing ROS, and it was known as a standalone tool. Now rosdep is installed in ROS by default. To initialize rosdep, you have to use the following commands:

```
$ sudo rosdep init
$ rosdep update
```

Setting up the environment

Congratulations! If you are at this step, you have an installed version of ROS on your system! To start using it, the system needs to know the location of the executable or binary files as well as the other commands. To do so, normally you need to execute the next script; if you also install another ROS distro, you can work with both just by calling the script of the one you need each time, since this script simply sets your environment. Here we use the one for ROS Hydro, but just replace Hydro with Fuerte or Groovy if you want to try other distros:

```
$ source /opt/ros/hydro/setup.bash
```

If you type `roscore` in the shell, you will see something starting up. This is the best test for finding out if you have ROS, and if it is installed correctly.

Notice that if you open another shell and type `roscore` or other ROS commands, it does not work. This is because it is necessary to execute the script again to configure the global variables, the path where ROS is installed, and so on.

It is very easy to solve this; you just need to add the script at the end of your `.bashrc` script file so that when you start a new shell, the script will execute and you will have the environment configured.

The `.bashrc` file is within the user home (`/home/USERNAME/.bashrc`). It has the configuration of the shell or terminal, and each time the user opens the terminal, this file is loaded. So you can add commands or configuration to make the user's life easy. For this reason, we will add the script at the end of the `.bashrc` file, to avoid keying it in each time we open a terminal. We do this with the following command:

```
$ echo "source /opt/ros/hydro/setup.bash" >> ~/.bashrc
```

To see the results, you have to execute the file using the next command, or close the current terminal and open another.

```
$ source ~/.bashrc
```

Some users need more than a single ROS distribution installed in their system. Your `~/.bashrc` must only source the `setup.bash` of the version you are currently using, since the last call will override the environment set of the others. So you have several distros living in the same system and need to switch between them.

For example, you might have the following lines in your `.bashrc` file:

...
source /opt/ros/hydro/setup.bash
source /opt/ros/fuerte/setup.bash
source /opt/ros/electric/setup.bash
...

The ROS Electric version will be executed in this case. So you have to make sure that the version you are running is the last one in the file.

If you want to check the version used in a terminal, you can do so easily using the `echo $ROS_DISTRO` command.

Getting rosinstall

Now, the next step is to install a command tool that will help us install other packages with a single command. This tool is based in Python, but don't worry, you don't need to know Python to use it. You will learn how to use this tool in the upcoming chapters:

To install this tool on Ubuntu, run the following command:

```
$ sudo apt-get install python-rosinstall
```

And that is all! You have a complete ROS system installed in your system. When I finish a new installation of ROS, I personally like to test two things: that `roscore` works, and `turtlesim`.

If you want to do the same,, type the following commands in different shells:

```
$ roscore
```
```
$ rosrun turtlesim turtlesim_node
```

And if everything is okay, you will see the following screenshot:

How to install VirtualBox and Ubuntu

VirtualBox is a general-purpose full virtualizer for x86 hardware, targeted at server, desktop, and embedded use. VirtualBox is free and supports all the major operating systems and pretty much every Linux flavor out there.

If you don't want to change the operating system of your computer to Ubuntu, tools such as VirtualBox help us virtualize a new operating system in our computers without making any changes.

In the following section, we are going to show you how to install VirtualBox and a new installation of Ubuntu. After this virtual installation, you should have a clean installation to restart your development machine if you have any problems, or to save all the setups necessary for your robot in the machine.

Downloading VirtualBox

The first step is to download the VirtualBox installation file. The latest version at the time of writing this book is 4.3.12; you can download it from `http://download.virtualbox.org/virtualbox/4.3.12/`. If you're using Windows, you can download it from `http://download.virtualbox.org/virtualbox/4.3.12/VirtualBox-4.3.12-93733-Win.exe`.

Once installed, you need to download the image of Ubuntu; for this tutorial we will use a copy of Ubuntu with ROS Hydro installed. You can download it from `http://nootrix.com/2014/04/virtualized-ros-hydro/`.

For this version, the Nootrix team are using torrent to download the virtual machine; I tried this way to download the file and it works perfectly.

You can find different virtual machines with Ubuntu and ROS preinstalled, but we are going to use this version because it is referred to in the official pages of ROS.

Creating the virtual machine

Creating a new virtual machine with the downloaded file is very easy; just proceed with the following steps. Open VirtualBox and click on **File | Import Appliance**. Then click on **Open appliance** and select the `ROSHydro.ova` file downloaded earlier:

In the windows that follow, you can configure the parameters of the new virtual machine. Keep the default configuration and change only the name for the virtual system. This name is how you distinguish this virtual machine from others. Our recommendation is to put a descriptive name, in our case the name of this book:

Chapter 1

Click on the **Import** button, and accept the software license agreement in the next window. You will see a progress bar. It means that VirtualBox is copying the file with the virtual image, and it is creating a new copy with the new name.

Notice that this process doesn't modify the original file `ROS.ova`, and you could create more virtual machines with different copies from the original file.

The process will take a few minutes depending on your computer. When it finishes, you can start your virtual machine by clicking on the **Start** button. Remember to select the right machine before you start it. In our case, we only have one but you could have more:

Sometimes, you will get an error as shown in the following screenshot. It is because your computer doesn't have the correct drivers to use the USB 2.0 controller. You can fix this by installing the Oracle VM VirtualBox Extension Pack, but you can also choose to disable the USB support to start using the virtual machine:

Getting Started with ROS Hydro

To disable the USB support, right-click over the virtual machine and select **Settings**. In the **General** tab, click on **Ports | USB** and uncheck the **Enable USB 2.0 (EHCI) Controller**, as shown in the following screenshot. Now you can restart the virtual machine and it should start without any problems.

Once the virtual machine starts, you should see the next window as seen in the following screenshot. It is the Ubuntu 12.04 OS with ROS installed:

When you finish these steps, you will have a full copy of ROS Hydro that can be used along with this book. You can run all the examples and stacks that we are going to work with. Unfortunately, VirtualBox has problems when working with real hardware, and it's possible that you may not be able to use this copy of ROS Hydro with the examples given in *Chapter 4*, *Using Sensors and Actuators with ROS*.

Installing ROS Hydro in BeagleBone Black (BBB)

BeagleBone Black is a low-cost development platform based on an ARM Cortex A8 processor. This board is fabricated with a Linux distribution called Ångström. Ångström was developed by a small group who wanted to unify Linux distribution for embedded systems. They wanted an operating system that was stable and user-friendly.

Texas Instruments designed BeagleBone Black thinking that the community of developers needed an on-board computer with some **general purpose input/output** (**GPIO**) pins. The BeagleBone Black platform is an evolution of the original BeagleBone. The main features of the board are an ARM Cortex A8 processor at 1 GHz with 512 MB RAM, and with Ethernet, USB, and HDMI connections and two headers of 46 pins GPIO. This GPIO can be set up as digital I/O, ADC, PWM, or for communication protocol like I2C, SPI, or UART. The GPIO is an easy way to communicate with sensors and actuators directly from the BeagleBone without intermediaries. The following is a labeled image of BeagleBone:

When the BeagleBone board came out, it was not possible to install ROS on the Ångström distribution. For this reason, it was common to install an operating system based on Ubuntu on the BeagleBone. There are different versions of Ubuntu ARM compatible with the BeagleBone Black and ROS; we recommend you use an image of Ubuntu ARM 13.04 raring armhf on the platform to work with ROS.

Now, a ROS version for Ångström distribution is ready to be installed; you can do it following the installation steps given at `http://wiki.ros.org/hydro/Installation/Angstrom`. Despite this possibility, we have chosen to install ROS on Ubuntu ARM because these distributions are more common and can be used on other ARM-based boards such as UDOO, ODROID U3, ODROID X2, or Gumstick.

The ARM technology is booming with the use of mobile devices such as smartphones and tablets. Apart from the increasing computer power of the ARM cortex, the great level of integration and low consumption have made this technology suitable for autonomous robotic systems. In the last few years, multiple ARM platforms for developers have been launched in the market. Some of them have features similar to the BeagleBone Black like the Raspberry PI or the Gumstick Overo. Additionally, more powerful boards like Gumstick DuoVero with a Dual Core ARM Cortex A9 or some quad core boards like Odroid U3, Odroid X2 or UDOO are now available.

Prerequisites

Before installing ROS on Beaglebone Black, we have to achieve some prerequisites. As this book is focused on ROS, we will list them without entering into detail. There is a lot of information about Beaglebone Black and Ubuntu ARM available on websites, forums, and books that you can check out.

First, we have to install an Ubuntu ARM distribution compatible with ROS. So, an image of Ubuntu ARM is needed. You can obtain an Ubuntu 13.04 Raring armhf using wget with the following command:

```
$ wget https://rcn-ee.net/deb/flasher/raring/BBB-eMMC-flasher-ubuntu-13.04-2013-10-08.img
```

Download the Ubuntu 13.04 armhf image and install it on your SD card. You can get more details on how to install Ubuntu on Bealgebone Black on eLinux at `http://elinux.org/Beagleboard:Ubuntu_On_BeagleBone_Black#Ubuntu_Raring_On_Micro_SD`.

The process described in the preceding webpage works fine, but we have to be careful with the version of Ubuntu used. As the website is periodically updated, they are now using Ubuntu 14.04, which is not compatible with ROS. We will use an Ubuntu 13.04 Raring armhf as mentioned earlier.

Chapter 1

Once we have Ubuntu ARM on our platform, the Beaglebone Black network interfaces must be configured to provide access to the network. So, you will have to configure the network settings such as IP, DNS, and gateway.

Remember that the easiest way could be mounting the SD card in another computer and editing `/etc/network/interfaces`.

After setting up the network, we should install the packages, programs, and libraries that ROS will need such as CMake, Python, or Vim using the following commands:

```
$ sudo apt-get install cmake python-catkin-pkg python-empy python-nose python-setuptools libgtest-dev build-essential
```

```
$ sudo apt-get install g++ curl pkg-config libv4l-dev libjpeg-dev build-essential libssl-dev vim
```

The operating system for Beaglebone Black is set up for micro SD cards with 1-4 GHz. This memory space is very limited if we want to use a great part of the ROS Hydro packages. So in order to solve this situation, we can use SD cards with larger space and expand the file system to occupy all the space available with re-partitioning.

So if we want to work with a bigger memory space, it is recommended to expand the Beaglebone Black memory file system. This process is further explained at http://elinux.org/Beagleboard:Expanding_File_System_Partition_On_A_microSD.

You can do this by following the commands listed next:

1. We need to become a super user, so we will type the following command and our password:

   ```
   $ sudo su
   ```

2. We will look at the partitions of our SD card:

   ```
   $ fdisk /dev/mmcblk0
   ```

3. On typing p, the two partitions of the SD card will be shown:

   ```
   $ p
   ```

4. After this, we will delete one partition by typing 'd' and then, we will type 2 to indicate that we want to delete /dev/mmcblk0p2:

   ```
   $ d
   $ 2
   ```

5. On typing n, a new partition will be created; if we type p it will be a primary partition. We will indicate that we want to number it as the second partition by typing 2:

   ```
   $ n
   $ p
   $ 2
   ```

6. You can write these changes by typing w if everything is right, or eliminate the changes with *Ctrl* + *Z*:

   ```
   $ w
   ```

7. We should reboot the board after finishing:

   ```
   $ reboot
   ```

8. Once again, become a super user once the reboot is complete:

   ```
   $ sudo su
   ```

9. And finally, run the following command to execute the expansion of the memory file system of the operating system.

   ```
   $ resize2fs /dev/mmcblk0p2
   ```

Now we should be ready to install ROS. At this point, the process of installation is pretty similar to the PC installation previously explained in this chapter. So, we should be familiar with it. We will see that the main difference when installing ROS on BeagleBone Black is that we can't install the ROS full-desktop; we must install it package by package.

Setting up the local machine and source.list file

Now you will start setting up your local machine:

```
$ sudo update-locale LANG=C LANGUAGE=C LC_ALL=C LC_MESSAGES=POSIX
```

After this, we will configure the source lists depending on the Ubuntu version that we have installed in BeagleBone Black. The number of Ubuntu versions compatible with BeagleBone Black are limited, and only active builds can be found for Ubuntu 13.04 raring armhf, the most popular version of Ubuntu ARM.

- Ubuntu 13.04 Raring armhf:

  ```
  $ sudo sh -c 'echo "deb http://packages.namniart.com/repos/ros raring main" > /etc/apt/sources.list.d/ros-latest.list'
  ```

- Ubuntu 12.10 Quantal armhf:

  ```
  $ sudo sh -c 'echo "deb http://packages.namniart.com/repos/ros quantal main" > /etc/apt/sources.list.d/ros-latest.list'
  ```

- Ubuntu 12.04 Precise armhf:

  ```
  $ sudo sh -c 'echo "deb http://packages.namniart.com/repos/ros precise main" > /etc/apt/sources.list.d/ros-latest.list'
  ```

Setting up your keys

As explained previously, this step is needed to confirm that the origin of the code is correct and that no-one has modified the code or programs without the knowledge of the owner:

```
$ wget http://packages.namniart.com/repos/namniart.key -O - | sudo apt-key add -
```

Installing the ROS packages

Before the installation of ROS packages, we must update the system to avoid problems of library dependencies.

```
$ sudo apt-get update
```

This part of the installation is slightly different for the Beaglebone Black. There are a lot of libraries and packages in ROS and not all of them compile fully on an ARM. So, it is not possible to make a full-desktop installation. It is recommended to install package by package to ensure that they will work on an ARM platform.

You can try to install ROS-base, known as ROS Bare Bones. ROS-base installs the ROS package along with the build and communications libraries but does not include the GUI tools:

```
$ sudo apt-get install ros-hydro-ros-base
```

We can install specific ROS packages by using the following command:

```
$ sudo apt-get install ros-hydro-PACKAGE
```

If we need to find the ROS packages available for BeagleBone Black, you can run the following command:

```
$ apt-cache search ros-hydro
```

For example, the following packages are the basics that work with ROS and can be installed individually using `apt-get` install:

```
$ sudo apt-get install ros-hydro-ros
$ sudo apt-get install ros-hydro-roslaunch
$ sudo apt-get install ros-hydro-rosparam
$ sudo apt-get install ros-hydro-rosservice
```

Although theoretically, not all the packages of ROS are supported by BeagleBone Black, in practice, we have been able to migrate entire projects developed on PC to BeagleBone Black. We tried a lot of packages, and we could only not install rviz.

Initializing rosdep for ROS

The `rosdep` command-line tool must be installed and initialized before you can use ROS. This allows you to easily install libraries and solving system dependencies for the source you want to compile, and is required to run some core components in ROS. You can use the following commands to install and initialize `rosdep`:

```
$ sudo apt-get install python-rosdep
$ sudo rosdep init
$ rosdep update
```

Setting up the environment in BeagleBone Black

If you have arrived at this step, congratulations because you have installed ROS in your BeagleBone Black. The ROS environment variables can be added to your bash, so they will be added every time a shell is launched:

```
$ echo "source /opt/ros/hydro/setup.bash" >> ~/.bashrc
$ source ~/.bashrc
```

We have to be careful if we have more than one version of ROS in our system. The `bashrc` setup must use the variables of the version being used only.

If we want to set up the environment in the current shell, we will run the following command:

```
$ source /opt/ros/hydro/setup.bash
```

Getting rosinstall for BeagleBone Black

`Rosinstall` is a common command-line tool in ROS that helps us to install packages easily. It can be installed on Ubuntu with the following command line:

```
$ sudo apt-get install python-rosinstall
```

Summary

In this chapter, we have installed ROS Hydro on different devices (PC, VirtualBox, and BeagleBone Black) in Ubuntu. With these steps, you have everything necessary installed on your system to start working with ROS and you can also practice the examples in this book. You also have the option of installing ROS using the source code. This option is for advanced users and we recommend you use only the repository as installation as it is more common and normally does not give errors or problems.

It is a good idea to play around with ROS and its installation on a virtual machine. That way, if you have problems with the installation or with something else, you can reinstall a new copy of your operating system and start again.

Normally, with virtual machines, you will not have access to real hardware, for example, sensors or actuators. Anyway, you can use it for testing the algorithms.

2
ROS Architecture and Concepts

Once you have installed ROS, you certainly must be thinking, "OK, I have installed it, and now what?" In this chapter, you will learn the structure of ROS and the parts it is made up of. Furthermore, you will start to create nodes and packages and use ROS with examples using Turtlesim.

The ROS architecture has been designed and divided into three sections or levels of concepts:

- The Filesystem level
- The Computation Graph level
- The Community level

The first level is the Filesystem level. In this level, a group of concepts are used to explain how ROS is internally formed, the folder structure, and the minimum number of files that it needs to work.

The second level is the Computation Graph level where communication between processes and systems happens. In this section, we will see all the concepts and systems that ROS has to set up systems, handle all the processes, communicate with more than a single computer, and so on.

The third level is the Community level where there are certain tools and concepts to share knowledge, algorithms, and code from any developer. This level is important because ROS can grow quickly with great support from the community.

Understanding the ROS Filesystem level

When you start to use or develop projects with ROS, you will see that although this concept can sound strange in the beginning, you will become familiar with it with time.

Similar to an operating system, an ROS program is divided into folders, and these folders have files that describe their functionalities:

- **Packages**: Packages form the atomic level of ROS. A package has the minimum structure and content to create a program within ROS. It may have ROS runtime processes (nodes), configuration files, and so on.
- **Package manifests**: Package manifests provide information about a package, licenses, dependencies, compilation flags, and so on. A package manifest is managed with a file called `package.xml`.
- **Metapackages**: When you want to aggregate several packages in a group, you will use metapackages. In ROS Fuerte, this form for ordering packages was called Stacks. To maintain the simplicity of ROS, the stacks were removed, and now, metapackages make up this function. In ROS, there exist a lot of these metapackages; one of them is the navigation stack.
- **Metapackage manifests**: Metapackage manifests (`package.xml`) are similar to a normal package but with an export tag in XML. It also has certain restrictions in its structure.

- **Message (msg) types**: A message is the information that a process sends to other processes. ROS has a lot of standard types of messages. Message descriptions are stored in my_package/msg/MyMessageType.msg.
- **Service (srv) types**: Service descriptions, stored in my_package/srv/MyServiceType.srv, define the request and response data structures for services provided by each process in ROS.

In the following screenshot, you can see the content of the turtlesim package. What you see is a series of files and folders with code, images, launch files, services, and messages. Keep in mind that the screenshot was edited to show a short list of files; the real package has more.

```
turtlesim/
├── CHANGELOG.rst
├── CMakeLists.txt
├── images
│   ├── files
│   └── hydro.svg
├── include
│   └── turtlesim
│       ├── turtle_frame.h
│       └── turtle.h
├── launch
│   └── multisim.launch
├── msg
│   ├── Color.msg
│   └── Pose.msg
├── package.xml
├── src
│   ├── turtle.cpp
│   └── turtlesim.cpp
├── srv
│   ├── Kill.srv
│   └── TeleportRelative.srv
```

The workspace

Basically, the workspace is a folder where we have packages, edit the source files or compile packages. It is useful when you want to compile various packages at the same time and is a good place to have all our developments localized.

A typical workspace is shown in the following screenshot. Each folder is a different space with a different role:

```
catkin_ws/
├── build
│   ├── catkin
│   ├── catkin_generated
│   ├── Makefile
│   └── ...
├── devel
│   ├── bin
│   ├── setup.zsh
│   └── ...
└── src
    ├── CMakeLists.txt -> /opt/ros/hydro/share/catkin/cmake/toplevel.cmake
    ├── ros_tutorials-hydro-devel
    └── ...
```

- **The Source space**: In the Source space (the `src` folder), you put your packages, projects, clone packages, and so on. One of the most important files in this space is `CMakeLists.txt`. The `src` folder has this file because it is invoked by CMake when you configure the packages in the workspace. This file is created with the `catkin_init_workspace` command.
- **The Build space**: In the `build` folder, CMake and catkin keep the cache information, configuration, and other intermediate files for our packages and projects.
- **The Development (devel) space**: The `devel` folder is used to keep the compiled programs. This is used to test the programs without the installation step. Once the programs are tested, you can install or export the package to share with other developers.

You have two options with regard to building packages with catkin. The first one is to use the standard CMake workflow. With this, you can compile one package at a time, as shown in the following commands:

```
$ cmake packageToBuild/
$ make
```

> **Downloading the example code**
>
> You can download the example code files from your account at http://www.packtpub.com for all the Packt Publishing books you have purchased. If you purchased this book elsewhere, you can visit http://www.packtpub.com/support and register to have the files e-mailed directly to you. You can also download these code files from https://github.com/AaronMR/ROS_Book_Hydro.

If you want to compile all your packages, you can use the `catkin_make` command line, as shown in the following commands:

```
$ cd workspace
$ catkin_make
```

Both commands build the executables in the build space directory configured in ROS.

Another interesting feature of ROS are its overlays. When you are working with a package of ROS, for example, Turtlesim, you can do it with the installed version, or you can download the source file and compile it to use your modified version.

ROS permits you to use your version of this package instead of the installed version. This is very useful information if you are working on an upgrade of an installed package. At this moment, perhaps you don't understand the utility of this, but in the next chapters, we will use this feature to create our own plugins.

Packages

Usually, when we talk about packages, we refer to a typical structure of files and folders. This structure looks as follows:

- `include/package_name/`: This directory includes the headers of the libraries that you would need.
- `msg/`: If you develop nonstandard messages, put them here.
- `scripts/`: These are executable scripts that can be in Bash, Python, or any other scripting language.
- `src/`: This is where the source files of your programs are present. You can create a folder for nodes and nodelets or organize it as you want.
- `srv/`: This represents the service (`srv`) types.
- `CMakeLists.txt`: This is the CMake build file.
- `package.xml`: This is the package manifest.

To create, modify, or work with packages, ROS gives us tools for assistance, some of which are as follows:

- `rospack`: This command is used to get information or find packages in the system.
- `catkin_create_pkg`: This command is used when you want to create a new package.
- `catkin_make`: This command is used to compile a workspace.

- `rosdep`: This command installs the system dependencies of a package.
- `rqt_dep`: This command is used to see the package dependencies as a graph. If you want to see the package dependencies as a graph, you will find a plugin called package graph in rqt. Select a package and see the dependencies.

To move between packages and their folders and files, ROS gives us a very useful package called `rosbash`, which provides commands that are very similar to Linux commands. The following are a few examples:

- `roscd`: This command helps us change the directory. This is similar to the `cd` command in Linux.
- `rosed`: This command is used to edit a file.
- `roscp`: This command is used to copy a file from a package.
- `rosd`: This command lists the directories of a package.
- `rosls`: This command lists the files from a package. This is similar to the `ls` command in Linux.

The `package.xml` file must be in a package, and it is used to specify information about the package. If you find this file inside a folder, probably this folder is a package or a metapackage.

If you open the `package.xml` file, you will see information about the name of the package, dependencies, and so on. All of this is to make the installation and the distribution of these packages easy.

Two typical tags that are used in the `package.xml` file are `<build_depend>` and `<run _depend>`.

The `<build_depend>` tag shows what packages must be installed before installing the current package. This is because the new package might use a functionality of another package.

The `<run_depend>` tag shows the packages that are necessary to run the code of the package. The following screenshot is an example of the `package.xml` file:

```xml
<?xml version="1.0"?>
<package>
  <name>example</name>
  <version>0.0.1</version>
  <description>
    this is a example.
  </description>
  <maintainer email="test@test.com">test</maintainer>
  <license>BSD</license>

  <url type="website">http://www.test.com</url>
  <author>test</author>

  <buildtool_depend>catkin</buildtool_depend>
  <build_depend>geometry_msgs</build_depend>

  <run_depend>geometry_msgs</run_depend>
</package>
```

Metapackages

As we have shown earlier, metapackages are special packages with only one file inside; this file is `package.xml`. This package does not have other files, such as code, includes, and so on.

Metapackages are used to refer to others packages that are normally grouped following a feature-like functionality, for example, navigation stack, `ros_tutorials`, and so on.

You can convert your stacks and packages from ROS Fuerte to Hydro and catkin using certain rules for migration. These rules can be found at `http://wiki.ros.org/catkin/migrating_from_rosbuild`.

ROS Architecture and Concepts

In the following screenshot, you can see the content from the `package.xml` file in the `ros_tutorials` metapackage. You can see the `<export>` tag and the `<run_depend>` tag. These are necessary in the package manifest, which is shown in the following screenshot:

```xml
<?xml version="1.0"?>
<package>
...
    <buildtool_depend>catkin</buildtool_depend>
...
    <run_depend>roscpp_tutorials</run_depend>
    <run_depend>rospy_tutorials</run_depend>
    <run_depend>turtlesim</run_depend>
...
    <export>
      <metapackage/>
    </export>
...
</package>
```

If you want to locate the `ros_tutorials` metapackage, you can use the following command:

`$ rosstack find ros_tutorials`

The output will be a path, such as `/opt/ros/hydro/share/ros_tutorials`.

To see the code inside, you can use the following command line:

`$ vim /opt/ros/hydro/share/ros_tutorials/package.xml`

Remember that Hydro uses metapackages, not stacks, but the `rosstack find` command line works to find metapackages.

Messages

ROS uses a simplified message description language to describe the data values that ROS nodes publish. With this description, ROS can generate the right source code for these types of messages in several programming languages.

ROS has a lot of messages predefined, but if you develop a new message, it will be in the `msg/` folder of your package. Inside that folder, certain files with the `.msg` extension define the messages.

A message must have two principal parts: fields and constants. Fields define the type of data to be transmitted in the message, for example, `int32`, `float32`, and `string`, or new types that you have created earlier, such as `type1` and `type2`. Constants define the name of the fields.

An example of a `msg` file is as follows:

```
int32 id
float32 vel
string name
```

In ROS, you can find a lot of standard types to use in messages, as shown in the following table list:

Primitive type	Serialization	C++	Python
bool (1)	unsigned 8-bit int	uint8_t(2)	bool
int8	signed 8-bit int	int8_t	int
uint8	unsigned 8-bit int	uint8_t	int(3)
int16	signed 16-bit int	int16_t	int
uint16	unsigned 16-bit int	uint16_t	int
int32	signed 32-bit int	int32_t	int
uint32	unsigned 32-bit int	uint32_t	int
int64	signed 64-bit int	int64_t	long
uint64	unsigned 64-bit int	uint64_t	long
float32	32-bit IEEE float	float	float
float64	64-bit IEEE float	double	float
string	ascii string (4)	std::string	string
time	secs/nsecs signed 32-bit ints	ros::Time	rospy.Time
duration	secs/nsecs signed 32-bit ints	ros::Duration	rospy.Duration

A special type in ROS is the header type. This is used to add the time, frame, and so on. This permits you to have the messages numbered, to see who is sending the message, and to have more functions that are transparent for the user and that ROS is handling.

The header type contains the following fields:

```
uint32 seq
time stamp
string frame_id
```

You can see the structure using the following command:

```
$ rosmsg show std_msgs/Header
```

Thanks to the header type, it is possible to record the timestamp and frame of what is happening with the robot, as we will see in the upcoming chapters.

In ROS, there exist tools to work with messages. The `rosmsg` tool prints out the message definition information and can find the source files that use a message type.

In the upcoming sections, we will see how to create messages with the right tools.

Services

ROS uses a simplified service description language to describe ROS service types. This builds directly upon the ROS `msg` format to enable request/response communication between nodes. Service descriptions are stored in `.srv` files in the `srv/` subdirectory of a package.

To call a service, you need to use the package name, along with the service name; for example, you will refer to the `sample_package1/srv/sample1.srv` file as `sample_package1/sample1`.

There are tools that exist to perform functions with services. The `rossrv` tool prints out the service descriptions and packages that contain the `.srv` files, and finds source files that use a service type.

If you want to create a service, ROS can help you with the service generator. These tools generate code from an initial specification of the service. You only need to add the `gensrv()` line to your `CMakeLists.txt` file.

In the upcoming sections, you will learn how to create your own services.

Understanding the ROS Computation Graph level

ROS creates a network where all the processes are connected. Any node in the system can access this network, interact with other nodes, see the information that they are sending, and transmit data to the network:

The basic concepts in this level are nodes, the master, Parameter Server, messages, services, topics, and bags, all of which provide data to the graph in different ways and are explained in the following list:

- **Nodes**: Nodes are processes where computation is done. If you want to have a process that can interact with other nodes, you need to create a node with this process to connect it to the ROS network. Usually, a system will have many nodes to control different functions. You will see that it is better to have many nodes that provide only a single functionality, rather than have a large node that makes everything in the system. Nodes are written with a ROS client library, for example, roscpp or rospy.

- **The master**: The master provides the registration of names and the lookup service to the rest of the nodes. It also sets up connections between the nodes. If you don't have it in your system, you can't communicate with nodes, services, messages, and others. In a distributed system, you will have the master in one computer, and you can execute nodes in this or other computers

- **Parameter Server**: Parameter Server gives us the possibility of using keys to store data in a central location. With this parameter, it is possible to configure nodes while it's running or to change the working of the nodes.

- **Messages**: Nodes communicate with each other through messages. A message contains data that sends information to other nodes. ROS has many types of messages, and you can also develop your own type of message using standard messages.

[33]

- **Topics**: Each message must have a name to be routed by the ROS network. When a node is sending data, we say that the node is publishing a topic. Nodes can receive topics from other nodes simply by subscribing to the topic. A node can subscribe to a topic, and it isn't necessary that the node that is publishing this topic should exist. This permits us to decouple the production from the consumption. It's important that the name of the topic be unique to avoid problems and confusion between topics with the same name.
- **Services**: When you publish topics, you are sending data in a many-to-many fashion, but when you need a request or an answer from a node, you can't do it with topics. Services give us the possibility of interacting with nodes. Also, services must have a unique name. When a node has a service, all the nodes can communicate with it, thanks to ROS client libraries.
- **Bags**: Bags are a format to save and play back the ROS message data. Bags are an important mechanism to store data, such as sensor data, that can be difficult to collect but is necessary to develop and test algorithms. You will use bags a lot while working with complex robots.

In the following figure, you can see the graphic representation of this level. It represents a real robot working in real conditions. In the graph, you can see the nodes, the topics, which node is subscribed to a topic, and so on. This graph does not represent messages, bags, Parameter Server, and services. It is necessary for other tools to see a graphic representation of them. The tool used to create the graph is rqt_graph; you will learn more about it in *Chapter 3, Visualization and Debug Tools*.

These concepts are implemented in the ros_comm repository.

Nodes and nodelets

Nodes are executables that can communicate with other processes using topics, services, or the Parameter Server. Using nodes in ROS provides us with fault tolerance and separates the code and functionalities, making the system simpler.

ROS has another type of node called nodelets. These special nodes are designed to run multiple nodes in a single process, with each nodelet being a thread (light process). This way, we avoid using the ROS network among them but permit communication with other nodes. With that, nodes can communicate more efficiently, without overloading the network. Nodelets are especially useful for camera systems and 3D sensors, where the volume of data transferred is very high.

A node must have a unique name in the system. This name is used to permit the node to communicate with another node using its name without ambiguity. A node can be written using different libraries, such as `roscpp` and `rospy`; `roscpp` is for C++ and `rospy` is for Python. Throughout this book, we will use `roscpp`.

ROS has tools to handle nodes and give us information about it, such as `rosnode`. The `rosnode` tool is a command-line tool used to display information about nodes, such as listing the currently running nodes. The supported commands are as follows:

- `rosnode info NODE`: This prints information about a node
- `rosnode kill NODE`: This kills a running node or sends a given signal
- `rosnode list`: This lists the active nodes
- `rosnode machine hostname`: This lists the nodes running on a particular machine or lists machines
- `rosnode ping NODE`: This tests the connectivity to the node.
- `rosnode cleanup`: This purges the registration information from unreachable nodes

In the upcoming sections, you will learn how to use these commands with examples.

A powerful feature of ROS nodes is the possibility of changing parameters while you start the node. This feature gives us the power to change the node name, topic names, and parameter names. We use this to reconfigure the node without recompiling the code so that we can use the node in different scenes.

An example of changing a topic name is as follows:

```
$ rosrun book_tutorials tutorialX topic1:=/level1/topic1
```

This command will change the topic name `topic1` to `/level1/topic1`. I am sure that you don't understand this at this moment, but you will find the utility of it in the upcoming chapters.

To change parameters in the node, you can do something similar to changing the topic name. For this, you only need to add an underscore (_) to the parameter name; for example:

```
$ rosrun book_tutorials tutorialX _param:=9.0
```

The preceding command will set `param` to the float number `9.0`.

Bear in mind that you cannot use names that are reserved by the system. They are as follows:

- `__name`: This is a special, reserved keyword for the name of the node
- `__log`: This is a reserved keyword that designates the location where the node's log file should be written
- `__ip` and `__hostname`: These are substitutes for `ROS_IP` and `ROS_HOSTNAME`
- `__master`: This is a substitute for `ROS_MASTER_URI`
- `__ns`: This is a substitute for `ROS_NAMESPACE`

Topics

Topics are buses used by nodes to transmit data. Topics can be transmitted without a direct connection between nodes, which means that the production and consumption of data are decoupled. A topic can have various subscribers and can also have various publishers, but you can take care about publishing the same topic with different nodes because it can create conflicts.

Each topic is strongly typed by the ROS message type used to publish it, and nodes can only receive messages from a matching type. A node can subscribe to a topic only if it has the same message type.

The topics in ROS can be transmitted using TCP/IP and UDP. The TCP/IP-based transport is known as **TCPROS** and uses the persistent TCP/IP connection. This is the default transport used in ROS.

The UDP-based transport is known as **UDPROS** and is a low-latency, lossy transport. So, it is best suited to tasks such as teleoperation.

ROS has a tool to work with topics called `rostopic`. It is a command-line tool that gives us information about the topic or publishes data directly on the network. This tool has the following parameters:

- `rostopic bw /topic`: This displays the bandwidth used by the topic.
- `rostopic echo /topic`: This prints messages to the screen.
- `rostopic find message_type`: This finds topics by their type.
- `rostopic hz /topic`: This displays the publishing rate of the topic.
- `rostopic info /topic`: This prints information about the active topic, topics published, ones it is subscribed to, and services.
- `rostopic list`: This prints information about active topics.
- `rostopic pub /topic type args`: This publishes data to the topic. It allows us to create and publish data in whatever topic we want, directly from the command line.
- `rostopic type /topic`: This prints the topic type, that is, the type of message it publishes.

We will learn to use it in the upcoming sections.

Services

When you need to communicate with nodes and receive a reply, you cannot do it with topics; you need to do it with services.

Services are developed by the user, and standard services don't exist for nodes. The files with the source code of the messages are stored in the `srv` folder.

Similar to topics, services have an associated service type that is the package resource name of the `.srv` file. As with other ROS filesystem-based types, the service type is the package name and the name of the `.srv` file. For example, the `chapter2_tutorials/srv/chapter2_srv1.srv` file has the `chapter2_tutorials/chapter2_srv1` service type.

ROS has two command-line tools to work with services: `rossrv` and `rosservice`. With `rossrv`, we can see information about the services' data structure, and it has exactly the same usage as `rosmsg`.

With `rosservice`, we can list and query services. The supported commands are as follows:

- `rosservice call /service args`: This calls the service with the arguments provided
- `rosservice find msg-type`: This finds services by service type
- `rosservice info /service`: This prints information about the service
- `rosservice list`: This lists the active services
- `rosservice type /service`: This prints the service type
- `rosservice uri /service`: This prints the ROSRPC URI service

Messages

A node sends information to another node using messages that are published by topics. The message has a simple structure that uses standard types or types developed by the user.

Message types use the following standard ROS naming convention; the name of the package, then /, and then the name of the .msg file. For example, `std_msgs/ msg/ String.msg` has the `std_msgs/String` message type.

ROS has the `rosmsg` command-line tool to get information about messages. The accepted parameters are as follows:

- `rosmsg show`: This displays the fields of a message
- `rosmsg list`: This lists all messages
- `rosmsg package`: This lists all of the messages in a package
- `rosmsg packages`: This lists all of the packages that have the message
- `rosmsg users`: This searches for code files that use the message type
- `rosmsg md5`: This displays the MD5 sum of a message

Bags

A bag is a file created by ROS with the .bag format to save all of the information of the messages, topics, services, and others. You can use this data later to visualize what has happened; you can play, stop, rewind, and perform other operations with it.

The bag file can be reproduced in ROS just as a real session can, sending the topics at the same time with the same data. Normally, we use this functionality to debug our algorithms.

To use bag files, we have the following tools in ROS:

- `rosbag`: This is used to record, play, and perform other operations
- `rqt_bag`: This is used to visualize data in a graphic environment
- `Rostopic`: This helps us see the topics sent to the nodes

The ROS master

The ROS master provides naming and registration services to the rest of the nodes in the ROS system. It tracks publishers and subscribers to topics as well as services. The role of the master is to enable individual ROS nodes to locate one another. Once these nodes have located each other, they communicate with each other in a peer-to-peer fashion. You can see in a graphic example the steps performed in ROS to advertise a topic, subscribe to a topic, and publish a message, in the following diagram:

The master also provides Parameter Server. The master is most commonly run using the `roscore` command, which loads the ROS master, along with other essential components.

Parameter Server

Parameter Server is a shared, multivariable dictionary that is accessible via a network. Nodes use this server to store and retrieve parameters at runtime.

Parameter Server is implemented using XMLRPC and runs inside the ROS master, which means that its API is accessible via normal XMLRPC libraries. XMLRPC is a **Remote Procedure Call (RPC)** protocol that uses XML to encode its calls and HTTP as a transport mechanism.

ROS Architecture and Concepts

Parameter Server uses XMLRPC data types for parameter values, which include the following:

- 32-bit integers
- Booleans
- Strings
- Doubles
- ISO8601 dates
- Lists
- Base64-encoded binary data

ROS has the `rosparam` tool to work with Parameter Server. The supported parameters are as follows:

- `rosparam list`: This lists all the parameters in the server
- `rosparam get parameter`: This gets the value of a parameter
- `rosparam set parameter value`: This sets the value of a parameter
- `rosparam delete parameter`: This deletes a parameter
- `rosparam dump file`: This saves Parameter Server to a file
- `rosparam load file`: This loads a file (with parameters) on Parameter Server

Understanding the ROS Community level

The ROS Community level concepts are the ROS resources that enable separate communities to exchange software and knowledge. These resources include the following:

- **Distributions**: ROS distributions are collections of versioned metapackages that you can install. ROS distributions play a similar role to Linux distributions. They make it easier to install a collection of software, and they also maintain consistent versions across a set of software.
- **Repositories**: ROS relies on a federated network of code repositories, where different institutions can develop and release their own robot software components.
- **The ROS Wiki**: The ROS Wiki is the main forum for documenting information about ROS. Anyone can sign up for an account, contribute their own documentation, provide corrections or updates, write tutorials, and more.

- **Bug Ticket System**: If you find a problem or want to propose a new feature, ROS has this resource to do it.
- **Mailing lists**: The ROS user-mailing list is the primary communication channel about new updates to ROS as well as a forum to ask questions about the ROS software.
- **ROS Answers**: Users can ask questions on forums using this resource.
- **Blog**: You can find regular updates, photos, and news at http://www.ros.org/news.

Tutorials to practice with ROS

It is time for you to practice what you have learned until now. In the upcoming sections, you will see examples for you to practice along with the creation of packages, using nodes, using Parameter Server, and moving a simulated robot with Turtlesim.

Navigating by ROS Filesystem

We have command-line tools to navigate through the filesystem. We are going to explain the most used ones.

To get information and move to packages and stacks, we will use `rospack`, `rosstack`, `roscd`, and `rosls`.

We use `rospack` and `rosstack` to get information about packages and stacks, the path, the dependencies, and so on.

For example, if you want to find the path of the `turtlesim` package, you will use the following command:

```
$ rospack find turtlesim
```

You will then obtain the following output:

```
/opt/ros/hydro/share/turtlesim
```

The same thing happens with the metapackages that you have installed in the system. An example of this is as follows:

```
$ rosstack find ros_comm
```

You will obtain the path for the `ros_comm` metapackage as follows:

```
/opt/ros/hydro/share/ros_comm
```

To list the files inside the pack or stack, you will use the following command:

```
$ rosls turtlesim
```

The following is the output of the preceding command:

```
cmake    images    srv    package.xml    msg
```

If you want to go inside the folder, you will use `roscd` as follows:

```
$ roscd turtlesim
$ pwd
```

The new path will be as follows:

```
/opt/ros/hydro/share/turtlesim
```

Creating our own workspace

Before we do anything, we are going to create our own workspace. In this workspace, we will have all the code that we will use in this book.

To see the workspace that ROS is using, use the following command:

```
$ echo $ROS_PACKAGE_PATH
```

You will see output similar to the following:

```
/opt/ros/hydro/share:/opt/ros/hydro/stacks
```

The folder that we are going to create is in `~/dev/catkin_ws/src/`. To add this folder, we use the following commands:

```
$ mkdir -p ~/dev/catkin_ws/src
$ cd ~/dev/catkin_ws/src
$ catkin_init_workspace
```

Once we've created the workspace folder, there are no packages inside—only `CMakeList.txt`. The next step is building the workspace. To do this, we use the following commands:

```
$ cd ~/dev/catkin_ws
$ catkin_make
```

Now, if you type the `ls` command in the directory, you can see new folders created with the previous command. These are the `build` and `devel` folders.

To finish the configuration, use the following command:

```
$ source devel/setup.bash
```

This step is only to reload the `setup.bash` file. You will obtain the same result if you close and open a new shell. You should have this command line in the end in your `~/.bashrc` file because we used it in *Chapter 1, Getting Started with ROS Hydro*. If not, you can add it using the following command:

```
$ echo "source /opt/ros/hydro/setup.bash" >> ~/.bashrc
```

Creating a ROS package and metapackage

As said earlier, you can create a package manually. To avoid tedious work, we will use the `catkin_create_pkg` command-line tool.

We will create the new package in the workspace created previously using the following commands:

```
$ cd ~/dev/catkin_ws/src
$ catkin_create_pkg chapter2_tutorials std_msgs roscpp
```

The format of this command includes the name of the package and the dependencies that will have the package, in our case `std_msgs` and `roscpp`. This is shown in the following command:

```
Catkin_create_pkg [package_name] [depend1] [depend2] [depend3]
```

The following dependencies are included:

- `std_msgs`: This contains common message types representing primitive data types and other basic message constructs, such as MultiArray.
- `roscpp`: This is a C++ implementation of ROS. It provides a client library that enables C++ programmers to quickly interface with ROS topics, services, and parameters.

If everything is right, you will see the following screenshot:

```
Created file chapter2_tutorials/package.xml
Created file chapter2_tutorials/CMakeLists.txt
Created folder chapter2_tutorials/include/chapter2_tutorials
Created folder chapter2_tutorials/src
Successfully created files in /home/aaronmr/dev/catkin_ws/src/chapter2_tutorials.
Please adjust the values in package.xml.
```

ROS Architecture and Concepts

As we saw earlier, you can use the `rospack`, `roscd`, and `rosls` commands to retrieve information about the new package. The following are the dependencies used:

- `rospack profile`: This command informs you about the newly added packages to the ROS system. It is useful after installing any new package.
- `rospack find chapter2_tutorials`: This command helps us find the path.
- `rospack depends chapter2_tutorials`: This command helps us see the dependencies.
- `rosls chapter2_tutorials`: This command helps us see the content.
- `roscd chapter2_tutorials`: This command changes the actual path.

Building an ROS package

Once you have your package created and you have some code, it is necessary to build the package. When you build the package, what happens really is that the code is compiled.

To build a package, we will use the `catkin_make` tool, as follows:

$ cd ~/dev/catkin_ws/

$ catkin_make

In a few seconds, you will see something similar to the following screenshot:

```
Base path: /home/aaronmr/dev/catkin_ws
Source space: /home/aaronmr/dev/catkin_ws/src
Build space: /home/aaronmr/dev/catkin_ws/build
Devel space: /home/aaronmr/dev/catkin_ws/devel
Install space: /home/aaronmr/dev/catkin_ws/install
...
-- BUILD_SHARED_LIBS is on
-- ~~~~~~~~~~~~~~~~~~~~~~~~~~~~~~~~~~~~~~~~~~~~~~~~~~
-- ~~  traversing 29 packages in topological order:
-- ~~  - chapter2_tutorials
...
-- ~~~~~~~~~~~~~~~~~~~~~~~~~~~~~~~~~~~~~~~~~~~~~~~~~~
-- +++ processing catkin package: 'chapter2_tutorials'
-- ==> add_subdirectory(chapter2_tutorials)
...
[100%] Built target ..........
```

If you don't encounter any failures, the package is compiled.

Remember that you should run the `catkin_make` command line in the `workspace` folder. If you try to do it in any other folder, the command will fail. An example of this is provided in the following command lines:

```
$ roscd chapter2_tutorials/
$ catkin_make
```

When you are in the `chapter2_tutorials` folder and try to build the package using `catkin_make`, you will get the following error:

```
The specified base path "/home/your_user/dev/catkin_ws/src/chapter2_tutorials" contains a CMakeLists.txt but "catkin_make" must be invoked in the root of workspace
```

If you execute `catkin_make` in the `catkin_ws` folder, you will obtain a good compilation.

Playing with ROS nodes

As we explained in the *Nodes and nodelets* section, nodes are executable programs, and these executables are in the `devel` space. To practice, and learn about, nodes, we are going to use a typical package called `turtlesim`.

If you have installed the desktop installation, you will have the `turtlesim` package preinstalled; if not, install it with the following command:

```
$ sudo apt-get install ros-hydro-ros-tutorials
```

Before starting with anything, you must start `roscore` using the following command:

```
$ roscore
```

To get information on nodes, we have the `rosnode` tool. To see what parameters are accepted, type the following command:

```
$ rosnode
```

You will obtain a list of accepted parameters, as shown in the following screenshot:

```
rosnode is a command-line tool for printing information about ROS Nodes.

Commands:
        rosnode ping    test connectivity to node
        rosnode list    list active nodes
        rosnode info    print information about node
        rosnode machine list nodes running on a particular machine or list machines
        rosnode kill    kill a running node
        rosnode cleanup purge registration information of unreachable nodes

Type rosnode <command> -h for more detailed usage, e.g. 'rosnode ping -h'
```

[45]

ROS Architecture and Concepts

If you want a more detailed explanation of the use of these parameters, use the following command:

    $ rosnode <param> -h

Now that `roscore` is running, we are going to get information about the nodes that are running, using the following command:

    $ rosnode list

You see that the only node running is `/rosout`. It is normal because this node runs whenever `roscore` is run.

We can get all the information about this node using parameters. Try to use the following commands for more information:

    $ rosnode info
    $ rosnode ping
    $ rosnode machine
    $ rosnode kill
    $ rosnode cleanup

Now, we are going to start a new node with `rosrun` using the following command:

    $ rosrun turtlesim turtlesim_node

We will then see a new window appear with a little turtle in the middle, as shown in the following screenshot:

Chapter 2

If we see the node list now, we will see a new node with the name /turtlesim. You can see information about the node using rosnode info nameNode.

You can see a lot of information that can be used to debug your programs, using the following command:

```
$ rosnode info /turtlesim
```

The preceding command line prints the following information:

```
Node [/turtlesim]
Publications:
 * /turtle1/color_sensor [turtlesim/Color]
 * /rosout [rosgraph_msgs/Log]
 * /turtle1/pose [turtlesim/Pose]


Subscriptions:
 * /turtle1/cmd_vel [unknown type]


Services:
 * /turtle1/teleport_absolute
 * /turtlesim/get_loggers
 * /turtlesim/set_logger_level
 * /reset
 * /spawn
 * /clear
 * /turtle1/set_pen
 * /turtle1/teleport_relative
 * /kill


contacting node http://127.0.0.1:43753/ ...
Pid: 32298
Connections:
 * topic: /rosout
 * to: /rosout
 * direction: outbound
 * transport: TCPROS
```

[47]

In the information, we can see the Publications (*topics*), Subscriptions (*topics*), and Services (*srv*) that the node has and the unique name of each.

Now, let's see how you interact with the node using topics and services.

Learning how to interact with topics

To interact and get information about topics, we have the rostopic tool. This tool accepts the following parameters:

- rostopic bw TOPIC: This displays the bandwidth used by topics
- rostopic echo TOPIC: This prints messages to the screen
- rostopic find TOPIC: This finds topics by their type
- rostopic hz TOPIC: This displays the publishing rate of topics
- rostopic info TOPIC: This prints information about active topics
- rostopic list: This lists the active topics
- rostopic pubs TOPIC: This publishes data to the topic
- rostopic type TOPIC: This prints the topic type

If you want see more information on these parameters, use -h as follows:

$ rostopic bw -h

With the pub parameter, we can publish topics that can subscribe to any node. We only need to publish the topic with the correct name. We will do this test later; we are now going to use a node that will do this work for us:

$ rosrun turtlesim turtle_teleop_key

With this node, we can move the turtle using the arrow keys, as illustrated in the following screenshot:

Why does the turtle move when `turtle_teleop_key` is executed?

If you want to see information about the `/teleop_turtle` and `/turtlesim` nodes, we can see in the following code that there exists a topic called `/turtle1/cmd_vel [geometry_msgs/Twist]` in the `Publications` section of the node, and in the `Subscriptions` section of the second node, there is `/turtle1/cmd_vel [geometry_msgs/Twist]`:

```
$ rosnode info /teleop_turtle


Node [/teleop_turtle]
...
Publications:
 * /turtle1/cmd_vel [geometry_msgs/Twist]



$ rosnode info /turtlesim


Node [/turtlesim]
...
```

```
Subscriptions:
 * /turtle1/cmd_vel [geometry_msgs/Twist]
...
```

This means that the first node is publishing a topic that the second node can subscribe to. You can see the topic list using the following command line:

```
$ rostopic list
```

The output will be as follows:

```
/rosout
/rosout_agg
/turtle1/color_sensor
/turtle1/cmd_vel
/turtle1/pose
```

With the `echo` parameter, you can see the information sent by the node. Run the following command line and use the arrow keys to see the data that is being sent:

```
$ rostopic echo /turtle1/cmd_vel
```

You will see something similar to the following output:

```
---
linear:
    x: 0.0
    y: 0.0
    z: 0.0
angular:
    x: 0.0
    y: 0.0
    z: 2.0
---
```

You can see the type of message sent by the topic using the following command line:

```
$ rostopic type /turtle1/cmd_vel
```

You will see something similar to the following output:

```
Geometry_msgs/Twist
```

If you want to see the message fields, you can do it with the next command:

```
$ rosmsg show geometry_msgs/Twist
```

You will see something similar to the following output:

```
geometry_msgs/Vector3 linear
   float64 x
   float64 y
   float64 z
geometry_msgs/Vector3 angular
   float64 x
   float64 y
   float64 zfloat32 angular
```

These tools are useful because, with this information, we can publish topics using the `rostopic pub [topic] [msg_type] [args]` command:

```
$ rostopic pub /turtle1/cmd_vel  geometry_msgs/Twist -r 1 -- "linear:
   x: 1.0
   y: 0.0
   z: 0.0
angular:
   x: 0.0
   y: 0.0
   z: 1.0"
```

You will see the turtle doing a curve, as shown in the following screenshot:

Learning how to use services

Services are another way through which nodes can communicate with each other. Services allow nodes to send a request and receive a response.

The tool that we are going to use to interact with services is called `rosservice`. The accepted parameters for this command are as follows:

- `rosservice args /service`: This prints the service arguments
- `rosservice call /service`: This calls the service with the arguments provided
- `rosservice find msg-type`: This finds services by their service type
- `rosservice info /service`: This prints information about the service
- `rosservice list`: This lists the active services
- `rosservice type /service`: This prints the service type
- `rosservice uri /service`: This prints the ROSRPC URI service

Chapter 2

We are going to list the services available for the `turtlesim` node using the following command, so if it is not working, run `roscore` and run the `turtlesim` node:

`$ rosservice list`

You will obtain the following output:

```
/clear
/kill
/reset
/rosout/get_loggers
/rosout/set_logger_level
/spawn
/teleop_turtle/get_loggers
/teleop_turtle/set_logger_level
/turtle1/set_pen
/turtle1/teleport_absolute
/turtle1/teleport_relative
/turtlesim/get_loggers
/turtlesim/set_logger_level
```

If you want to see the type of any service, for example, the `/clear` service, use the following command:

`$ rosservice type /clear`

You will see something similar to the following output:

`std_srvs/Empty`

To invoke a service, you will use `rosservice call [service] [args]`. If you want to invoke the `/clear` service, use the following command:

`$ rosservice call /clear`

In the `turtlesim` window, you will now see that the lines created by the movements of the turtle will be deleted.

Now, we are going to try another service, for example, the /spawn service. This service will create another turtle in another location with a different orientation. To start with, we are going to see the following type of message:

```
$ rosservice type /spawn | rossrv show
```

You will see something similar to the following output:

```
float32 x
float32 y
float32 theta
string name
---
string name
```

The preceding command is the same as the following commands. If you want to know why these lines are the same, search in Google about *piping Linux*:

```
$ rosservice type /spawn
```

You will see something similar to the following output:

```
turtlesim/Spawn
```

Type in the following command:

```
$ rossrv show turtlesim/Spawn
```

You will see something similar to the following output:

```
float32 x
float32 y
float32 theta
string name
---
string name
```

With these fields, we know how to invoke the service. We need the position of x and y, the orientation (theta), and the name of the new turtle:

```
$ rosservice call /spawn 3 3 0.2 "new_turtle"
```

We then obtain the following result:

Using Parameter Server

Parameter Server is used to store data that is accessible to all nodes. ROS has a tool called `rosparam` to manage Parameter Server. The accepted parameters are as follows:

- `rosparam set parameter value`: This sets the parameter
- `rosparam get parameter`: This gets the parameter
- `rosparam load file`: This loads parameters from the file
- `rosparam dump file`: This dumps parameters to the file
- `rosparam delete parameter`: This deletes the parameter
- `rosparam list`: This lists the parameter names

For example, we can see the parameters in the server that are used by all nodes:

```
$ rosparam list
```

We obtain the following output:

```
/background_b
/background_g
/background_r
/rosdistro
/roslaunch/uris/host_aaronmr_laptop__60878
/rosversion
/run_id
```

The background parameters are of the `turtlesim` node. These parameters change the color of the windows that are initially blue. If you want to read a value, you will use the `get` parameter:

```
$ rosparam get /background_b
```

To set a new value, you will use the `set` parameter:

```
$ rosparam set /background_b 100
```

Another important feature of `rosparam` is the `dump` parameter. With this parameter, you can save or load the contents of Parameter Server.

To save Parameter Server, use `rosparam dump [file_name]` as follows:

```
$ rosparam dump save.yaml
```

To load a file with new data for Parameter Server, use `rosparam load [file_name] [namespace]` as follows:

```
$ rosparam load load.yaml namespace
```

Creating nodes

In this section, we are going to learn how to create two nodes: one to publish data and the other to receive this data. This is the basic way of communicating between two nodes, that is, to handle data and do something with this data.

Navigate to the `chapter2_tutorials/src/` folder using the following command:

```
$ roscd chapter2_tutorials/src/
```

Create two files with the names example1_a.cpp and example1_b.cpp. The example1_a.cpp file will send the data with the node name, and the example1_b.cpp file will show the data in the shell. Copy the following code inside the example1_a.cpp file or download it from the repository:

```cpp
#include "ros/ros.h"
#include "std_msgs/String.h"
#include <sstream>

int main(int argc, char **argv)
{
  ros::init(argc, argv, "example1_a");
  ros::NodeHandle n;
  ros::Publisher chatter_pub = n.advertise<std_msgs::String>("message", 1000);
  ros::Rate loop_rate(10);
  while (ros::ok())
  {
    std_msgs::String msg;
    std::stringstream ss;
    ss << " I am the example1_a node ";
    msg.data = ss.str();
    //ROS_INFO("%s", msg.data.c_str());
    chatter_pub.publish(msg);
    ros::spinOnce();
    loop_rate.sleep();
  }
  return 0;
}
```

Here is a further explanation of the preceding code:

```cpp
#include "ros/ros.h"
#include "std_msgs/String.h"
#include <sstream>
```

The headers to be included are ros/ros.h, std_msgs/String.h, and sstream. Here, ros/ros.h includes all the files necessary to use the node with ROS, and std_msgs/String.h includes the header that denotes the type of message we are going to use.

```cpp
ros::init(argc, argv, "example1_a");
```

Initiate the node and set the name; remember that the name must be unique:

```cpp
ros::NodeHandle n;
```

ROS Architecture and Concepts

This is the handler of our process.

```
ros::Publisher chatter_pub = n.advertise<std_msgs::String>("message",
1000);
```

Set a publisher and tell the master the name of the topic and the type. The name is `message`, and the second parameter is the buffer size. If the topic is publishing data quickly, the buffer will keep at 1,000.

```
ros::Rate loop_rate(10);
```

Set the frequency to send the data, which in this case is 10 Hz.

```
while (ros::ok())
{
```

The `ros::ok()` line stops the node if *Ctrl + c* is pressed or if ROS stops all the nodes:

```
std_msgs::String msg;
std::stringstream ss;
ss << " I am the example1_a node ";
msg.data = ss.str();
```

In this part, we create a variable for the message with the correct type to send the data:

```
chatter_pub.publish(msg);
```

Here, the message is published:

```
ros::spinOnce();
```

We have a subscriber in this part, where ROS updates and reads all the topics:

```
loop_rate.sleep();
```

Sleep for the necessary time to get a 10 Hz frequency.

Now, we will create the other node. Copy the following code inside the `example1_b.cpp` file or download it from the repository:

```
#include "ros/ros.h"
#include "std_msgs/String.h"

void chatterCallback(const std_msgs::String::ConstPtr& msg)
{
  ROS_INFO("I heard: [%s]", msg->data.c_str());
}

int main(int argc, char **argv)
```

```
{
  ros::init(argc, argv, "example1_b");
  ros::NodeHandle n;
  ros::Subscriber sub = n.subscribe("message", 1000, chatterCallback);
  ros::spin();
  return 0;
}
```

Let's explain the code:

```
#include "ros/ros.h"
#include "std_msgs/String.h"
```

Include the headers and the type of message to use for the topic:

```
void messageCallback(const std_msgs::String::ConstPtr& msg)
{
  ROS_INFO("I heard: [%s]", msg->data.c_str());
}
```

This function is called every time that the node receives a message. This is where we do something with the data; in this case, we show it in the shell:

```
ros::Subscriber sub = n.subscribe("message", 1000, messageCallback);
```

Create a subscriber and start to listen to the topic with the name message. The buffer will be of 1,000, and the function to handle the message will be messageCallback:

```
ros::spin();
```

The ros::spin() line is a loop where the node starts to read the topic and when a message arrives, messageCallback is called. When the user presses *Ctrl* + *c*, the node exits the loop and ends.

Building the node

As we are using the chapter2_tutorials package, we are going to edit the CMakeLists.txt file. You can use your favorite editor or the rosed tool. This will open the file with the Vim editor:

```
$ rosed chapter2_tutorials CMakeLists.txt
```

ROS Architecture and Concepts

At the end of the file, we will copy the following lines:

```
include_directories(
  include
  ${catkin_INCLUDE_DIRS}
)

add_executable(chap2_example1_a src/example1_a.cpp)
add_executable(chap2_example1_b src/example1_b.cpp)

add_dependencies(chap2_example1_a chapter2_tutorials_generate_messages_cpp)
add_dependencies(chap2_example1_b chapter2_tutorials_generate_messages_cpp)

target_link_libraries(chap2_example1_a ${catkin_LIBRARIES})
target_link_libraries(chap2_example1_b ${catkin_LIBRARIES})
```

Now, to build the package and compile all the nodes, use the `catkin_make` tool as follows:

```
$ cd ~/dev/catkin_ws/
$ catkin_make chapter2_tutorials
```

If ROS is not running on your computer, you will have to use the following command:

```
$ roscore
```

You can check whether ROS is running using the `rosnode list` command as follows:

```
$ rosnode list
```

Now, run both nodes in different shells:

```
$ rosrun chapter2_tutorials example1_a

$ rosrun chapter2_tutorials example1_b
```

If you check the shell where the `example1_b` node is running, you will see something similar to the following screenshot:

```
...
[ INFO] [1403252419.452448698]: I heard: [ I am the example1_a node ]
[ INFO] [1403252419.552163326]: I heard: [ I am the example1_a node ]
[ INFO] [1403252419.653701929]: I heard: [ I am the example1_a node ]
[ INFO] [1403252419.752261663]: I heard: [ I am the example1_a node ]
[ INFO] [1403252419.854459847]: I heard: [ I am the example1_a node ]
...
```

Everything that is happening can be viewed in the following diagram. You can see that the example1_a node is publishing the message topic, and the example2_b node is subscribing to the topic.

You can use rosnode and rostopic to debug and see what the nodes are doing. Try the following commands:

```
$ rosnode list
$ rosnode info /example1_a
$ rosnode info /example1_b
$ rostopic list
$ rostopic info /message
$ rostopic type /message
$ rostopic bw /message
```

Creating msg and srv files

In this section, we are going to learn how to create msg and srv files for use in our nodes. They are files where we put a specification about the type of data to be transmitted and the values of this data. ROS will use these files to create the necessary code for us to implement the msg and srv files to be used in our nodes.

Let's start with the msg file first.

In the example used in the *Building the node* section, we created two nodes with a standard type message. Now, we are going to learn how to create custom messages with the tools that ROS has.

First, create a new msg folder in our chapter2_tutorials package, create a new chapter2_msg1.msg file and the following lines:

```
int32 A
int32 B
int32 C
```

Now, edit package.xml and remove <!--   --> from the <build_depend>message_generation</build_depend> and <run_depend>message_runtime</run_depend> lines.

Edit `CMakeList.txt` and add the `message_generation` line as follows:

```
find_package(catkin REQUIRED COMPONENTS
  roscpp
  std_msgs
  message_generation
)
```

Find the next lines, uncomment, and add the name of the new message as follows:

```
## Generate messages in the 'msg' folder
add_message_files(
      FILES
      chapter2_msg1.msg
)

## Generate added messages and services with any dependencies listed here
 generate_messages(
    DEPENDENCIES
    std_msgs
  )
```

And now, you can compile using the following lines:

```
$ cd ~/dev/catkin_ws/
$ catkin_make
```

To check whether all is OK, you can use the `rosmsg` command:

```
$ rosmsg show chapter2_tutorials/chapter2_msg1
```

If you see the same content as that of the `chapter2_msg1.msg` file, all is OK.

Now, we are going to create a `srv` file. Create a new folder in the `chapter2_tutorials` folder with the name `srv`, create a new `chapter2_srv1.srv` file, and add the following lines:

```
int32 A
int32 B
int32 C
---
int32 sum
```

To compile the new `msg` and `srv` files, you have to uncomment the following lines in the `package.xml` and `CMakeLists.txt` files. These lines permit the configuration of the messages and services and tell ROS how and what to build.

[62]

First of all, open the `package.xml` folder from your `chapter2_tutorials` package as follows:

`$ rosed chapter2_tutorials package.xml`

Search for the following lines and uncomment them:

```
<build_depend>message_generation</build_depend>
<run_depend>message_runtime</run_depend>
```

Open `CMakeLists.txt` using the following command:

`$ rosed chapter2_tutorials CMakeLists.txt`

Find the following lines, uncomment them, and complete them with the correct data:

```
catkin_package(
CATKIN_DEPENDS message_runtime
)
```

To generate messages, you need to add the `message_generation` line in the `find_package` section:

```
find_package(catkin REQUIRED COMPONENTS
    roscpp
    std_msgs
    message_generation
)
```

Add the names of the message and service files in the `add_message_files` section, as follows:

```
## Generate messages in the 'msg' folder
add_message_files(
    FILES
    chapter2_msg1.msg
)

## Generate services in the 'srv' folder
add_service_files(
    FILES
    chapter2_srv1.srv
)
```

ROS Architecture and Concepts

Uncomment the `generate_messages` section to make sure that the generation of messages and services can be done:

```
## Generate added messages and services with any dependencies listed here
 generate_messages(
    DEPENDENCIES
    std_msgs
 )
```

You can test whether all is OK using the `rossrv` tool as follows:

```
$ rossrv show chapter2_tutorials/chapter2_srv1
```

If you see the same content as that of the `chapter2_srv1.srv` file, all is OK.

Using the new srv and msg files

First, we are going to learn how to create a service and how to use it in ROS. Our service will calculate the sum of three numbers. We need two nodes: a server and a client.

In the `chapter2_tutorials` package, create two new nodes with the following names: `example2_a.cpp` and `example2_b.cpp`. Remember to put the files in the `src` folder.

In the first file, `example2_a.cpp`, add the following code:

```
#include "ros/ros.h"
#include "chapter2_tutorials/chapter2_srv1.h"

bool add(chapter2_tutorials::chapter2_srv1::Request  &req,
         chapter2_tutorials::chapter2_srv1::Response &res)
{
  res.sum = req.A + req.B + req.C;
  ROS_INFO("request: A=%ld, B=%ld C=%ld", (int)req.A, (int)req.B, (int)req.C);
  ROS_INFO("sending back response: [%ld]", (int)res.sum);
  return true;
}

int main(int argc, char **argv)
{
  ros::init(argc, argv, "add_3_ints_server");
```

```
    ros::NodeHandle n;

    ros::ServiceServer service = n.advertiseService("add_3_ints", add);
    ROS_INFO("Ready to add 3 ints.");
    ros::spin();

    return 0;
}
```

Let's explain the code:

```
#include "ros/ros.h"
#include "chapter2_tutorials/chapter2_srv1.h"
```

These lines include the necessary headers and the `srv` file that we created:

```
bool add(chapter2_tutorials::chapter2_srv1::Request  &req,
         chapter2_tutorials::chapter2_srv1::Response &res)
```

This function will add three variables and send the result to the other node:

```
ros::ServiceServer service = n.advertiseService("add_3_ints", add);
```

Here, the service is created and advertised over ROS.

In the second file, `example2_b.cpp`, add this code:

```
#include "ros/ros.h"
#include "chapter2_tutorials/chapter2_srv1.h"
#include <cstdlib>

int main(int argc, char **argv)
{
  ros::init(argc, argv, "add_3_ints_client");
  if (argc != 4)
  {
    ROS_INFO("usage: add_3_ints_client A B C ");
    return 1;
  }

  ros::NodeHandle n;
  ros::ServiceClient client = n.serviceClient<chapter2_
tutorials::chapter2_srv1>("add_3_ints");
  chapter2_tutorials::chapter2_srv1 srv;
  srv.request.A = atoll(argv[1]);
  srv.request.B = atoll(argv[2]);
  srv.request.C = atoll(argv[3]);
```

```
   if (client.call(srv))
   {
     ROS_INFO("Sum: %ld", (long int)srv.response.sum);
   }
   else
   {
     ROS_ERROR("Failed to call service add_3_ints");
     return 1;
   }

   return 0;
}
```

Let's explain the code:

```
ros::ServiceClient client = n.serviceClient<chapter2_
tutorials::chapter2_srv1>("add_3_ints");
```

Create a client for the service with the name add_3_ints.

```
chapter2_tutorials::chapter2_srv1 srv;
srv.request.A = atoll(argv[1]);
srv.request.B = atoll(argv[2]);
srv.request.C = atoll(argv[3]);
```

Here, we create an instance of our srv file and fill all the values to be sent. If you remember, the message has three fields.

```
if (client.call(srv))
```

With this line, the service is called and the data is sent. If the call succeeds, call() will return true, and if not, call() will return false.

To build the new nodes, edit CMakeList.txt and add the following lines:

```
add_executable(chap2_example2_a src/example2_a.cpp)
add_executable(chap2_example2_b src/example2_b.cpp)

add_dependencies(chap2_example2_a chapter2_tutorials_generate_
messages_cpp)
add_dependencies(chap2_example2_b chapter2_tutorials_generate_
messages_cpp)

target_link_libraries(chap2_example2_a ${catkin_LIBRARIES})
target_link_libraries(chap2_example2_b ${catkin_LIBRARIES})
```

Chapter 2

Now, execute the following command:

```
$ cd ~/dev/catkin_ws
$ catkin_make
```

To start the nodes, execute the following command lines:

```
$ rosrun chapter2_tutorials example2_a
$ rosrun chapter2_tutorials example2_b 1 2 3
```

You should see something similar to this output:

```
Node example2_a
[ INFO] [1355256113.014539262]: Ready to add 3 ints.
[ INFO] [1355256115.792442091]: request: A=1, B=2 C=3
[ INFO] [1355256115.792607196]: sending back response: [6]
Node example2_b
[ INFO] [1355256115.794134975]: Sum: 6
```

Now, we are going to create nodes with our custom msg file. The example is the same, that is, example1_a.cpp and example1_b.cpp, but with the new message, chapter2_msg1.msg.

The following code snippet is present in the example3_a.cpp file:

```
#include "ros/ros.h"
#include "chapter2_tutorials/chapter2_msg1.h"
#include <sstream>

int main(int argc, char **argv)
{
  ros::init(argc, argv, "example3_a");
  ros::NodeHandle n;
  ros::Publisher pub = n.advertise<chapter2_tutorials::chapter2_msg1>("message", 1000);
  ros::Rate loop_rate(10);
  while (ros::ok())
  {
    chapter2_tutorials::chapter2_msg1 msg;
    msg.A = 1;
    msg.B = 2;
    msg.C = 3;
    pub.publish(msg);
    ros::spinOnce();
    loop_rate.sleep();
```

```
    }
    return 0;
}
```

The following code snippet is present in the `example3_b.cpp` file:

```cpp
#include "ros/ros.h"
#include "chapter2_tutorials/chapter2_msg1.h"

void messageCallback(const chapter2_tutorials::chapter2_
msg1::ConstPtr& msg)
{
  ROS_INFO("I heard: [%d] [%d] [%d]", msg->A, msg->B, msg->C);
}

int main(int argc, char **argv)
{
  ros::init(argc, argv, "example3_b");
  ros::NodeHandle n;
  ros::Subscriber sub = n.subscribe("message", 1000, messageCallback);
  ros::spin();
  return 0;
}
```

If we run both nodes now, we will see something similar to the following output:

```
...
[ INFO] [1355270835.920368620]: I heard: [1] [2] [3]
[ INFO] [1355270836.020326372]: I heard: [1] [2] [3]
[ INFO] [1355270836.120367449]: I heard: [1] [2] [3]
[ INFO] [1355270836.220266466]: I heard: [1] [2] [3]
...
```

The launch file

The launch file is a useful feature in ROS to launch more than one node. In these sections, we have created nodes, and we have been executing them in different shells. Imagine working with 20 nodes and the nightmare of executing each one in a shell!

With the launch file, we can do it in the same shell by launching a configuration file with the extension .launch.

To practice with this utility, we are going to create a new folder in our package as follows:

```
$ roscd chapter2_tutorials/
$ mkdir launch
$ cd launch
$ vim chapter2.launch
```

Now, put the following code inside the chapter2.launch file:

```
<?xml version="1.0"?>
<launch>
   <node name ="example1_a" pkg="chapter2_tutorials" type="example1_a"/>
   <node name ="example1_b" pkg="chapter2_tutorials" type="example1_b"/>
</launch>
```

This file is simple although you can write a very complex file if you want, for example, to control a complete robot, such as PR2 or Robonaut. Both are real robots and they are simulated in ROS.

The file has a launch tag; inside this tag, you can see the node tag. The node tag is used to launch a node from a package, for example, the example1_a node from the chapter2_tutorials package.

This launch file will execute two nodes—the first two examples of this chapter. If you remember, the example1_a node sends a message to the example1_b node. To launch the file, you can use the following command:

```
$ roslaunch chapter2_tutorials chapter2.launch
```

ROS Architecture and Concepts

You will see something similar to the following screenshot on your screen:

```
started roslaunch server http://127.0.0.1:40930/

SUMMARY
========

PARAMETERS
 * /rosdistro
 * /rosversion

NODES
  /
    example1_a (chapter2_tutorials/example1_a)
    example1_b (chapter2_tutorials/example1_b)

auto-starting new master
process[master]: started with pid [19889]
ROS_MASTER_URI=http://localhost:11311

setting /run_id to b334800a-f940-11e3-989f-080027b05884
process[rosout-1]: started with pid [19902]
started core service [/rosout]
process[example1_a-2]: started with pid [19914]
process[example1_b-3]: started with pid [19925]
```

The running nodes are listed in the screenshot. You can also see the running nodes using the following command:

```
$ rosnode list
```

You will see the three nodes listed as follows:

```
/example1_a
/example1_b
/rosout
```

When you launch a launch file, it is not necessary to execute it before the `roscore` command; `roslaunch` does it for us.

Remember that the `example1_b` node prints in the screen the message received from the other node. If you take a look, you won't see anything. This is because `example1_b` prints the message using `ROS_INFO`, and when you run only a node in a shell, you can see it, but when you run a launch file, you can't.

Now, to see the message printed in the screen, you can use the `rqt_console` utility. You will learn more about this utility in the following chapters. Now, run the following command:

```
$ rqt_console
```

You will see the message sent by `example1_b`, as shown in the following screenshot:

On the line, you can see the message, the node that has sent it, and the path of the source file.

Dynamic parameters

Another utility in ROS is the Dynamic Reconfigure utility. Normally, when you are programming a new node, you initialize the variables with data that can only be changed within the node. If you want to change these values dynamically from outside the node, you can use Parameter Server, services, or topics. If you are working in a PID node to control a motor, for example, you should use the Dynamic Reconfigure utility.

In this section, you will learn how to configure a basic node with this feature. Add the necessary lines in the `CMakeLists.txt` and `package.xml` files.

To use Dynamic Reconfigure, you should write a configuration file and save it in the `cfg` folder in your package. Create the folder and a new file as follows:

```
$ roscd chapter2_tutorials
$ mkdir cfg
$ vim chapter2.cfg
```

ROS Architecture and Concepts

Write the following code in the `chapter2.cfg` file:

```python
#!/usr/bin/env python
PACKAGE = "chapter2_tutorials"

from dynamic_reconfigure.parameter_generator_catkin import *

gen = ParameterGenerator()

gen.add("double_param", double_t, 0, "A double parameter", .1, 0,   1)
gen.add("str_param", str_t, 0, "A string parameter", "Chapter2_dynamic_reconfigure")
gen.add("int_param", int_t, 0, "An Integer parameter", 1,  0, 100)
gen.add("bool_param",  bool_t, 0, "A Boolean parameter",  True)

size_enum = gen.enum([ gen.const("Low", int_t, 0, "Low is 0"),
                       gen.const("Medium", int_t, 1, "Medium is 1"),
                       gen.const("High", int_t, 2, "Hight is 2")],
                     "Select from the list")

gen.add("size", int_t, 0, "Select from the list", 1, 0, 3, edit_method=size_enum)

exit(gen.generate(PACKAGE, "chapter2_tutorials", "chapter2_"))
```

Let's explain the code:

```python
#!/usr/bin/env python
PACKAGE = "chapter2_tutorials"

from dynamic_reconfigure.parameter_generator_catkin import *
```

These lines initialize ROS and import the parameter generator:

```python
gen = ParameterGenerator()
```

This line initializes the parameter generator, and thanks to it, we can start to add parameters in the following lines:

```python
gen.add("double_param", double_t, 0, "A double parameter", .1, 0,   1)
gen.add("str_param", str_t, 0, "A string parameter", "Chapter2_dynamic_reconfigure")
gen.add("int_param", int_t, 0, "An Integer parameter", 1,  0, 100)
gen.add("bool_param",  bool_t, 0, "A Boolean parameter",  True)
```

These lines add different parameter types and set the default values, description, range, and so on. The parameter has the following arguments:

```
gen.add(name, type, level, description, default, min, max)
```

- `name`: This is the name of the parameter
- `type`: This is the type of the value stored
- `level`: This is a bitmask that is passed to the callback
- `description`: This is a little description that describes the parameter
- `default`: This is the default value when the node starts
- `min`: This is the minimum value for the parameter
- `max`: This is the maximum value for the parameter

The names of the parameters must be unique, and the values have to be in the range and have `min` and `max` values:

```
exit(gen.generate(PACKAGE, "chapter2_tutorials", "chapter2_"))
```

The last line generates the necessary files and exits the program. Notice that the `.cfg` file was written in Python. This book is for C++ snippets, but we will sometimes use Python snippets.

It is necessary to change the permissions for the file because the file will be executed by ROS. To make the file executable and runnable by any user, we will use the `chmod` command with the `a+x` parameter as follows:

$ chmod a+x cfg/chapter2.cfg

Open `CMakeList.txt` and add the following lines:

```
find_package(catkin REQUIRED COMPONENTS
  roscpp
  std_msgs
  message_generation
  dynamic_reconfigure
)

generate_dynamic_reconfigure_options(
  cfg/chapter2.cfg
)

add_dependencies(example4 chapter2_tutorials_gencfg)
```

ROS Architecture and Concepts

Now, we are going to write our new node with Dynamic Reconfigure support. Create a new file in your `src` folder as follows:

```
$ roscd chapter2_tutorials
$ vim src/example4.cpp
```

Write the following code snippet in the file:

```cpp
#include <ros/ros.h>
#include <dynamic_reconfigure/server.h>
#include <chapter2_tutorials/chapter2Config.h>

void callback(chapter2_tutorials::chapter2Config &config, uint32_t level) {
  ROS_INFO("Reconfigure Request: %d %f %s %s %d",
        config.int_param,
        config.double_param,
        config.str_param.c_str(),
        config.bool_param?"True":"False",
        config.size);
}

int main(int argc, char **argv) {
  ros::init(argc, argv, "example4_dynamic_reconfigure");

  dynamic_reconfigure::Server<chapter2_tutorials::chapter2Config> server;
  dynamic_reconfigure::Server<chapter2_tutorials::chapter2Config>::CallbackType f;

  f = boost::bind(&callback, _1, _2);
  server.setCallback(f);

  ros::spin();
  return 0;
}
```

Let's explain the code and note the important lines:

```cpp
#include <ros/ros.h>
#include <dynamic_reconfigure/server.h>
#include <chapter2_tutorials/chapter2Config.h>
```

These lines include the headers for ROS, Parameter Server, and our `config` file created earlier:

```
void callback(chapter2_tutorials::chapter2Config &config, uint32_t
level) {
  ROS_INFO("Reconfigure Request: %d %f %s %s %d",
         config.int_param,
         config.double_param,
         config.str_param.c_str(),
         config.bool_param?"True":"False",
         config.size);
}
```

The callback function will print the new values for the parameters. The way to access the parameters is, for example, `config.int_param`. The name of the parameter must be the same as the one that you configured in the `example2.cfg` file:

```
dynamic_reconfigure::Server<chapter2_tutorials::chapter2Config>
server;
```

The server is initialized in the line where we pass the `chapter2_Config` configuration file:

```
dynamic_reconfigure::Server<chapter2_tutorials::chapter2Config>::Call
backType f;

f = boost::bind(&callback, _1, _2);
server.setCallback(f);
```

Now, we send the callback function to the server. When the server gets a reconfiguration request, it will call the callback function.

Once we are done with the explanation, we need to add lines to the `CMakeLists.txt` file as follows:

```
add_executable(chap2_example4 src/example4.cpp)

add_dependencies(chap2_example4 chapter2_tutorials_gencfg)

target_link_libraries(chap2_example4 ${catkin_LIBRARIES})
```

Now, you have to compile and run the node and the Dynamic Reconfigure GUI as follows:

```
$ roscore
$ rosrun chapter2_tutorials example4
$ rosrun rqt_reconfigure rqt_reconfigure
```

ROS Architecture and Concepts

When you execute the last command, you will see a new window where you can modify dynamically the parameters of the node, as shown in the following screenshot:

Each time you modify a parameter with the slider, the checkbox, and so on, you will see the changes made in the shell where the node is running. You can see an example in the following screenshot:

```
[ INFO] [1403367196.752115948]: Reconfigure Request: 20 0.800000 qwert True 1
[ INFO] [1403367196.942722848]: Reconfigure Request: 20 0.800000 qwerty True 1
[ INFO] [1403367196.973132691]: Reconfigure Request: 20 0.800000 qwerty True 1
[ INFO] [1403367197.183714401]: Reconfigure Request: 20 0.800000 qwertyu True 1
[ INFO] [1403367197.217819018]: Reconfigure Request: 20 0.800000 qwertyu True 1
[ INFO] [1403367203.160337570]: Reconfigure Request: 1 0.800000 qwertyu True 1
[ INFO] [1403367203.188864110]: Reconfigure Request: 1 0.800000 qwertyu True 1
```

Thanks to Dynamic Reconfigure, you can program and test your nodes more efficiently and in a fast way. Using the program with hardware is a good choice and you will learn more about it in the next chapters.

Summary

This chapter provided you with general information about the ROS architecture and how it works. You saw certain concepts, tools, and samples of how to interact with nodes, topics, and services. In the beginning, all of these concepts might look complicated and without use, but in the upcoming chapters, you will start to understand their applications.

It is useful to practice using these terms and tutorials before continuing because, in the upcoming chapters, we will assume that you know all of the concepts and uses.

Remember that if you have queries about something and you cannot find the solution in this book, you can use the official resources of ROS from `http://www.ros.org`. Additionally, you can ask the ROS community questions at `http://answers.ros.org`.

In the next chapter, you will learn how to debug and visualize data using ROS tools. This will help you to find problems, know whether what ROS is doing is correct, and better define what your expectations from it are.

3
Visualization and Debug Tools

ROS has a good number of tools that allow the user and the developer to visualize and debug the code in order to detect and solve issues with both hardware and software. This comprises a message logging system similar to `log4cxx`, diagnostic messages and also visualization and inspection tools that show which nodes are running and how are they connected.

In this chapter, we will also show you how to debug an ROS node with the GDB debugger. The message logging API will be explained, and advice will be given on how to choose the logging level. Then, we will explain the set of ROS tools that are meant to inspect which processes are running and what information is communicated among them. For instance, the following figure shows a tool that visualizes the graph of the system, where the nodes are the processes running and the edges represent the data workflow through communication topics. This tool is `rqt_graph`, and in this case, it show the nodes and topics for the REEM robot running on a Gazebo simulation.

Visualization and Debug Tools

You can see multiple controllers for the arms, torso, head, **MoveIt!** `move_group` node, pick and place action servers, and `play_motion` node for pre-recorded movements. Other nodes publish `joint_states`, spawn the robot controllers, and control the joystick to move the mobile base.

Similarly, this chapter will show you how to plot scalar data in a time series, visualize images from a video stream, and represent different types of data in a 3D representation using (the widely known) `rviz` (or `rqt_rviz`) shown in the following screenshot:

The preceding screenshot shows the REEM robot, which can be run in simulation with the following command:

```
$ roslaunch reem_2dnav_gazebo reem_navigation.launch
```

> **Downloading the example code**
>
> You can download the example code files from your account at http://www.packtpub.com for all the Packt Publishing books you have purchased. If you purchased this book elsewhere, you can visit http://www.packtpub.com/support and register to have the files e-mailed directly to you. You can also download these code files from https://github.com/AaronMR/ROS_Book_Hydro.

Note that, before you install it, you follow the instructions provided at http://wiki.ros.org/Robots/REEM.

In the next sections, we will do the following:

- We will look at how to debug our code in ROS.
- We will look at how to use logging messages in our code, with different severity levels, names, conditions, and throttling options. Here, we will explain the `rqt_logger_level` and `rqt_console` interfaces, which allow setting the severity level of a node and visualizing the message, respectively.
- We will look at how to inspect the state of the ROS system by listing the nodes running, the topics, services, and actions they use to transfer messages among them, and the parameters declared in the ROS master server. We will explain `rqt_graph`, which shows nodes and topics in a directed graph representation, and `rqt_reconfigure`, which allows changing dynamic parameters.
- We will look at how to visualize diagnostics information using the `runtime_monitor` and `robot_monitor` interfaces.
- We will look at how to plot scalar data from messages using `rqt_plot`. For nonscalar data, we will explain other `rqt` tools available in ROS, such as `rqt_image_view` to visualize images and `rqt_rviz` to show multiple data in a 3D representation. We also show how to visualize markers and interactive markers.
- We will explain what frames are and how they are integrated into ROS messages and visualization tools. We also explain how to use `rqt_tf_tree` to visualize the **Transform Frame (tf)** tree.
- We will look at how to save messages and replay them for simulation or evaluation purposes. We also explain the `rqt_bag` interface.
- Finally, other `rqt_gui` interfaces are explained as well as how to arrange them in a single GUI.

Most of the `rqt` tools can be run by simply putting their name in the terminal, such as `rqt_console`, but in some cases, this does not work and we must use `rosrun rqt_reconfigure rqt_reconfigure`, which always works; note that the name seems to be repeated but it is actually the package name and the node name one after the other.

Debugging ROS nodes

ROS nodes can be debugged as regular programs. They run as a process in the operative system and have a PID. Therefore, you can debug them as with any program using standard tools, such as gdb. Similarly, you can check for memory leaks with valgrind or profile the performance of your algorithm with callgrind. However, remember that in order to run a node, you must run the following command:

```
$ rosrun chapter3_tutorials example1
```

Unfortunately, you cannot run the command in the following way:

```
$ gdb rosrun chapter3_tutorials example1
```

In the next sections, we will explain how to call these tools for an ROS node to overcome this issue. Later, we will see how to add a logging message to our code in order to make it simple to diagnose problems that, in practice, helps to diagnose basic problems even without debugging the binaries. Similar, later on, we will discuss ROS introspection tools that allow detecting broken connections between nodes easily. Therefore, although here we will show you a bottom-up overview, in practice, we follow a top-down approach to diagnose issues.

Using the GDB debugger with ROS nodes

In order to debug a C/C++ node with the gdb debugger, all we have to know is the location of the node executable. With the ROS hydro and catkin packages, the node executable is placed inside the devel/lib/<package> folder within the workspace. For example, in order to run the example1 node from the chapter3_tutorials package in gdb, we have to proceed as follows, starting from the workspace folder (~/dev/catkin_ws):

```
$ cd devel/lib/chapter3_tutorials
```

If you have run catkin_make install, you can also navigate to the install/lib/chapter3_tutorials directory using the following code:

```
$ cd install/lib/chapter3_tutorials
```

Visualization and Debug Tools

Now we can run the node executable inside `gdb` with the following command:

`$ gdb example1`

> Remember that you must have `roscore` running before you start your node because it will need the master/server running.

Once `roscore` is running, you can start your node in `gdb` by pressing the *R* key (and *Enter*), and you can also list the associated source code with the *L* key as well as setting breakpoints or any of the functionalities that `gdb` comes with. If everything is correct, you should see the following output in the `gdb` terminal after running the node:

```
(gdb) r
Starting program: ~/dev/catkin_ws/devel/lib/chapter3_tutorials /example1
[Thread debugging using libthread_db enabled]
Using host libthread_db library "/lib/x86_64-linux-gnu/libthread_db.so.1".
[New Thread 0x7ffff2664700 (LWP 3204)]
[New Thread 0x7ffff1e63700 (LWP 3205)]
[New Thread 0x7ffff1662700 (LWP 3206)]
[New Thread 0x7ffff0e61700 (LWP 3211)]
[DEBUG] [1356342615.325647326]: This is a simple DEBUG message!
[DEBUG] [1356342615.326124607]: This is a DEBUG message with an argument: 3.140000
[DEBUG] [1356342615.326254667]: This is DEBUG stream message with an argument: 3.14
[Thread 0x7ffff0e61700 (LWP 3211) exited]
[Thread 0x7ffff1662700 (LWP 3206) exited]
[Thread 0x7ffff2664700 (LWP 3204) exited]
[Thread 0x7ffff1e63700 (LWP 3205) exited]
[Inferior 1 (process 3200) exited normally]
```

Attaching a node to GDB while launching ROS

We might get a `launch` file that starts the node, as in this example:

```
<launch>
  <node pkg="chapter3_tutorials" type="example1" name="example1"/>
</launch>
```

In order to attach it to `gdb`, we must add `launch-prefix="xterm -e gdb --args"` as follows:

```
<launch>
<node pkg="chapter3_tutorials" type="example1" name="example1"
  launch-prefix="xterm -e gdb --args"/>
</launch>
```

Similarly, you can also add `output="screen"` to make the node output appear on the terminal. With this launch prefix, a new `xterm` terminal will be created with the node attached to `gdb`. Set breakpoints if needed, and then press the *C* or *R* key to run the node and debug it. For example, this is useful to obtain a backtrace (`bt`) if the node crashes.

Profiling a node with valgrind while launching ROS

Additionally, we can use the same attribute to attach the node to diagnosis tools. For example, we can run `valgrind` (see http://valgrind.org for further information) on our program to detect memory leaks and perform profiling analysis. Contrary to attaching to `gdb`, now we do not need to start `xterm` anew:

```
<launch>
<node pkg="chapter3_tutorials" type="example1"
  name="example1" output="screen"
  launch-prefix="valgrind"/>
</launch>
```

Visualization and Debug Tools

Enabling core dumps for ROS nodes

Although ROS nodes are actually regular executables, there is a tricky point to enable core dumps, which can later be used in a `gdb` session. First of all, we have to set an unlimited core size; the current value can be checked with `ulimit -a`. Note that this is also required for any executable and not just ROS nodes:

```
$ ulimit -c unlimited
```

Then, to allow core dumps to be created, we must set the core filename to use the `pid` process by default. Otherwise, they will not be created because at `$ROS_HOME`, there is already a `core` directory to prevent core dumps. Therefore, in order to create core dumps with the name and path `$ROS_HOME/core.PID`, we must run the following command:

```
$ echo 1 | sudo tee /proc/sys/kernel/core_uses_pid
```

Logging messages

It is a good practice to include messages that indicate what the program is doing. But we must do it without compromising on the efficiency of our software and the clarity of its output. In ROS, we have an API that covers both features, built on top of `log4cxx` (a port of the well-known `log4j` logger library). In brief, we have several levels of messages, which might have a name (named messages) and depend on a condition or even throttle. All of them have a null footprint on performance if they are masked by the current verbosity level (even at compile time). They also have full integration with other ROS tools to visualize and filter the messages from all the nodes running.

Outputting a logging message

ROS comes with a great number of functions/macros to output logging messages. It supports different levels, conditions, STL streams, throttling, and other features that we will see in this section. To start with something simple, an information message is printed with this code in C++:

```
$ ROS_INFO("My INFO message.");
```

In order to have access to these logging functions/macros, this header is enough:

```
#include <ros/ros.h>
```

This includes the following header (where the logging API is defined):

```
#include <ros/console.h>
```

As a result of running a program with the preceding message, we will get the following output:

```
[ INFO] [1356440230.837067170]: My INFO message.
```

All messages are printed with their level and the current timestamp (your output might differ for this reason), before the actual message, with both between square brackets. The timestamp is the `epoch` time, that is, the seconds and nanoseconds since January 1, 1970. Then, we have our message—always with a newline:

This function allows parameters in the same way as the C `printf` function does. For example, we can print the value of a floating point number in the variable `val` with this code:

```
float val = 1.23;
ROS_INFO("My INFO message with argument: %f", val);
```

Also, C++ STL streams are supported with `*_STREAM` functions. Therefore, the previous instruction is equivalent to the following using streams:

```
ROS_INFO_STREAM("My INFO message with argument: " << val);
```

Note that we did not specify any stream since the API takes care of that by redirecting to `cout/cerr`, a file, or both.

Setting the debug message level

ROS supports the following logging levels (in the increasing order of relevance):

- DEBUG
- INFO
- WARN
- ERROR
- FATAL

These names are part of the function used to output messages following this syntax:

```
ROS_<LEVEL>[_<OTHER>]
```

Each message is printed with a particular color. The colors are as follows:

```
DEBUG in green
INFO in white
WARN in yellow
ERROR in red
FATAL in purple
```

Each message level is meant to be used for a different purpose. Here, we suggest uses for the following levels:

- `DEBUG`: These messages are useful only when debugging
- `INFO`: These messages indicate significant steps or what the node is doing
- `WARN`: These messages warn you that something might be wrong, missed, or abnormal
- `ERROR`: These messages indicate errors although the node can still run
- `FATAL`: These error messages usually prevent the node from continuing to run

Configuring the debugging level of a particular node

By default, only messages of `INFO` or higher levels are shown. ROS uses the levels to filter the messages printed by a particular node. There are many ways to do so. Some of them are set at the time of compilation and some messages aren't even compiled below a given verbosity level; others can be changed before execution using a configuration file, and it is also possible to change that level dynamically using the `rqt_console` and `rqt_logger_level` tools.

It is possible to set the logging level at compile time in our source code, but this is very uncommon and not recommended because it requires us to modify the source code to change the logging level; please refer to *Learning ROS for Robotics Programming, Packt Publishing*, if you want to see how to do it.

Nevertheless, in some cases, we need to remove the overhead of all the logging functions below a given level. In that case, we want to be able to see those messages later because they get removed from the code and not just disabled. To do so, we must set `ROSCONSOLE_MIN_SEVERITY` to the minimum severity level desired or even none in order to avoid any message (even `FATAL`). The macros are as follows:

```
ROSCONSOLE_SEVERITY_DEBUG
ROSCONSOLE_SEVERITY_INFO
ROSCONSOLE_SEVERITY_WARN
```

```
ROSCONSOLE_SEVERITY_ERROR
ROSCONSOLE_SEVERITY_FATAL
ROSCONSOLE_SEVERITY_NONE
```

The `ROSCONSOLE_MIN_SEVERITY` macro is defined in `<ros/console.h>` to the DEBUG level if not given. Therefore, we can pass it as a built argument (with `-D`) or put it before all the headers. For example, to show only ERROR (or higher) messages, we will put this in our source code:

```
#define ROSCONSOLE_MIN_SEVERITY ROSCONSOLE_SEVERITY_ERROR
```

Alternatively, we can set this to all the nodes in a package setting this macro in `CMakeLists.txt` by adding this line:

```
add_definitions(-DROSCONSOLE_MIN_SEVERITY=ROSCONSOLE_SEVERITY_ERROR)
```

On the other hand, we have the more flexible solution of setting the minimum logging level in a configuration file. We create a `config` folder with a file, such as `chapter3_tutorials.config`, and this content (edit the file given since it is set to DEBUG):

```
log4j.logger.ros.chapter3_tutorials=ERROR
```

Then, we must set the `ROSCONSOLE_CONFIG_FILE` environment variable to point to our file. We can do this on a `launch` file that also runs the node. Therefore, we will extend the `launch` file shown earlier to do so with the `env` (environment variable) element as shown here:

```
<launch>
  <!-- Logger config -->
  <env name="ROSCONSOLE_CONFIG_FILE"
       value="$(find chapter3_tutorials)/config/chapter3_tutorials.config"/>

  <!-- Example 1 -->
  <node pkg="chapter3_tutorials" type="example1" name="example1"
        output="screen"/>
</launch>
```

The environment variable takes the configuration file shown previously, which contains the logging level specification for each named logger; in this case, it is for the package name.

Visualization and Debug Tools

Giving names to messages

By default, ROS assigns several names to the node loggers. The messages discussed until now will be named after the node's name. In complex nodes, we can give a name to those messages of a given module or functionality. This is done with ROS_<LEVEL>[_STREAM]_NAMED functions (see the `example2` node):

```
ROS_INFO_STREAM_NAMED(
  "named_msg",
  "My named INFO stream message; val = " << val
);
```

With named messages, we can set different initial logging levels for each named message using the configuration file and modify them individually later. We must use the name of the messages as children of the package in the specification; for example, for `named_msg` messages, we will use the following code:

```
log4j.logger.ros.chapter3_tutorials.named_msg=ERROR
```

Conditional and filtered messages

Conditional messages are printed only when a given condition is satisfied. To use them, we have the ROS_<LEVEL>[_STREAM]_COND[_NAMED] functions; note that they can be named messages as well (see the `example2` node for more examples and combinations):

```
ROS_INFO_STREAM_COND(
  val < 0.,
  "My conditional INFO stream message; val (" << val << ") < 0"
);
```

Filtered messages are similar to conditional message in essence, but they allow us to specify a user-defined filter that extends `ros::console::FilterBase`; we must pass a pointer to such a filter in the first argument of a macro with the format ROS_<LEVEL>[_STREAM]_FILTER[_NAMED]. The following example is taken from the `example2` node:

```
struct MyLowerFilter : public ros::console::FilterBase {
  MyLowerFilter( const double& val ) : value( val ) {}
  inline virtual bool isEnabled() { return value < 0.; }
  double value;
};

MyLowerFilter filter_lower( val );

ROS_INFO_STREAM_FILTER(&filter_lower,
  "My filter INFO stream message; val (" << val << ") < 0"
);
```

Showing messages in the once, throttle, and other combinations

It is also possible to control how many times a given message is shown. We can print it only once with ROS_<LEVEL>[_STREAM]_ONCE[_NAMED]:

```
for( int i = 0; i < 10; ++i ) {
  ROS_INFO_STREAM_ONCE("My once INFO stream message; i = " << i);
}
```

This code from the example2 node will show the message only once.

However, it is usually better to show the message with a certain frequency. For that, we have throttle messages. They have the same format as the once message, but here ONCE is replaced with THROTTLE, and they have a first argument, which is period, that is, it is printed only every period seconds:

```
for( int i = 0; i < 10; ++i ) {
  ROS_INFO_STREAM_THROTTLE(2,
    "My throttle INFO stream message; i = " << i);
  ros::Duration( 1 ).sleep();
}
```

Finally, note that named, conditional, and once/throttle messages can be used together with all the available levels.

Nodelets also have some support in terms of logging messages. Since they have their own namespace, they have a specific name to differentiate the message of one nodelet from another. Simply put, all the macros shown until now are valid, but instead of ROS_*, we have NODELET_*. These macros will only compile inside nodelets. Also, they operate by setting up a named logger with the name of the nodelet running so that you can differentiate between the outputs of two nodelets of the same type running in the same nodelet manager. They also have the advantage that you can turn one specific nodelet into the debug level instead of all the nodelets of a specific type.

Using rqt_console and rqt_logger_level to modify the debugging level on the fly

ROS provides a series of tools to manage logging messages. In ROS hydro, we have two separate GUIs: `rqt_logger_level` to set the logging level of the nodes or named loggers and `rqt_console` to visualize, filter, and analyze the logging messages.

In order to test this, we are going to use `example3`. Run `roscore` and `rqt_console` to see the logging messages:

```
$ rosrun rqt_console rqt_console
```

The following window will open:

Now run the node:

```
$ rosrun chapter3_tutorials example3
```

You will start seeing the logging messages, as the next screenshot shows. Note that `roscore` must be running and that you must press the recording button on `rqt_console`.

In `rqt_console`, the messages are collected and shown in a table where different columns separate the timestamp, the message itself, the severity level, and the node that produced that message, besides other information. You can fit the columns automatically by pressing the **Resize columns** button. If you double-click on a message, you can see all the information, including the line of code that generated it, as shown in the screenshot:

Visualization and Debug Tools

This interface allows pausing, saving, and loading previous/saved logging messages. We can clear the list of messages and filter them. In ROS `hydro`, excluding filtered ones, the messages have specific interfaces depending on the filter criteria. For instance, nodes can be filtered with a single rule, where we select the nodes we want to exclude. Additionally, in the same way, we can set highlighting filters. This is shown in the following screenshot:

As an example, the messages from the previous image are filtered by excluding those with a severity different than ERROR and FATAL.

Chapter 3

In order to set the severity of the loggers, we must run the following command:

```
$ rosrun rqt_logger_level rqt_logger_level
```

Here, we can select the node, then the named logger, and finally its severity. Once we modify it, the new messages received with a severity below the desired one will not appear in `rqt_console`:

Shown in the next screenshot is an example where we set the severity level to the minimum (DEBUG) for the named logger, `ros.chapter3_tutorials.named_msg`, of the `example3` node; remember that the named loggers are created by the `*_NAMED` logging functions:

As you can see, every node has several internal loggers by default, which are related to the ROS communication API, among others; in general, you should not reduce their severity.

Inspecting what is going on

When our system is running, we might have several nodes and many more topics publishing messages among nodes. Also, we might have nodes providing actions or services as well. For large systems, it is important to have tools that let us see what is running at a given time. ROS provides basic but powerful tools with this aim, from the CLI to GUI applications.

Listing nodes, topics, services, and parameters

In our honest opinion, we will start with the most basic level of introspection. We are going to see how to obtain the list of nodes running and topics and services available at a given time:

Obtain the list of all	Command
Nodes running	`rosnode list`
Topics of all nodes running	`rostopic list`
Services of all nodes running	`rosservice list`
Parameters on the server	`rosparam list`

We recommend that you go back to *Chapter 2, ROS Architecture and Concepts*, to see how these commands also allow us to obtain the message type sent by a particular topic as well as its fields, using `rosmsg show`.

Any of these commands can be combined with regular bash commands, such as `grep`, to look for the desired nodes, topics, services, or parameters. For example, action goal topics can be found using the following command:

```
$ rostopic list | grep goal
```

The `grep` bash command looks for text or patterns in a list of files or the standard output, which can be piped as shown in this example.

Chapter 3

Additionally, ROS provides several GUIs to play with topics and services. First, `rqt_top` shows the nodes running in an interface similar to a table of processes (ToP), which allows us to rapidly see all the nodes and resources they are using. For this screenshot, we have used the REEM simulation with the navigation stack running, as an example:

On the other hand, `rqt_topic` shows the debugging information about topics, including publishers, subscribers, the publishing rate, and messages published. You can view the message fields topic and select the topics you want to subscribe to, to analyze their bandwidth and rate (Hz) and see the latest message published; note that latched topics usually do not publish continuously, so you will not see any information about them. The following screenshot shows this:

Visualization and Debug Tools

Similarly, `rqt_publisher` allows us to manage multiple instances of `rostopic pub` commands in a single interface. It also supports Python expressions for the published messages and fixed values. In the next screenshot, we will see two example topics being published (we will see the messages using `rostopic echo <topic>` in two different terminals).

An alternative with a more flexible GUI is `rqt_ez_publisher`. For ROS `hydro`, you must install it manually using the following code from an empty workspace:

```
$ cd src
$ git clone https://github.com/OTL/rqt_ez_publisher.git
$ cd ..
$ catkin_make
$ source devel/setup.bash
```

For ROS `indigo`, it will come as a Debian package, so you will only have to run the following command:

```
$ sudo apt-get install ros-indigo-rqt-ez-publisher
```

Then, just run the following command:

```
$ rosrun rqt_ez_publisher rqt_ez_publisher
```

With the `example5` node running, you can publish messages that will be read by this node. In the next screenshot, we will select the `accel` and `temp` topics (and remove the `accel/y` and `accel/z` fields):

Note that with `repeat` enabled, the messages are continuously published; otherwise, the GUI only publishes the messages when you change the values.

And `rqt_service_caller` does the same thing for multiple instances of `rosservice call` commands. In the next screenshot, we will call the `/move_base/NavfnROS/make_plan` service, where we have to set up the request; for empty services, this is not needed as the `/global_localization` service from the `/amcl` node. After clicking on the **Call** button, we will obtain the response message. For this example, we have used the REEM simulation with the navigation stack running:

Inspecting the node's graph online with rqt_graph

The current state of an ROS session can be shown as a directed graph where the nodes running are the graph nodes and the edges are the publisher-subscriber connections among these nodes through the topics. This graph is drawn dynamically by `rqt_graph`:

```
$ rosrun rqt_graph rqt_graph
```

In order to illustrate how to inspect the nodes, topics, and services with `rqt_graph`, we are going to run the `example4` and `example5` nodes simultaneously with the following launch file:

```
$ roslaunch chapter3_tutorials example4_5.launch
```

The `example4` node publishes in two different topics and calls a service. Meanwhile, `example5` subscribes to those topics and also has the service server to attend the request queries and provide the response. Once the nodes are running, we have the node's topology in the next screenshot:

Visualization and Debug Tools

In this screenshot, we have the nodes connected by the topics. Since `Hide Debug` is selected, we do not see the ROS server node `rosout` as well as the `rosout` topic that publishes the logging messages for the diagnostic aggregator in the server, as we did previously. We can deselect this option to show the debug nodes/topics, so that the ROS server is shown as well as the `rqt_graph` node itself (see the next screenshot). It is useful to hide these nodes for large systems because it simplifies the graph. Also, with ROS `hydro`, the nodes in the same namespace are grouped, for example, the image pipeline nodes:

When there is a problem in the system, the nodes appear in red all the time (not just when we move the mouse over them). In those cases, among others, it is useful to select `all topics` to also show unconnected topics. This usually shows misspelled topic names that break connections among nodes.

When running nodes in different machines, `rqt_graph` shows its great high-level debugging capabilities since it shows whether the nodes see each other from one machine to the other, enumerating the connections.

Finally, we can enable statistics to see the message rate and bandwidth represented in the topic edge, with the rate written and the line width, as shown in the next figure. We must set this parameter before running `rqt_graph` in order to have this information available:

```
$ rosparam set enable_statistics true
```

Unfortunately, this parameter it is not available to ROS `hydro` yet. It will come with ROS `indigo` (the next distribution), and it will be probably backported to `hydro`.

Setting dynamic parameters

If a node implements a dynamic reconfigure parameter server, we can use `rqt_reconfigure` to modify them on the fly. Run the following example, which implements a dynamic reconfigure server with several parameters (see the `cfg` file in the `cfg` folder of the package).

```
$ roslaunch chapter3_tutorials example6.launch
```

With the dynamic reconfigure server running, open the GUI with the following command:

```
$ rosrun rqt_reconfigure rqt_reconfigure
```

Select the `example6` server in the left-hand side table list, and you will see its parameters, which you can modify directly. The parameter changes take effect immediately, running the code inside a callback method in the source code, which checks for the validity of the values. In this example, the parameters are printed every time they are changed, that is, when the callback method is executed. The following screenshot encapsulates this discussion:

Visualization and Debug Tools

Dynamic parameters were originally meant for drivers, so it was easy to modify them. For this reason, several drivers already implement them; nevertheless, they can be used for any other node. Examples of drivers that implement them are the `hokuyo_node` driver for the Hokuyo laser rangefinders or the Firewire `camera1394` driver. Indeed, in the case of Firewire cameras, it is common for drivers to support changing some configuration parameters of the sensor, such as the frame rate, shutter speed, and brightness, among others. The ROS driver for FireWire (IEEE 1394, a and b) cameras can be run with the following command:

```
$ rosrun camera1394 camera1394_node
```

Once the camera is running, we can configure its parameters with `rqt_reconfigure`, and we will see something similar to what's shown in the following screenshot:

Note that we will cover how to work with cameras in *Chapter 5*, *Computer Vision*, where we will also explain these parameters from a developer's point of view.

When something weird happens

ROS has several tools to detect potential problems in all the elements of a given package. Just move with `roscd` to the package you want to analyze. Then, run `roswtf`. For `chapter3_tutorials`, we have the following output. Note that if you have something running, the ROS graph would be analyzed too. We run the `roslaunch chapter3_tutorials example6.launch` command that yields the an output similar to the following screenshot:

In general, we should expect no error or warning, but even some of them are innocuous. In the preceding screenshot, we see that `roswtf` does not detect any error; it only issues a warning about `pip`, which sometimes might generate problems with the Python code installed in the system. Note that the purpose of `roswtf` is to signal potential problems, and then we are responsible to check whether they are real or meaningless ones, as in the previous case.

Another useful tool is `catkin_lint`, which helps to diagnose errors with `catkin`, usually in the `CMakeLists.txt` and `package.xml` files. For `chapter3_tutorials`, we have the following output:

```
$ catkin_lint -W2 --pkg chapter3_tutorials
```

Visualization and Debug Tools

With `-W2`, we see warnings that can be usually ignored, as the ones shown in the following screenshot:

Visualizing node diagnostics

ROS nodes can provide diagnostic information using the `diagnostics` topic. For that, there is an API that helps to publish diagnostic information in a standard way. The information follows the `diagnostic_msgs/DiagnositcStatus` message type, which allows us to specify a level (OK, WARN, ERROR), name, message, and hardware ID as well as a list of `diagnostic_msgs/KeyValue`, which are pairs of `key` and `value` strings.

The interesting part comes with the tools to collect and visualize this diagnostic information. At the basic level, `rqt_runtime_monitor` allows us to visualize the information directly published through the `diagnostics` topic. Run the `example7` node, which publishes information through the diagnostics topic and this visualization tool to see the diagnostic information:

```
$ roslaunch chapter3_tutorials example7.launch
$ rosrun rqt_runtime_monitor rqt_runtime_monitor
```

The preceding commands display the following output:

![Runtime Monitor window showing Stale (0), Errors (0), Warnings (0), Ok (1) with example7: status: ok]

When the system is large, we can aggregate diagnostic information using the `diagnostic_aggregator`. It processes and categorizes the `diagnostics` topic messages and republishes them on `diagnostics_agg`. These aggregated diagnostic messages can be visualized with `rqt_robot_monitor`. The diagnostic aggregator is configured with a configuration file, such as the following one (see `config/diagnostic_aggregator.yaml` in `chapter3_tutorials`), where we define different `analyzers`, in this case using an `AnalyzerGroup`:

```
type: AnalyzerGroup
path: Sensors
analyzers:
  status:
    type: GenericAnalyzer
    path: Status
    startswith: example7
    num_items: 1
```

The `launch` file used in the preceding code already runs the diagnostic `aggregator_node` with the preceding configuration, so you can run the following command:

$ **rosrun rqt_robot_monitor rqt_robot_monitor**

Now, we can compare the visualization of `rqt_runtime_monitor` with the one of `rqt_robot_monitor`, as shown in the following screenshot:

Plotting scalar data

Scalar data can be easily plotted with generic tools already available in ROS. Even nonscalar data can be plotted, but with each scalar field plotted separately. That is why we talk about scalar data, because most nonscalar structures are better represented with ad hoc visualizers, some of which we will see later; for instance, images, poses, orientation/attitude, and so on.

Creating a time series plot with rqt_plot

Scalar data can be plotted as a time series over the time provided by the timestamps of the messages. Then, in the *y* axis, we will plot our scalar data. The tool to do so is `rqt_plot`. It has a powerful argument syntax, which allows specifying several fields of a structured message in a concise manner as well; we can also add or remove topics or fields manually from the GUI.

To show `rqt_plot` in action, we are going to use the `example4` node since it publishes a scalar and a vector (nonscalar) in two different topics, which are `temp` and `accel`, respectively. The values put in these messages are synthetically generated, so they have no actual meaning, but they are useful for our plotting demonstration purposes. So, start by running the node using the following command:

```
$ rosrun chapter3_tutorials example4
```

To plot a message, we must know its format; use `rosmg show <msg type>` if you do not know it. In the case of scalar data, we always have a `data` field that has the actual value. Hence, for the `temp` topic, which is of the `Int32` type, we will run the following command:

```
$ rosrun rqt_plot rqt_plot /temp/data
```

With the node running, we will see a plot that changes over time, with the incoming messages, as shown in the following screenshot:

For `accel`, we have a `Vector3` message (as you can check with `rostopic type /accel`), which contains three fields that we can visualize in a single plot. The `Vector3` message has the x, y, and z fields. We can specify the fields separated by commas (,) or in the more concise manner shown in the following command:

```
$ rosrun rqt_plot rqt_plot /accel/x:y:z
```

Visualization and Debug Tools

The plot will look somewhat like the one in the following screenshot:

We can also plot each field in a separate axis. However, `rqt_plot` does not support this directly. Instead, we must use `rqt_gui` and arrange three plots manually, as shown in the following command and the screenshot after that:

```
$ rosrun rqt_gui rqt_gui
```

The `rqt_plot` GUI supports three plotting frontends. Before ROS hydro, only `matplotlib` was supported. Now, we can use QT frontends, which are faster and support more time series simultaneously. You can access and select them from the configuration button:

Image visualization

In ROS, we have a node that allows the display of images coming from a camera on-the-fly. This is an example of a topic with complex data, which is better visualized or analyzed with special tools. You only need a camera to do this, such as your laptop webcam. The `example8` node implements a basic camera capture program using `OpenCV` and ROS bindings to convert `cv::Mat` images into ROS `Image` messages that can be published in a topic. This node publishes the camera frames in the `/camera` topic.

We are only going to run the node with a `launch` file created to do so. The code inside the node is still new for the reader, but in the next chapters, we will cover how to work with cameras and images in ROS, so we will be able to come back to this node and understand it:

```
$ roslaunch chapter3_tutorials example8.launch
```

Once the node is running, we can list the topics (`rostopic list`) and see that the `/camera` topic is there. A straightforward way to verify that we are actually capturing images is to see at which frequency we are receiving images in the topic with `rostopic hz /camera`. It should be something in the region of 30 Hz usually. This is shown in the following screenshot:

```
enrique@pc-acer[hydro]:svn:
~/svn/ros_book_hydro_ws/src/ros_book_v2/chapter3_tutorials$ rostopic hz /camera
subscribed to [/camera]
average rate: 10.728
        min: 0.084s max: 0.099s std dev: 0.00474s window: 10
average rate: 10.746
        min: 0.084s max: 0.099s std dev: 0.00441s window: 21
average rate: 10.725
        min: 0.084s max: 0.099s std dev: 0.00426s window: 31
average rate: 10.710
        min: 0.084s max: 0.100s std dev: 0.00409s window: 42
average rate: 10.702
        min: 0.084s max: 0.100s std dev: 0.00398s window: 53
```

Visualizing a single image

We cannot use `rostopic echo /camera` because, as it's an image, the amount of information in plain text would be very huge and not human readable. Hence, we are going to use the following command:

```
$ rosrun image_view image_view image:=/camera
```

This is the `image_view` node, which shows the images in the given topic (the `image` argument) in a window. This way, we can visualize every image or frame published in a topic in a very simple and flexible manner—even over a network. If you press the right-hand side button of your mouse on the window, you can save the current frame in the disk, usually in your home directory or `~/.ros`.

ROS hydro also has `rqt_image_view`, which supports viewing multiple images in a single window but does not allow the saving of images by pressing the right-hand side button. We can select the `image` topic manually on the GUI, or as we do with `image_view`:

```
$ rosrun rqt_image_view rqt_image_view
```

The preceding command yields an output shown in the following screenshot:

ROS provides a camera calibration interface built on top of the OpenCV calibration API. We will cover this in *Chapter 5*, *Computer Vision*, when we see how to work with cameras. There, we will see monocular and stereo cameras as well as the ROS image pipeline (image_proc and stereo_image_proc), which allow the rectification of the camera image distortion and compute the depth image disparity for stereo pairs, so that we obtain a point cloud.

3D visualization

There are certain devices (such as stereo cameras, 3D lasers, the Kinect sensor, and so on) that provide 3D data—usually in the form of point clouds (organized/ordered or not). For this reason, it is extremely useful to have tools that visualize this type of data. In ROS, we have rviz or rqt_rviz, which integrates an OpenGL interface with a 3D world that represents sensor data in a world representation, using the frame of the sensor that reads the measurements in order to draw such readings in the correct position with respect to each other.

Visualization and Debug Tools

Visualizing data in a 3D world using rqt_rviz

With `roscore` running, start `rqt_rviz` with (note that `rviz` is still valid in ROS hydro):

```
$ rosrun rqt_rviz rqt_rviz
```

We will see the graphical interface of the following screenshot, which has a simple layout:

On the left-hand side, we have the `Displays` panel, in which we have a tree list of the different elements in the world, which appears in the middle. In this case, we have certain elements already loaded. Indeed, this layout is saved in the `config/example9.rviz` file, which can be loaded in the **File | Open Config** menu.

Below the **Displays** area, we have the **Add** button that allows adding more elements by topic or type. Also note that there are global options, which are basically a tool to set the fixed frame in the world, with respect to which the others might move. Then, we have `Axes` and a `Grid` as a reference for the rest of the elements. In this case, for the `example9` node, we are going to see `Marker` and `PointCloud2`.

Finally, on the status bar, we have information regarding the time, and on the right-hand side, there are menus. The **Tools** properties allows us to configure certain plugin parameters, such as, the `2D Nav Goal` and `2D Pose Estimate` topic names. The **Views** menu gives different view types, where `Orbit` and `TopDownOrtho` are generally enough; one for a 3D view and the other for a 2D top view. Another menu shows elements selected on the environment. At the top, we also have a menu bar with the current operation mode (`Interact`, `Move`, `Measure`, and so on.) and certain plugins.

Now we are going to run the `example9` node using the following screenshot:

```
$ roslaunch chapter3_tutorials example9.launch
```

In `rqt_rviz`, we are going to set `frame_id` of the marker, which is `frame_marker`, in the fixed frame. We will see a red cubic marker moving, as shown in the following screenshot:

Visualization and Debug Tools

Similarly, if we set the fixed frame to `frame_pc`, we will see a point cloud that represents a plane of 200 x 100 points, as shown in the following screenshot:

The list of supported built-in types in `rqt_viz` includes `Camera` and `Image`, which are shown in a window—similar to `image_view`. In the case of `Camera`, its calibration is used, and in the case of stereo images, they allow us to overlay the point cloud. We can also see the `LaserScan` data from range lasers, `Range` cone values from IR/sonar sensors, or `PointCloud2` from 3D sensors, such as the Kinect sensor.

For the navigation stack, which we will cover the in next chapters, we have several data types, such as `Odometry` (which plots the robot odometry poses), `Path` (which draws the path plan followed by the robot), `Pose` objects, `PoseArray` for particle clouds with the robot pose estimate, the **Occupancy Grid Map** (**OGM**) as a `Map`, and `costmaps` (which are of the `Map` type in ROS hydro and were `GridCell` before).

Among other types, it is also worth mentioning the `RobotModel`, which shows the CAD model of all the robot parts, taking the transformation among the frames of each element into account. Indeed, `tf` elements can also be drawn, which is very useful to debug the frames in the system; we will see an example in the next section. In `RobotModel`, we also have the links that belong to the robot URDF description with the option to draw a trail showing how they move over time.

Basic elements can also be represented, such as a `Polygon` for the robot footprint; several kind of `Markers`, which support basic geometric elements, such as cubes, spheres, lines, and so on; and even `InteractiveMarker` objects, which allow the user to set a pose (position and orientation) on the 3D world. Run the `example8` node to see an example of a simple interactive marker:

```
$ roslaunch chapter3_tutorials example10.launch
```

You will see a marker that you can move in the interactive mode of `rqt_rviz`. Its pose can be used to modify the pose of another element in the system, such as the joint of a robot:

The relationship between topics and frames

All topics must have a frame if they are publishing data from a particular sensor that has a physical location in the real world. For example, a laser is located in a position with respect to the base link of the robot (usually at the middle of the traction wheels in wheeled robots). If we use the laser scans to detect obstacles in the environment or to build a map, we must use the transformation the laser and the base link. In ROS, stamped messages have `frame_id`, apart from the timestamp (which is also extremely important to put or synchronize different messages). A `frame_id` gives a name to the frame it belongs to.

However, the frames themselves are meaningless. We need the transformation among them. Actually, we have the tf frame, which usually has the base_link frame as its root (or map if the navigation stack is running). Then, in rqt_rviz, we can see how this and other frames move with respect to each other.

Visualizing frame transformations

To illustrate how to visualize frame transformations, we are going to use the turtlesim example. Run the following command to start the demonstration:

```
$ roslaunch turtle_tf turtle_tf_demo.launch
```

This is a very basic example with the purpose of illustrating the tf visualization in rqt_rviz; note that, for the different possibilities offered by the tf API, you should see later chapters of this book. For now, it is enough to know that it allows us to make computations in one frame and then transform them to another, including time delays. It is also important to know that tf is published at a certain frequency in the system, so it is like a subsystem where we can traverse the tf tree to obtain the transformation between any frames in it; we can do it in any node of our system just by consulting tf.

If you receive an error, it is probably because the listener died on the launch startup because another node that was required was still not ready, so please run the following command on another terminal to start it again:

```
$ rosrun turtle_tf turtle_tf_listener
```

Now you should see a window with two turtles, where one follows the other. You can control one of the turtles with the arrow keys as long as you have the focus on the terminal where you run the launch file. The following screenshot shows how one turtle has been following the other after moving the one we control with the keyboard for some time:

Each turtle has its own frame, so we can see it in `rqt_rviz`:

```
$ rosrun rqt_rviz rqt_rviz
```

Now, instead of viewing the `turtlesim` window, we are going to see how the turtles' frames move in `rqt_rviz` as we move our turtle with the arrow keys. We have to set the fixed frame to `/world` and then add the `tf` tree to the left-hand side area. We will see that we have the `/turtle1` and `/turtle2` frames, both as children of the root `/world` frame. In the world representation, the frames are shown as axes, and the parent-child links are shown with a yellow arrow that has a pink end. Also set the view type to `TopDownOrtho`, so it is easier to see how the frames move because they only move on the 2D ground plane. You might also find it useful to translate the world center, which is done with the mouse with the *Shift* key pressed.

In the next screenshot, you can see how the two turtle frames are shown with respect to the `/world` frame. You can change the fixed frame to experiment with this example and `tf`. Note that `config/example_tf.rviz` is provided to give the basic layout for this example:

Saving and playing back data

Usually, when we work with robotic systems, the resources are shared, not always available, or the experiments cannot be done regularly because of the cost or time required for preparing and performing them or because they are difficult to reproduce. For this reason, it is a good practice to record the data of the experiment session for later analysis and to work, develop, and test our algorithms. However, the process of saving good data so that we can reproduce the experiment offline is not trivial. Fortunately, in ROS, we have powerful tools that have already solved this problem.

ROS can save all the messages published on any topic. It has the ability to create a bag file that contains the messages as they are with all their fields and timestamps. That allows the reproduction of the experiment offline with its real conditions on the robot as the latency of messages transmission. What's more, ROS tools do all this efficiently, with a high bandwidth, and in an adequate manner to organize the saved data.

In the next section, we will explain the tools provided by ROS to save and play back the data stored in bag files, which use a binary format designed for and by ROS developers. We will also see how to manage these files, that is, inspect the content (number of messages, topics, and so on), compress them, and split or merge several of them.

What is a bag file?

A bag file is a container of messages sent by topics that were recorded during a session using a robot or nodes. In brief, they are the logging files for the messages transferred during the execution of our system, and they allow us to play back everything, even with the time delays, since all messages are recorded with a timestamp—not only the timestamp in the header, but also for the packets that have it. The difference between the timestamp used to record and the one in the header is that the first one is set once the message is recorded, while the other is set by the producer/publisher of the message.

The data stored in a bag file is in the binary format. The particular structure of this container allows for an extremely fast recording bandwidth, which is the most important concern when saving data. Also, the size of the bag file is relevant but usually at the expense of speed. Anyway, we have the option to compress the file on the fly with the bz2 algorithm; just use the -j parameter when you record with rosbag record as you will see in the sequel.

Every message is recorded along with the topic that published it. Therefore, we can specify which topics to record or just record all (with -a). Later, when we play the bag file back, we can also select a particular subset of topics of the ones in the bag file by indicating the name of the topics we want to be published.

Recording data in a bag file with rosbag

The first thing we have to do is simply record some data. We are going to use a very simple system as an example—our example4 node. Hence, we will first run the node:

```
$ rosrun chapter3_tutorials example4
```

Now we have two options. First, we can record all the topics with the following command:

```
$ rosbag record -a
```

Otherwise, we can record only specific topics. In this case, it makes sense to record only the example4 topics, so we will run the following command:

```
$ rosbag record /temp /accel
```

By default, when we run the above command, the rosbag program subscribes to the node and starts recording the message in a bag file in the current directory with the data as the name. Once you have finished the experiment or you want to stop recording, you only have to hit *Ctrl + C*. The following is an example of a recording session and the resulting bag file:

```
[ INFO] [1404248014.668263731]: Subscribing to /temp
[ INFO] [1404248014.671339658]: Subscribing to /accel
[ INFO] [1404248014.674950564]: Recording to 2014-07-01-22-54-34.bag.
```

You can see more options with rosbag help record, which include the bag file size, the duration of the recording, options to split the files in several ones of a given size, and so on. As we mentioned before, the file can be compressed on the fly (the -j option). In our honest opinion, this is only useful for a small bandwidth, because it also consumes CPU time, and it might produce message dropping. If messages are dropped, we can increase the buffer (-b) size for the recorder in MB, which defaults to 256 MB, but can be increased to some GB if the bandwidth is very high (especially with images).

Visualization and Debug Tools

It is also possible to include the call to `rosbag record` into a `launch` file, which is useful when we want to set up a recorder for certain topics. To do so, we must add the following node:

```
<node pkg="rosbag" type="record" name="bag_record"
      args="/temp /accel"/>
```

Note that the topics and other arguments to the command are passed using the `args` argument. Also, it is important to say that when it is run from the `launch` file, the `bag` file is created by default in `~/.ros` unless we give the name of the file with `-o` (prefix) or `-O` (full name).

Playing back a bag file

Now that we have a `bag` file recorded, we can use it to play back all the messages of the topics inside it; note that we need `roscore` running and usually nothing else. Then, we will move to the folder with the `bag` file we want to play (there are two examples in the `bag` folder of this chapter's tutorials) and run this command:

```
$ rosbag play 2014-07-01-22-54-34.bag
```

We will see the following output:

```
[ INFO] [1404248314.594700096]: Opening 2014-07-01-22-54-34.bag

Waiting 0.2 seconds after advertising topics... done.

Hit space to toggle paused, or 's' to step.
 [RUNNING]  Bag Time: 1404248078.757944   Duration: 2.801764 / 39.999515
```

In the terminal in which we play the `bag` file, we can pause (hit space) or move step by step (hit s). As usual, press *Ctrl* + *C* to finish it immediately. Once we reach the end of the file, it will close, but there is an option to loop (`-l`), which sometimes might be useful.

Automatically, we will see the topics with `rostopic list`, as follows:

`/accel`

`/clock`

`/rosout`

`/rosout_agg`

`/temp`

The `/clock` topic appears because we can simulate the system clock to simulate a faster playback. This can be configured using the `-r` option. The `/clock` topic publishes the time for the simulation at a configurable frequency with the `--hz` argument (it defaults to 100 Hz).

Also, we can specify a subset of the topics in the file to be published. This is done with the `--topics` option.

Inspecting all the topics and messages in a bag file

There are two main ways to see what we have inside a `bag` file. The first one is very simple. We just type `rosbag info <bag_file>`, and the result is something similar to the one shown in the following screenshot:

```
~/svn/ros_book_hydro_ws/src/ros_book_v2/chapter3_tutorials/bag$ rosbag info 2014-07-01-22-54-34.bag
path:        2014-07-01-22-54-34.bag
version:     2.0
duration:    40.0s
start:       Jul 01 2014 22:54:35.96 (1404248075.96)
end:         Jul 01 2014 22:55:15.96 (1404248115.96)
size:        10.9 KB
messages:    82
compression: none [1/1 chunks]
types:       geometry_msgs/Vector3 [4a842b65f413084dc2b10fb484ea7f17]
             std_msgs/Int32       [da5909fbe378aeaf85e547e830cc1bb7]
topics:      /accel    41 msgs    : geometry_msgs/Vector3
             /temp     41 msgs    : std_msgs/Int32
```

We have information about the `bag` file itself, such as the creation date, duration, size, the number of messages inside, and the compression (if any). Then, we have the list of data types inside the file and finally the list of topics, with their corresponding name, number of messages, and type.

Visualization and Debug Tools

The second way to inspect a `bag` file is extremely powerful. It is a GUI named `rqt_bag` that also allows playing back the files, viewing the images (if any), plotting scalar data, and also the RAW structure of the messages; it is the replacement of rxbag. We only have to pass the name of the `bag` file, and we will see something similar to the following screenshot (for the previous `bag` file):

We have a timeline for all the topics, where each message appears with a mark. In the case of images, we can enable the thumbnails to see them in the timeline.

In the next screenshot, we can see how to access the `RAW`, `Plot`, and `Image` (if the topic is of the `Image` type) views for the topics in the file. This pop-up menu appears with a right-click over the timeline. The following screenshot corresponds to the old rxbag because this functionality has been recently added to `rqt_bag` and might still not be available in your Debian repository:

As an alternative, we can use `rqt_gui` and put the `rqt_bag` and `rqt_plot` plugins in the same window; the layout of the following screenshot can be imported from the perspective given in the `config/bag_plot.perspective` folder. However, we have to use `Publish All` and play to actually see the plot, which differs from the `rxbag` behavior. For `/accel`, we can plot all the fields in a single axis. To do so, once we have the plot view, we add each field by pressing the + button/icon. Note that we can remove them later or create different axes. As mentioned before, the plot is not generated for all the values in the file, but it simply shows the data that is played back and published:

Remember that with the `rxbag` behavior, we must press the play button at least once to be able to plot the data. Then we can play, pause, stop, and move to the beginning or the end of the file.

The images are straightforward, and a simple window appears with the current frame with options to save them as image files in the disk.

Since the first version of `rqt_bag` did not have the preview/visualization features mentioned previously, you will still need rxbag compiled for ROS hydro or just upgrade to the latest ROS hydro version of `rqt_bag` (or clone the `hydro-devel` branch from the GitHub repository and compile).

Using the rqt_gui and rqt plugins

Since ROS Fuerte, the `rx` applications or tools are deprecated, and we should instead use the `rqt` nodes. They are basically the same, and only a few of them incorporate small updates, bug fixes, and new features. The following table shows the equivalences for the tools shown in this chapter (the ROS hydro `rqt` tool and the one it replaces from previous ROS distributions):

ROS hydro rqt tool	Replaces (ROS fuerte or before)
rqt_console and rqt_logger_level	rxconsole
rqt_graph	rxgraph
rqt_reconfigure rqt_reconfigure	dynamic_reconfigure reconfigure_gui
rqt_plot	rxplot
rqt_image_view	image_view
rqt_bag	rxbag

In ROS hydro, there are even more standalone plugins, such as a shell (rqt_shell), a topic publisher (rqt_publisher), a message type viewer (rqt_msg), and much more (the most important ones have been covered in this chapter). Even rqt_viz is a plugin, which replaces rviz, and can also be integrated into the new rqt_gui interface. We can run this GUI and add and arrange several plugins manually on the window, as it has been seen in several examples in this chapter:

```
$ rosrun rqt_gui rqt_gui
```

Summary

After reading and running the code of this chapter, you learned to use many tools that help you to develop robotic systems faster, debug errors, and visualize your results, so that you can evaluate their quality or validate them. Some of the specific concepts and tools you will exploit the most in your life as a robot developer have been summarized here.

Now you know how to include logging messages in your code with different levels of verbosity, which will help you to debug errors in your nodes. For this purpose, you can also use the powerful tools included in ROS, such as the `rqt_console` interface. Additionally, you can also inspect or list the nodes running, topics published, and services provided in the whole system. This includes the inspection of the node graph using `rqt_graph`.

Regarding the visualization tools, you should be able to plot scalar data using `rqt_plot` for a more intuitive analysis of certain variables published by your nodes. Similarly, you can view more complex types (nonscalar ones). This includes images and 3D data using `rqt_image_view` and `rqt_rviz`, respectively. Similarly, you can use tools to calibrate and rectify the camera images.

Finally, recording and playing back the messages of the topics available are now in your hands with `rosbag`. You also know how to view the contents of a `bag` file with `rqt_bag`. This allows you to record the data from your experiments and process them later with your AI or robotics algorithms.

In the next chapter, you will use many of the tools covered here to visualize data of very different types. Several sensors are presented along with the instructions to use them in ROS and visualize their output data.

4
Using Sensors and Actuators with ROS

When you think of a robot, you would probably think of a human-sized one with arms, a lot of sensors, and a wide field of locomotion systems.

Now that we know how to write small programs in ROS and manage them, we are going to work with sensors and actuators—things that can interact with the real world.

You can find a wide list of devices supported by ROS at `http://www.ros.org/wiki/Sensors`.

In this chapter, we will deal with the following topics:

- Cheap and common sensors for your projects
- 3D sensors, such as Kinect and laser rangefinders
- Using Arduino to connect more sensors and actuators

We know that it is impossible to explain all the types of sensors in this chapter. For this reason, we have selected some of the most commonly used ones and those that are affordable to most users—regular, sporadic, or amateur.

Sensors and actuators can be organized into different categories: rangefinders, cameras, pose estimation devices, and so on. They will help you find what you are looking for more quickly.

Using a joystick or a gamepad

I am sure that, at one point or another, you have used a joystick or a gamepad of a video console.

A joystick is nothing more than a series of buttons and potentiometers. With this device, you can perform or control a wide range of actions.

In ROS, a joystick is used to telecontrol a robot to change its velocity or direction.

Before we start, we are going to install some packages. To install these packages in Ubuntu, execute the following command:

```
$ sudo apt-get install ros-hydro-joystick-drivers
$ rosstack profile & rospack profile
```

> **Downloading the example code**
> You can download the example code files from your account at http://www.packtpub.com for all the Packt Publishing books you have purchased. If you purchased this book elsewhere, you can visit http://www.packtpub.com/support and register to have the files e-mailed directly to you. You can also download these code files from https://github.com/AaronMR/ROS_Book_Hydro.

In these packages, you will find code to learn how to use the joystick and a guide to create our packages.

First of all, connect your joystick to your computer. Now, we are going to check whether the joystick is recognized, using the following command:

```
$ ls /dev/input/
```

We will see the following output:

```
by-id     event0    event2    event4    event6    event8    js0      mouse0
by-path   event1    event3    event5    event7    event9    mice
```

The port created is `js0`; with the `jstest` command, we can check whether it is working, by using the following command:

```
$ sudo jstest /dev/input/js0
```

```
Axes:  0:  0  1:  0  2:  0  Buttons:  0:off  1:off  2:off  3:off  4:off
5:off  6:off  7:off  8:off  9:off  10:off
```

Our joystick, Logitech Attack 3, has 3 axes and 11 buttons, and if we move the joystick, the values change.

Once you have checked the joystick, we are going to test it in ROS. To do this, you can use the `joy` and `joy_node` packages:

```
$ rosrun joy joy_node
```

If everything is OK, you will see the following output:

```
[ INFO] [1357571588.441808789]: Opened joystick: /dev/input/js0.
deadzone_: 0.050000.
```

How does joy_node send joystick movements?

With the `joy_node` package active, we are going to see the messages sent by this node. This will help us understand how it sends information about axes and buttons.

To see the messages sent by the node, we can use this command:

```
$ rostopic echo /joy
```

And then, we can see each message sent:

```
---
header:
seq: 157
```

```
stamp:
  secs: 1357571648
  nsecs: 430257462
  frame_id: ''
axes: [-0.0, -0.0, 0.0]
buttons: [0, 0, 0, 0, 0, 0, 0, 0, 0, 0, 0]
---
```

You will see two main vectors: one for axes and the other for buttons. Obviously, these vectors are used to publish the states of the buttons and axes of the real hardware.

If you want to know the message type, type the following command line in a shell:

`$ rostopic type /joy`

You will then obtain the type used by the message; in this case, it is `sensor_msgs/Joy`.

Now, to see the fields used in the message, use the following command line:

`$ rosmsg show sensor_msgs/Joy`

You will see the following output:

```
std_msgs/Header header
  uint32 seq
  time stamp
  string frame_id
float32[] axes
int32[] buttons
```

This is the message structure that you must use if you want to use a joystick with your developments. In the next section, you will learn how to write a node that subscribes to the joystick topic and how to generate moving commands to move `turtlesim`.

Using joystick data to move a turtle in turtlesim

Now, we are going to create a node that gets data from `joy_node` and `Published` topics to control `turtlesim`.

First, it is necessary to know the name of the topic where we will publish the messages. So, we are going to start `turtlesim` and do some investigation:

`$ rosrun turtlesim turtlesim_node`

Chapter 4

To see the topic list, use the following command line:

`$ rostopic list`

You will then see the following output, where `turtle1/command_velocity` is the topic we will use:

```
/rosout
/rosout_agg
/turtle1/cmd_vel
/turtle1/color_sensor
/turtle1/pose
```

Now, we need to know the topic type. Use the following command line to see it:

`$ rostopic type /turtle1/cmd_vel`

You will see this output:

`geometry_msgs/Twist`

To know the contents of this message, execute the following command line:

`$ rosmsg show geometry_msgs/Twist`

You will then see the two fields that are used to send the velocity:

```
geometry_msgs/Vector3 linear
  float64 x
  float64 y
  float64 z
geometry_msgs/Vector3 angular
  float64 x
  float64 y
  float64 z
```

OK, now that we have localized the topic and the structure to use, it is time to create a program to generate velocity commands using data from the joystick.

Using Sensors and Actuators with ROS

Create a new file, c4_example.1.cpp, in the chapter4_tutorials/src directory and type in the following code snippet:

```cpp
#include<ros/ros.h>
#include<geometry_msgs/Twist.h>
#include<sensor_msgs/Joy.h>
#include<iostream>
using namespace std;

class TeleopJoy{
public:
  TeleopJoy();
private:
  void callBack(const sensor_msgs::Joy::ConstPtr& joy);
  ros::NodeHandle n;
  ros::Publisher pub;
 ros::Subscriber sub;
  int i_velLinear, i_velAngular;
};


TeleopJoy::TeleopJoy()
{
  n.param("axis_linear",i_velLinear,i_velLinear);
  n.param("axis_angular",i_velAngular,i_velAngular);
  pub = n.advertise<geometry_msgs::Twist>("/turtle1/cmd_vel",1);
  sub = n.subscribe<sensor_msgs::Joy>("joy", 10, &TeleopJoy::callBack, this);
}


void TeleopJoy::callBack(const sensor_msgs::Joy::ConstPtr& joy)
{
  geometry_msgs::Twist vel;
  vel.angular.z = joy->axes[i_velAngular];
  vel.linear.x = joy->axes[i_velLinear];
  pub.publish(vel);
}

int main(int argc, char** argv)
{
  ros::init(argc, argv, "teleopJoy");
  TeleopJoy teleop_turtle;
  ros::spin();
}
```

Now, we are going to break the code to explain how it works. In the main function, we create an instance of the `TeleopJoy` class:

```
int main(int argc, char** argv)
{
  ...
   TeleopJoy teleop_turtle;
  ...
```

In the constructor, four variables are initialized. The first two variables are filled using data from Parameter Server. These variables are joystick axes. The next two variables are the advertiser and the subscriber. The advertiser will publish a topic with the `geometry_msgs::Twist` type. The subscriber will get data from the topic with the name `Joy`. The node that is handling the joystick sends this topic:

```
TeleopJoy::TeleopJoy()
{
  n.param("axis_linear",i_velLinear,i_velLinear);
  n.param("axis_angular",i_velAngular,i_velAngular);
  pub = n.advertise<geometry_msgs::Twist>("/turtle1/cmd_vel",1);
  sub = n.subscribe<sensor_msgs::Joy>("joy", 10, &TeleopJoy::callBack, this);
}
```

Each time the node receives a message, the `callBack` function is called. We create a new variable with the name `vel`, which will be used to publish data. The values of the axes of the joystick are assigned to the `vel` variable. In this part, you can create a process with the data received before publishing it:

```
void TeleopJoy::callBack(const sensor_msgs::Joy::ConstPtr& joy)
{
  geometry_msgs::Twist vel;
  vel.angular.z = joy->axes[i_velAngular];
  vel.linear.x = joy->axes[i_velLinear];
  pub.publish(vel);
}
```

Finally, the topic is published using `pub.publish(vel)`.

We are going to create a launch file for this example. In the launch file, we declare data for Parameter Server and launch the `joy` and `example1` nodes.

Copy the following code step to a new file, `example1.launch`, in the `chapter4_tutorials/src` directory:

```
<launch>

<node pkg="turtlesim" type="turtlesim_node" name="sim"/>
<node pkg="chapter4_tutorials" type="c4_example1" name="c4_example1" />
<param name="axis_linear" value="1" type="int" />
<param name="axis_angular" value="0" type="int" />

<node respawn="true" pkg="joy"type="joy" name="teleopJoy">
  <param name="dev" type="string" value="/dev/input/js0" />
  <param name="deadzone" value="0.12" />
</node>

</launch>
```

You will notice that, in the launch file, there are three different nodes: `c4_example1`, `sim`, and `joy`.

There are four parameters in the launch file; these parameters will add data to Parameter Server, and it will be used by our node. The `axis_linear` and `axis_angular` parameters will be used to configure the axes of the joystick. If you want to change the axes configuration, you only need to change the value and put the number of the axes you want to use. The `dev` and `deadzone` parameters will be used to configure the port where the joystick is connected, and the dead zone is the region of movement that is not recognized by the device.

To run the launch file, use the following command line:

`$ roslaunch chapter4_tutorials example1.launch`

You can see whether everything is fine by checking the running nodes and the topic list by using the `rosnode` list and the `rostopic` list. If you want to see it graphically, use `rqt_graph`.

Using a laser rangefinder – Hokuyo URG-04lx

In mobile robotics, it is very important to know where the obstacles are, the outline of a room, and so on. Robots use maps to navigate and move across unknown spaces. The sensor used for these purposes is LIDAR. This sensor is used to measure distances between the robot and objects.

In this section, you will learn how to use a low-cost version of LIDAR that is widely used in robotics. This sensor is the Hokuyo URG-04lx rangefinder. You can obtain more information about it at `http://www.hokuyo-aut.jp/`. The Hokuyo rangefinder is a device used to navigate and build maps in real time:

The Hokuyo URG-04lx model is a low-cost rangefinder commonly used in robotics. It has a very good resolution and is very easy to use. To start with, we are going to install the drivers for the laser:

```
$ sudo apt-get install ros-hydro-hokuyo-node
$ rosstack profile && rospack profile
```

Once installed, we are going to check whether everything is OK. Connect your laser and check whether the system can detect it and whether it is configured correctly:

```
$ ls -l /dev/ttyACM0
```

When the laser is connected, the system sees it, so the result of the preceding command line is the following output:

```
crw-rw---- 1 root dialout 166, 0 Jan 13 11:09 /dev/ttyACM0
```

In our case, we need to reconfigure the laser device to give ROS the access to use it; that is, we need to give the appropriate permissions:

```
$ sudo chmod a+rw /dev/ttyACM0
```

Check the reconfiguration with the following command line:

```
$ ls -l /dev/ttyACM0
crw-rw-rw- 1 root dialout 166, 0 Jan 13 11:09 /dev/ttyACM0
```

Using Sensors and Actuators with ROS

Once everything is OK, we are going to switch on the laser. Start `roscore` in one shell, and, in another shell, execute the following command:

`$ rosrun hokuyo_node hokuyo_node`

If everything is fine, you will see the following output:

`[ INFO] [1358076340.184643618]: Connected to device with ID: H1000484`

Understanding how the laser sends data in ROS

To check whether the node is sending data, use `rostopic` as shown here:

`$ rostopic list`

You will see the following topics as the output:

`/diagnostics`

`/hokuyo_node/parameter_descriptions`

`/hokuyo_node/parameter_updates`

`/rosout`

`/rosout_agg`

`/scan`

The `/scan` topic is the topic where the node is publishing. The type of data used by the node is shown here:

`$ rostopic type /scan`

You will then see the message type used to send information about the laser:

`sensor_msgs/LaserScan`

You can see the structure of the message by using the following command:

`$ rosmsg show sensor_msgs/LaserScan`

To learn a little bit more about how the laser works and what data it is sending, we are going to use the `rostopic` command to see a real message:

`$ rostopic echo /scan`

Then, you will see the following message sent by the laser:

```
---
header:
```

```
seq: 3895
stamp:
  secs: 1358076731
  nsecs: 284896750
  frame_id: laser
...
ranges: [1.1119999885559082, 1.1119999885559082, 1.1109999418258667, ...]
intensities: []
---
```

This data is difficult to understand for humans. If you want to see the data in a more friendly and graphical way, it is possible to do so using `rviz`. Type the following command line in a shell to launch `rviz` with the correct configuration file:

```
$ rosrun rviz rviz -d `rospack find chapter4_tutorials`/rviz/laser.rviz
```

The following screenshot shows a graphical representation of the message:

You will see the contour on the screen. If you move the laser sensor, you will see the contour changing.

Using Sensors and Actuators with ROS

Accessing the laser data and modifying it

Now, we are going to make a node get the laser data, do something with it, and publish the new data. Perhaps, this will be useful at a later date, and with this example, you will learn how to do it.

Copy the following code snippet to the c4_example2.cpp file in your /chapter4_tutorials/src directory:

```
#include <ros/ros.h>
#include "std_msgs/String.h"
#include <sensor_msgs/LaserScan.h>

#include<stdio.h>
using namespace std;
class Scan2{
  public:
  Scan2();
  private:
  ros::NodeHandle n;
  ros::Publisher scan_pub;
  ros::Subscriber scan_sub;
  void scanCallBack(const sensor_msgs::LaserScan::ConstPtr& scan2);
};
Scan2::Scan2()
{
  scan_pub = n.advertise<sensor_msgs::LaserScan>("/scan2",1);
  scan_sub = n.subscribe<sensor_msgs::LaserScan>("/scan",1, &Scan2::scanCallBack, this);
}

void Scan2::scanCallBack(const sensor_msgs::LaserScan::ConstPtr& scan2)
{
  int ranges = scan2->ranges.size();
  //populate the LaserScan message
  sensor_msgs::LaserScan scan;
  scan.header.stamp = scan2->header.stamp;
  scan.header.frame_id = scan2->header.frame_id;
  scan.angle_min = scan2->angle_min;
  scan.angle_max = scan2->angle_max;
  scan.angle_increment = scan2->angle_increment;
  scan.time_increment = scan2->time_increment;
  scan.range_min = 0.0;
  scan.range_max = 100.0;
```

```
      scan.ranges.resize(ranges);
      for(int i = 0; i < ranges; ++i)
      {
         scan.ranges[i] = scan2->ranges[i] + 1;
      }
      scan_pub.publish(scan);
   }
   int main(int argc, char** argv)
   {
      ros::init(argc, argv, "example2_laser_scan_publisher");
      Scan2 scan2;
      ros::spin();
   }
```

We are going to break the code and see what it is doing.

In the `main` function, we initialize the node with the name `example2_laser_scan_publisher` and create an instance of the class that we have created in the file.

In the constructor, we will create two topics: one of them will subscribe to the other topic, which is the original data from the laser. The second topic will publish the newly modified data from the laser.

This example is very simple; we are only going to add 1 unit to the data received from the laser topic and publish it again. We do that in the `scanCallBack()` function. Take the input message and copy all the fields to another variable. Then, take the field where the data is stored and add the 1 unit. Once the new value is stored, publish the new topic:

```
   void Scan2::scanCallBack(const sensor_msgs::LaserScan::ConstPtr&
   scan2)
   {
       ...
   sensor_msgs::LaserScan scan;
       scan.header.stamp = scan2->header.stamp;
    ...
    ...
       scan.range_max = 100.0;
   scan.ranges.resize(ranges);

   for(int i = 0; i < ranges; ++i){
       scan.ranges[i] = scan2->ranges[i] + 1;
       }

   scan_pub.publish(scan);
   }
```

Using Sensors and Actuators with ROS

Creating a launch file

To launch everything, we are going to create a launch file, `example2.launch`:

```
<launch>
  <node pkg="hokuyo_node" type="hokuyo_node" name="hokuyo_node"/>
  <node pkg="rviz" type="rviz" name="rviz"
  args="-d $(find chapter4_tutorials)/rviz/laser.rviz"/>

  <node pkg="chapter4_tutorials" type="c4_example2" name="c4_example2"
/>
</launch>
```

Now, if you launch the `example2.launch` file, three nodes will start: `hokuyo_node`, `rviz`, and `c4_example2`. You will see the `rviz` screen with the two-laser contour. The green contour is the new data, as shown in the following screenshot:

Using the Kinect sensor to view objects in 3D

The Kinect sensor is a flat, black box that sits on a small platform when placed on a table or shelf near the television you're using with your Xbox 360. This device has the following three sensors that we can use for vision and robotics tasks:

- A color VGA video camera to see the world in color
- A depth sensor, which is an infrared projector and a monochrome CMOS sensor working together, to see objects in 3D
- A multiarray microphone that is used to isolate the voices of the players from the noise in the room

In ROS, we are going to use two of these sensors: the RGB camera and the depth sensor. In the latest version of ROS, you can even use three.

Before we start using it, we need to install the packages and drivers. Use the following command lines to install them:

```
$ sudo apt-get install ros-hydro-openni-camera ros-hydro-openni-launch
$ rosstack profile && rospack profile
```

Once the packages and drivers are installed, plug in the Kinect sensor, and we will run the nodes to start using it. In a shell, start `roscore`. In another shell, run the following command lines:

```
$ rosrun openni_camera openni_node
$ roslaunch openni_launch openni.launch
```

If everything goes well, you will not see any error messages.

How does Kinect send data from the sensors, and how do we see it?

Now, we are going to see what we can do with these nodes. List the topics that you have created by using this command:

```
$ rostopic list
```

Then, you will see a lot of topics, but the most important ones for us are the following:

...
/camera/rgb/image_color
/camera/rgb/image_mono
/camera/rgb/image_raw
/camera/rgb/image_rect
/camera/rgb/image_rect_color
...

We will see a lot of topics created by nodes. If you want to see one of the sensors, for example, the RGB camera, you can use the `/camera/rgb/image_color` topic. To see the image from the sensor, we are going to use the `image_view` package. Type the following command in a shell:

```
$ rosrun image_view image_view image:=/camera/rgb/image_color
```

Note that we need to rename (remap) the image topic to `/camera/rgb/image_color` by using the parameter's image. If everything is fine, a new window appears that shows the image from Kinect.

If you want to see the depth sensor, you can do so just by changing the topic in the last command line:

```
$ rosrun image_view image_view image:=/camera/depth/image
```

You will then see an image similar to the following screenshot:

Another important topic is the one that sends the point cloud data. This kind of data is a 3D representation of the depth image. You can find this data in `/camera/depth/points`, `/camera/depth_registered/points` and other topics.

We are going to see the type of message this is. To do this, use `rostopic type`. To see the fields of a message, we can use `rostopic type /topic_name | rosmsg show`. In this case, we are going to use the `/camera/depth/points` topic:

```
$ rostopic type /camera/depth/points | rosmsg show
```

To see the official specification of the message, visit http://ros.org/doc/api/sensor_msgs/html/msg/PointCloud2.html.

If you want to visualize this type of data, run `rviz` in a new shell and add a new `PointCloud2` data visualization, as shown here:

```
$ rosrun rviz rviz
```

Click on **Add**, order topics by display type, and select `PointCloud2`. Once you have added a `PointCloud2` display type, you have to select the name of the `camera/depth/points` topic.

Using Sensors and Actuators with ROS

On your computer, you will see a 3D image in real time; if you move in front of the sensor, you will see yourself moving in 3D, as you can see in the following screenshot:

Creating an example to use Kinect

Now, we are going to implement a program to generate a node that filters the point cloud from the Kinect sensor. This node will apply a filter to reduce the number of points in the original data. It will make a down sampling of the data.

Create a new file, `c4_example3.cpp`, in your `chapter4_tutorials/src` directory and type in the following code snippet:

```
#include <ros/ros.h>
#include <sensor_msgs/PointCloud2.h>
// PCL specific includes
#include <pcl_conversions/pcl_conversions.h>
#include <pcl/point_cloud.h>
#include <pcl/point_types.h>
```

```
#include <pcl/filters/voxel_grid.h>

#include <pcl/io/pcd_io.h>

ros::Publisher pub;

void cloud_cb (const pcl::PCLPointCloud2ConstPtr& input)
{
  pcl::PCLPointCloud2 cloud_filtered;
  pcl::VoxelGrid<pcl::PCLPointCloud2> sor;
  sor.setInputCloud (input);
  sor.setLeafSize (0.01, 0.01, 0.01);
  sor.filter (cloud_filtered);
  // Publish the dataSize
  pub.publish (cloud_filtered);
}

int main (int argc, char** argv)
{
  // Initialize ROS
  ros::init (argc, argv, "my_pcl_tutorial");
  ros::NodeHandle nh;
  // Create a ROS subscriber for the input point cloud
  ros::Subscriber sub = nh.subscribe ("/camera/depth/points", 1, cloud_cb);
  // Create a ROS publisher for the output point cloud
  pub = nh.advertise<sensor_msgs::PointCloud2> ("output", 1);
  // Spin
  ros::spin ();
}
```

This sample is based on the tutorial of **Point Cloud Library** (**PCL**). You can see it at http://pointclouds.org/documentation/tutorials/voxel_grid.php#voxelgrid.

All the work is done in the cb() function. This function is called when a message arrives. We create a sor variable with the VoxelGrid type, and the range of the grid is changed in sor.setLeafSize(). These values will change the grid used for the filter. If you increment the value, you will obtain less resolution and fewer points on the point cloud:

```
cloud_cb (const sensor_msgs::PointCloud2ConstPtr& input)
{
...
  pcl::VoxelGrid<sensor_msgs::PointCloud2> sor;
```

```
    ...
    sor.setLeafSize(0.01f,0.01f,0.01f);
    ...
}
```

If we open `rviz` now with the new node running, we will see the new point cloud in the window, and you will directly notice that the resolution is less than that of the original data, as shown in the following screenshot:

On `rviz`, you can see the number of points that a message has. For original data, we can see that the number of points is 2,19,075. With the new point cloud, we obtain 16,981 points. As you can see, it is a huge reduction of data.

At `http://pointclouds.org/`, you will find more filters and tutorials on how you can use this kind of data.

Using servomotors – Dynamixel

In mobile robots, servomotors are widely used. This kind of actuator is used to move sensors, wheels, and robotic arms. A low-cost solution is to use RC servomotors. It provides a movement range of 180 degrees and a high torque for the existing servomotors.

The servomotor that we will explain in this section is a new type of servomotor designed and used for robotics. This is the Dynamixel servomotor.

Dynamixel is a lineup, high-performance, networked actuator for robots developed by ROBOTIS, a Korean manufacturer. ROBOTIS is also the developer and manufacturer of OLLO, Bioloid, and DARwIn-OP DXL. These robots are used by numerous companies, universities, and hobbyists due to their versatile expansion capability, powerful feedback functions, position, speed, internal temperature, input voltage, and their simple daisy chain topology for simplified wiring connections.

In the following image, you can see Dynamixel AX-12 and the USB interface. Both are used in this example.

First, we are going to install the necessary packages and drivers. Type the following command line in a shell:

```
$ sudo apt-get install ros-hydro-dynamixel-motor
$ rosstack profile && rospack profile
```

Once the necessary packages and drivers are installed, connect the dongle to the computer and check whether it is detected. Normally, it will create a new port with the name `ttyUSBX` inside your `/dev/` folder. If you see this port, everything is OK, and now we can let the nodes play a little with the servomotor.

In a shell, start `roscore`, and in another shell, type the following command line:

```
$ roslaunch dynamixel_tutorials controller_manager.launch
```

If the motors are connected, you will see the motors detected by the driver. In our case, a motor with the ID 6 is detected and configured:

```
process[dynamixel_manager-1]: started with pid [3966]
```

```
[INFO] [WallTime: 1359377042.681841] pan_tilt_port: Pinging motor IDs 1 through 25...
```

```
[INFO] [WallTime: 1359377044.846779] pan_tilt_port: Found 1 motors - 1 AX-12 [6], initialization complete.
```

How does Dynamixel send and receive commands for the movements?

Once you have launched the `controller_manager.launch` file, you will see a list of topics. Remember to use the following command line to see these topics:

```
$ rostopic list
```

These topics will show the state of the motors configured, as follows:

```
/diagnostics
/motor_states/pan_tilt_port
/rosout
/rosout_agg
```

If you see `/motor_states/pan_tilt_port` with the `rostopic echo` command, you will see the state of all the motors, which, in our case, is only the motor with the ID 6; however, we cannot move the motors with these topics, so we need to run the next launch file to do it.

This launch file will create the necessary topics to move the motors, as follows:

```
$ roslaunch dynamixel_tutorials controller_spawner.launch
```

The topic list will have two new topics added to the list. One of the new topics will be used to move the servomotor, as follows:

```
/diagnostics
/motor_states/pan_tilt_port
/rosout
/rosout_agg
/tilt_controller/command
/tilt_controller/state
```

To move the motor, we are going to use the `/tilt_controller/command` that will publish a topic with the `rostopic` pub command. First, you need to see the fields of the topic and the type. To do that, use the following command lines:

```
$ rostopic type /tilt_controller/command
```

```
std_msgs/Float64
```

As you can see, it is a `Float64` variable. This variable is used to move the motor to a position measured in radians. So, to publish a topic, use the following commands:

```
$ rostopic pub /tilt_controller/command std_msgs/Float64 -- 0.5
```

Once the command is executed, you will see the motor moving, and it will stop at 0.5 radians or 28.6478898 degrees.

Creating an example to use the servomotor

Now, we are going to show you how you can move the motor using a node. Create a new file, `c4_example4.cpp`, in your `/chapter4_tutorials/src` directory with the following code snippet:

```cpp
#include<ros/ros.h>
#include<std_msgs/Float64.h>
#include<stdio.h>

using namespace std;

class Dynamixel{
  private:
    ros::NodeHandle n;
```

```cpp
    ros::Publisher pub_n;
  public:
    Dynamixel();
    int moveMotor(double position);
};

Dynamixel::Dynamixel(){
  pub_n = n.advertise<std_msgs::Float64>("/tilt_controller/
command",1);
}
int Dynamixel::moveMotor(double position)
{
  std_msgs::Float64 aux;
  aux.data = position;
  pub_n.publish(aux);
  return 1;
}

int main(int argc,char** argv)
{
  ros::init(argc, argv, "example4_move_motor");
  Dynamixel motors;

  float counter = -180;
  ros::Rate loop_rate(100);
  while(ros::ok())
  {
    if(counter < 180)
    {
      motors.moveMotor(counter*3.14/180);
      counter++;
    }else{
      counter = -180;
    }
    loop_rate.sleep();
  }
}
```

This node will move the motor continuously from -180 to 180 degrees. It is a simple example, but you can use it to make complex movements or control more motors. We assume that you understand the code and that it is not necessary to explain it. Note that you are publishing data to the /tilt_controller/command topic; this is the name of the motor.

Using Arduino to add more sensors and actuators

Arduino is an open source electronics prototyping platform based on flexible, easy-to-use hardware and software. It's intended for artists, designers, hobbyists, and anyone interested in creating interactive objects or environments. The following image shows how an Arduino board looks:

ROS can use this type of device with the rosserial package. Basically, Arduino is connected to the computer using a serial connection, and data is transmitted using this port. With rosserial, you can also use a lot of devices controlled by a serial connection, for example, GPS, servo controllers, and so on.

First, we need to install the packages. To do this, we use the following command lines:

```
$ sudo apt-get install ros-hydro-rosserial-arduino
$ sudo apt-get install ros-hydro-rosserial
```

Then, for the catkin workspace, we need to clone the rosserial repository into the workspace. The rosserial messages are created and ros_lib is compiled with the following command lines:

```
$ cd ~/dev/catkin_ws/src/
$ git clone https://github.com/ros-drivers/rosserial.git
$ cd ~/dev/catkin_ws/
```

```
$ catkin_make
$ catkin_make install
$ source install/setup.bash
```

OK, we assume that you have the Arduino IDE installed. If not, just follow the steps described at http://arduino.cc/en/Main/Software. For Ubuntu 12.04, you can use this command to install it:

```
$ sudo apt-get update && sudo apt-get install arduino arduino-core
```

Once you have the package and the IDE installed, it is necessary to copy ros_lib from the rosserial package to the sketchbook/libraries folder, which is created on your computer after running the Arduino IDE. Then, you have to run make_libraries.py:

```
$ cd ~/sketchbook/libraries
$ rosrun rosserial_arduino make_libraries.py .
```

Creating an example program to use Arduino

Now, we are going to upload an example program from the IDE to Arduino. Select the Hello World sample and upload the sketch:

The code in the preceding screenshot is very similar to the following code. In the following code, you can see an `include` line with the `ros.h` library. This library is the `rosserial` library, which we have installed before. Also, you can see a library with the message to send with a topic; in this case, it is the `std_msgs/String` type.

The following code snippet is present in the `c4_example5_1.ino` file:

```
#include <ros.h>
#include <std_msgs/String.h>

ros::NodeHandle  nh;

std_msgs::String str_msg;
ros::Publisher chatter("chatter", &str_msg);

char hello[19] = "chapter4_tutorials";

void setup()
{
  nh.initNode();
  nh.advertise(chatter);
}

void loop()
{
  str_msg.data = hello;
  chatter.publish( &str_msg );
  nh.spinOnce();
delay(1000);
}
```

The Arduino code is divided into two functions: `setup()` and `loop()`. The `setup()` function is executed once and is usually used for setting up the board. After `setup()`, the `loop()` function runs continuously. In the `setup()` function, the name of the topic is set; in this case, it is called `chatter`. Now, we need to start a node to hear the port and publish the topics sent by Arduino on the ROS network. Type the following command in a shell. Remember to run `roscore`:

```
$ rosrun rosserial_python serial_node.py /dev/ttyACM0
```

Now, you can see the messages sent by Arduino with the `rostopic echo` command:

```
$ rostopic echo chatter
```

Using Sensors and Actuators with ROS

You will see the following data in the shell:

```
data: chapter4_tutorials
```

The last example is about the data sent from Arduino to the computer. Now, we are going to use an example where Arduino will subscribe to a topic and will change the LED state connected to the pin number 13. The name of the example that we are going to use is `blink`; you can find this in the Arduino IDE by navigating to **File** | **Examples** | **ros_lib** | **Blink**.

The following code snippet is present in the `c4_example5_2.ino` file:

```
#include <ros.h>
#include <std_msgs/Empty.h>

ros::NodeHandle nh;
void messageCb( const std_msgs::Empty& toggle_msg){
digitalWrite(13, HIGH-digitalRead(13));   // blink the led
}

ros::Subscriber<std_msgs::Empty> sub("toggle_led", &messageCb );

void setup()
{
  pinMode(13, OUTPUT);
  nh.initNode();
  nh.subscribe(sub);
}

void loop()
{
  nh.spinOnce();
  delay(1);
}
```

Remember to launch the node to communicate with the Arduino board:

```
$ rosrun rosserial_python serial_node.py /dev/ttyACM0
```

Now, if you want to change the LED status, you can use the `rostopic pub` command to publish the new state:

```
$ rostopic pub /toggle_led std_msgs/Empty "{}" -once


publishing and latching message for 3.0 seconds
```

You will notice that the LED has changed its status; if the LED was on, it will now turn off. To change the status again, you only have to publish the topic once more:

```
$ rostopic pub /toggle_led std_msgs/Empty "{}" -once
```

```
publishing and latching message for 3.0 seconds
```

Now, you can use all the devices available to Arduino on ROS. This is very useful because you have access to cheap sensors and actuators to implement your robots.

> When we were writing the chapter, we noticed that Arduino does not work with `rosserial`, for instance, in the case of Arduino Leonardo. So, be careful with the selection of the device to use with this package.
>
> We didn't face any problems while working with Arduino UNO R3, Mega, Arduino Duemilanove, or Arduino Nano.

Using an ultrasound range sensor with Arduino

An I/O board such as Arduino can be connected to multiple sensors and actuators. In this section, we will program Arduino to control **HC-SR04**, an ultrasonic range sensor to be used in ROS. HC-SR04 sensors are low-cost and are commonly employed to measure distances between robots and obstacles.

This device is a **Printed Circuit Board** (PCB) with two piezoelectric transducers that are similar to microphones and piezoelectric headphones, but for the fact that they work in the ultrasonic range. One of the transducers is used as an emitter and the other as a receiver. The principle for measuring distance with this sensor is based on the echolocation system of animals such as bats. The sensor will emit ultrasound. If the ultrasound bounces against an obstacle, it will return to the sensor. Knowing the speed of sound in the air, we will measure the time between the emission and the reception of the sound to calculate the distance to the obstacle.

Using Sensors and Actuators with ROS

The HC-SR04 sensor has four male pins, **VCC** will be connected to 5V, GND will be connected to GND, the trigger will be connected to pin number 7, and **ECHO** will be connected to pin number 3. The trigger is used to activate the emission of ultrasound; when we write in pin number 7, a logical, high-level sensor will emit ultrasound waves. The echo pin will be at a high level if the sensor receives an ultrasound, as shown in the following diagram:

We will open `c4_examples5_2.ino` with the Arduino IDE and upload it to the board. The code is given here:

```
#include <ros.h>
#include <std_msgs/Int16.h>

ros::NodeHandle  nh;
std_msgs::Int16 range;
ros::Publisher range_pub("range", &range);
const int trigpin = 7;
const int echopin = 3;
long duration = 0;

void setup()
{
  nh.initNode();
```

[158]

```
    nh.advertise(range_pub);
  }

  void loop()
  {
    range.data = ping();
    range_pub.publish(&range);
    nh.spinOnce();
    delay(100);
  }

  long ping()
  {
  // Send out PING))) signal pulse
    pinMode(trigpin, OUTPUT);
    pinMode(echopin,INPUT);
    digitalWrite(trigpin, LOW);
    delayMicroseconds(2);
    digitalWrite(trigpin, HIGH);
    delayMicroseconds(10);
    digitalWrite(trigpin, LOW);
    //Get duration it takes to receive echo
    duration = pulseIn(echopin, HIGH);
    //Convert duration into distance
    return duration /29/2;
  }
```

We will include the `ros_lib` and `std_msgs/Int16` libraries, declare the `ros` handler and `std_msgs::Int16` named `"range"`. In this topic, Arduino will send the distance to the closest obstacle:

```
std_msgs::Int16 range;
ros::Publisher range_pub("range", &range);
```

In the `setup()` function, ROS is initialized and the message to be published is advertised as follows:

```
    nh.initNode();

    nh.advertise(range_pub);
```

In Arduino's `loop()` function, the `ping()` function is invoked to manage the ultrasonic sensor, the distance is calculated, and then the distance is published in centimeters. A delay of 100 ms is introduced to generate data at almost 10 hz:

```
range.data = ping();

range_pub.publish(&range);

nh.spinOnce();

delay(100);
```

The `ping()` function declares pin 7 as a digital output and pin 3 as a digital input. We will put pin number 7 to a low level to ensure that no sound is emitted and keep the channel clean. Then, it writes a digital high level during 10 microseconds.

After that, the `pulseIn()` Arduino function measures the time until the echo pin is at the high level, indicating that the ultrasound is received. This function returns the time in microseconds. Multiplying the duration of the pulse by the speed of sound, the distance is calculated. It's important to divide the distance by two because the sound pulse will go over two times the distance. First, it goes to the obstacle, and then it comes back to the sensor.

To run this node, we will execute `roscore` in a terminal. In a new one, we will execute the `rosserial` node to communicate with Arduino:

```
$ rosrun rosserial_python serial_node.py /dev/ttyACM0
```

Now, we should be prepared to use an ultrasound sensor in ROS.

As a curiosity, in the underwater robotics field, sonar technology is really fundamental; it plays the same role as a laser range sensor in ground robotics. As sound has better propagation features in water than it does in light, the sonar sensor is used to detect obstacles, to map, and to determine location.

How distance sensors send messages

If you have uploaded the code correctly to Arduino and `serial_node.py`, it's working well and we can see the topic name /range in the topic list:

```
$ rostopic list
```

You can learn about the type of the topic as usual by using the `rostopic` type:

```
$ rostopic type /range
std_msgs/Int16
```

If you want to check the data contained in the messages, we should type the following:

```
$ rostopic echo /range
```

You can play with this sensor, pointing it at objects at different distances.

Creating an example to use the ultrasound range

In this example, the ultrasound sensor will command the turtle of the `turtlesim` node. The example is programmed to behave depending on the distance to objects. This way, it is possible to avoid obstacles, publishing `geometry_msgs/Twist` in `turtlesim1/cmd_vel`. When the ultrasound finds an object too close, that is, less than 20 cm, the turtle will go backward. If an obstacle is found at a middle distance, that is, between 20 and 40 cm, the turtle will turn. If the obstacles are not found or if they are found at more than 40 cm, the turtle will go forward. You can open `c4_example5_2.cpp` to see the code:

```cpp
#include<ros/ros.h>
#include<geometry_msgs/Twist.h>
#include<std_msgs/Int16.h>
#include<iostream>
using namespace std;
ros::Publisher pub;
ros::Subscriber sub;

void rangeCallBack(const std_msgs::Int16 &range)
{
  geometry_msgs::Twist vel;
  if (range.data > 40)
  {
    vel.angular.z = 0;
    vel.linear.x = 1;
  }
  else if (range.data >20)
  {
    vel.angular.z = 1;
    vel.linear.x = 0;
  }
  else
  {
    vel.angular.z = 0;
    vel.linear.x = -1;
```

Using Sensors and Actuators with ROS

```
  }
  pub.publish(vel);
}


int main(int argc, char** argv)
{

  ros::init(argc, argv, "turtle_ultra_sound");
  ros::NodeHandle n;
  pub = n.advertise<geometry_msgs::Twist>("/turtle1/cmd_vel",1);
  sub = n.subscribe("range", 10, &rangeCallBack);
  ros::spin();
}
```

In the `main()` function, ROS is initialized and a publisher and a subscriber are declared. The publisher is `geometry_msgs::Twist /turtle1/cmd_vel` that controls the `turtlesim` node. The subscriber data comes from the ultrasound sensor, and each time a /range message is published, the /rangeCallBack function will run:

```
ros::init(argc, argv, "turtle_ultra_sound");
ros::NodeHandle n;
pub = n.advertise<geometry_msgs::Twist>("/turtle1/cmd_vel",1);
sub = n.subscribe("range", 10, &rangeCallBack);
ros::spin();
```

In /rangeCallBack, `std_msg::Int16` is expected, but `geometry_msgs::Twist` is declared. Depending on the range data, different values are assigned to /vel to model the three behaviors to avoid obstacles:

```
void rangeCallBack(const std_msgs::Int16 &range)
{
  geometry_msgs::Twist vel;
  if (range.data > 40)
  {
    vel.angular.z = 0;
    vel.linear.x = 1
  }
  ...
  pub.publish(vel);
}
```

To use this example, you should run `rosserial python`, the `turtlesim` node, and then `c4_example5_2`. Write the following commands in different terminals:

```
$ roscore
$ rosrun rosserial_python serial_node.py /dev/ttyACM0
$ rosrun chapter4_tutorials c4_example5_2
$ rosrun turtlesim turtlesim_node
```

Using the IMU – Xsens MTi

> *An inertial measurement unit, or IMU, is an electronic device that measures and reports on a craft's velocity, orientation, and gravitational forces, using a combination of accelerometers and gyroscopes, sometimes also magnetometers. IMUs are typically used to manoeuvre aircraft, including unmanned aerial vehicles (UAVs), among many others, and spacecraft, including satellites and landers.*
>
> *– Wikipedia*

In the following image, you can see the Xsens MTi, which is the sensor used in this section:

In this section, you will learn how to use it in ROS and how to use the topics published by the sensor. There is a small example with code to take data from the sensor and publish a new topic.

You can use a lot of IMU devices with ROS. In this section, we will use the Xsens IMU, which is necessary to install the right drivers. But if you want to use MicroStrain 3DM-GX2 or Wiimote with Wii Motion Plus, you need to download the following drivers:

- The drivers for the MicroStrain 3DM-GX2 IMU are available at http://www.ros.org/wiki/microstrain_3dmgx2_imu.
- The drivers for Wiimote with Wii Motion Plus are available at http://www.ros.org/wiki/wiimote.

To use our device, we are going to use `xsens_driver`. You can install it using the following command:

```
$ sudo apt-get install ros-hydro-xsens-driver
```

Using the following commands, we also need to install two packages because the driver depends on them:

```
$ rosstack profile
$ rospack profile
```

Now, we are going to start the IMU and see how it works. In a shell, launch the following command:

```
$ roslaunch xsens_driver xsens_driver.launch
```

This driver detects the USB port and the baud rate directly without any changes.

How does Xsens send data in ROS?

If everything is fine, you can see the topic list by using the `rostopic` command:

```
$ rostopic list
```

The node will publish three topics. We will work with `/imu/data` in this section. First of all, we are going to see the type and the data sent by this topic. To see the type and the fields, use the following command lines:

```
$ rostopic type /imu/data
$ rostopic type /imu/data | rosmsg show
```

The `/imu/data` topic is `sensor_msg/Imu`. The fields are used to indicate the orientation, acceleration, and velocity. In our example, we will use the orientation field. Check a message to see a real example of the data sent. You can do it with the following command:

```
$ rostopic echo /imu/data
```

You will see something similar to the following output:

```
---
header:
seq: 288
stamp:
  secs: 1330631562
  nsecs: 789304161
frame_id: xsens_mti_imu
orientation:
x: 0.00401890464127
y: -0.00402884092182
z: 0.679586052895
w: 0.73357373476
---
```

If you observe the orientation field, you will see four variables instead of three, as you would probably expect. This is because in ROS, the spatial orientation is represented using quaternions. You can find a lot of literature on the Internet about this concise and nonambiguous orientation representation.

We can observe the `imu` orientation in the `rviz` run and add the `imu` display type:

```
$ rosrun rviz rviz
```

Creating an example to use Xsens

Now that we know the type of data sent and what data we are going to use, let's start with the example.

In this example, we are going to use the IMU to move `turtlesim`. To do this, we need to take the data from the quaternion, convert it to Euler angles (`roll`, `pitch`, and `yaw`). We also need to take the rotation values around the *x* and *y* axes (roll and pitch) to move the turtle with a linear and angular movement.

The following code snippet is similar to the joystick code. Create a new file, `c4_example6.cpp`, in your `chapter4_tutorials/src/` directory and type in the following code:

```
#include<ros/ros.h>
#include<geometry_msgs/Twist.h>
#include<sensor_msgs/Imu.h>
#include<iostream>
```

```cpp
#include<tf/LinearMath/Matrix3x3.h>
#include<tf/LinearMath/Quaternion.h>

using namespace std;

class TeleopImu{
  public:
  TeleopImu();
  private:
  void callBack(const sensor_msgs::Imu::ConstPtr& imu);
  ros::NodeHandle n;
  ros::Publisher pub;
  ros::Subscriber sub;
};

TeleopImu::TeleopImu()
{
  pub = n.advertise<geometry_msgs::Twist>("/turtle1/cmd_vel",1);
  sub = n.subscribe<sensor_msgs::Imu>("imu/data", 10, &TeleopImu::callBack, this);
}

void TeleopImu::callBack(const sensor_msgs::Imu::ConstPtr& imu)
{
  geometry_msgs::Twist vel;
  tf::Quaternion bq(imu->orientation.x,imu->orientation.y,imu->orientation.z,imu->orientation.w);
  double roll,pitch,yaw;
  tf::Matrix3x3(bq).getRPY(roll,pitch,yaw);
  vel.angular.z = roll;
  vel.linear.x = pitch;
  pub.publish(vel);
}

int main(int argc, char** argv)
{
  ros::init(argc, argv, "teleopImu");
  TeleopImu teleop_turtle;
  ros::spin();
}
```

The node will subscribe to the `imu/data` topic and will publish a new topic with the movement commands for `turtlesim`:

```
TeleopImu::TeleopImu()
{
pub = n.advertise<geometry_msgs::Twist>("turtle1/cmd_vel",1);
sub = n.subscribe<sensor_msgs::Imu>("imu/data", 10,
&TeleopImu::callBack, this);
}
```

The important part of the code is the `callBack` function. Inside this callback method, the IMU topic is received and processed to create a new `geometry_msgs/Twist` topic. As you might remember, this type of message will control the velocity of `turtlesim`. The following code encapsulates this discussion:

```
void TeleopImu::callBack(const sensor_msgs::Imu::ConstPtr& imu)
{
...
tf::Matrix3x3(bq).getRPY(roll,pitch,yaw);
  vel.angular.z = roll;
    vel.linear.x = pitch;
pub.publish(vel);
}
```

The conversion of quaternions to Euler angles is done by means of the `Matrix3x3` class. Then, we use the accessor method, `getRPY`, provided by this class. Using this, we will get the roll, pitch, and yaw actions from the matrix about the fixed *x*, *y*, and *z* axes.

After that, we only need to assign the value of pitch and roll to the linear and angular velocity variables, respectively.

Now, if you run everything at the same time, you will see the turtle moving according to the IMU movements as if it were a joystick.

Using a low-cost IMU – 10 degrees of freedom

In this section, we will learn to use a low-cost sensor with 10 degrees of freedom (**DoF**). This sensor, which is similar to Xsens MTi, has an accelerometer (x3), a magnetometer (x3), a barometer (x1), and a gyroscope (x3). It is controlled with a simple I2C interface, and, in this example, it will be connected to Arduino Nano (http://arduino.cc/en/Main/ArduinoBoardNano).

This sensor is also used for similar uses. Xsens costs approximately $2,000, which is very expensive for normal users. The sensor explained in this section has an approximate cost of $20. The low price of this sensor permits its usage in a lot of projects. You can see this sensor in the following image. It is thin and has a few components:

This board has the following sensors:

- **ADXL345**: This is a three-axis accelerometer with a high resolution (13-bit) measurement of up to ±16 g. This sensor is widely used in mobile device applications. It measures the static acceleration of gravity in tilt-sensing applications as well as the dynamic acceleration resulting from motion or shock.
- **HMC5883L**: This sensor is designed for low-field magnetic sensing with a digital interface for devices such as low-cost compasses and magnetometers.
- **BMP085**: This is a high-precision barometric pressure sensor used in advanced mobile applications. It offers superior performance with an absolute accuracy up to to 0.03 hPa and has very low power consumption, 3 µA.
- **L3G4200D**: This is a three-axis gyroscope with a very high resolution (16-bit) measurement of up to 2,000 degrees per second (dps).This gyroscope measures how much the device is rotating around all three axes.

As we have said earlier, the board is controlled using the I2C protocol, and we will use Arduino to control it. In the following image, you can see the way to connect both the boards:

The only thing necessary to make it work is to connect the four wires. Connect GND and VCC from the sensor to GND and 5V in Arduino.

The **Serial Data Line (SDL)** must be connected to the analog pin **4**, and the **Serial Clock (SCK)** must be connected to the analog pin **5**. If you connect these pins wrongly, Arduino will not be able to communicate with the sensor.

Downloading the library for the accelerometer

Before using the sensor, it is necessary to download the right library for Arduino.

On the Internet, you can find a lot of libraries with different functionalities, but we will use the library that can be downloaded from `https://github.com/jenschr/Arduino-libraries`. Once you have downloaded the library, decompress it inside your sketchbook folder to load it.

You can find the libraries for the other sensors on the Internet. But to make your life easy, you can find all the necessary libraries to use the 10 DOF sensor in `chapter4_tutorials/libraries`. Inside each library, you can also find examples of how to use the sensor.

Programming Arduino Nano and the 10 DOF sensor

In this section, we are going to create a program in Arduino to take data from the accelerometers and publish it in ROS.

Using Sensors and Actuators with ROS

Open the Arduino IDE, create a new file with the name c4_example7.ino, and type in the following code:

```
#include <ros.h>
#include <std_msgs/Float32.h>

#include <Wire.h>
#include <ADXL345.h>

ADXL345 Accel;

ros::NodeHandle  nh;
std_msgs::Float32 velLinear_x;
std_msgs::Float32 velAngular_z;

ros::Publisher velLinear_x_pub("velLinear_x", &velLinear_x);
ros::Publisher velAngular_z_pub("velAngular_z", &velAngular_z);

void setup(){

  nh.initNode();
  nh.advertise(velLinear_x_pub);
  nh.advertise(velAngular_z_pub);

  Wire.begin();
  delay(100);
    Accel.set_bw(ADXL345_BW_12);

}

void loop(){

  double acc_data[3];
    Accel.get_Gxyz(acc_data);

  velLinear_x.data = acc_data[0];
  velAngular_z.data = acc_data[1];

  velLinear_x_pub.publish(&velLinear_x);
  velAngular_z_pub.publish(&velAngular_z);

  nh.spinOnce();
  delay(10);
}
```

Chapter 4

Let's break up the code and see the steps to take the data and publish it.

We are going to use two `Float32` variables to publish the data and it is necessary to include the following line in the program:

```
#include <std_msgs/Float32.h>
```

To be able to communicate with the sensor using the I2C Bus, we need to use the `Wire.h` library. This library is standard in Arduino:

```
#include <Wire.h>
```

To use the library downloaded before, we add the following `include` header:

```
#include <ADXL345.h>
```

We will use the `Accel` object to interact with the sensor:

```
ADXL345 Accel;
```

The data read from the sensor will be stored in the following variables: `velLinear_x`, which is used for linear velocity and the data is read from the accelerometer for the *x* axis, while `velAngular_z` is used for angular velocity and the data is read from the accelerometer for the *z* axis:

```
std_msgs::Float32 velLinear_x;
std_msgs::Float32 velAngular_z;
```

This program will publish two different topics—one for linear velocity and the other for angular velocity:

```
ros::Publisher velLinear_x_pub("velLinear_x", &velLinear_x);
ros::Publisher velAngular_z_pub("velAngular_z", &velAngular_z);
```

This is where the topic is created. Once you have executed these lines, you will see two topics in ROS with the names `velAngular_z` and `velLinear_x`:

```
nh.advertise(velLinear_x_pub);
nh.advertise(velAngular_z_pub);
```

The sensor and its bandwidth are initialized in this line as follows:

```
Accel.set_bw(ADXL345_BW_12);
```

The data returned by `get_Gxyz` is stored in a three-component vector:

```
double acc_data[3];
Accel.get_Gxyz(acc_data);
```

[171]

Using Sensors and Actuators with ROS

Finally, the data is published:

```
velLinear_x_pub.publish(&velLinear_x);
velAngular_z_pub.publish(&velAngular_z);
```

Creating an ROS node to use data from the 10 DOF sensor

In this section, we are going to create a new program to use data from the sensor and generate moving commands to move the turtle in turtlesim. The goal is to use the 10 DOF sensor board as the input for turtlesim and move the turtle by using the accelerometers.

So, create a new file inside the chapter4_tutorials/src directory with the name c4_example8.cpp and type in the following code:

```
#include<ros/ros.h>
#include<geometry_msgs/Twist.h>
#include<std_msgs/Float32.h>
class TeleopImu{
  public:
   TeleopImu();
   private:
     void velLinearCallBack(const std_msgs::Float32::ConstPtr& vx);
     void velAngularCallBack(const std_msgs::Float32::ConstPtr& wz);
     ros::NodeHandle n;
     ros::Publisher pub;
     ros::Subscriber velAngular_z_sub;
     ros::Subscriber velLinear_x_sub;
     geometry_msgs::Twist vel;
};

TeleopImu::TeleopImu()
{
  pub = n.advertise<geometry_msgs::Twist>("turtle1/cmd_vel",1);
  velLinear_x_sub = n.subscribe<std_msgs::Float32>("/velLinear_x", 1, &TeleopImu::velLinearCallBack, this);
  velAngular_z_sub = n.subscribe<std_msgs::Float32>("/velAngular_z", 1, &TeleopImu::velAngularCallBack, this);
}

void TeleopImu::velAngularCallBack(const std_msgs::Float32::ConstPtr& wz){
    vel.linear.x = -1 * wz->data;
```

```
      pub.publish(vel);
}



void TeleopImu::velLinearCallBack(const std_msgs::Float32::ConstPtr&
vx){
    vel.angular.z = vx->data;
    pub.publish(vel);
}



int main(int argc, char** argv)
{
    ros::init(argc, argv, "example8");
    TeleopImu teleop_turtle;
    ros::spin();
}
```

This code is similar to c4_example6.cpp that was used with the Xsens IMU; the only difference is the topic to subscribe, along with the type of data. In this case, we will subscribe to two topics created by Arduino Nano. These topics will be used to control turtlesim.

It is necessary to subscribe to the /velLinear_x and velAngular_z topics and we will do this as shown in the following lines:

```
velLinear_x_sub = n.subscribe<std_msgs::Float32>("/velLinear_x", 1,
&TeleopImu::velLinearCallBack, this);
velAngular_z_sub = n.subscribe<std_msgs::Float32>("/velAngular_z", 1,
&TeleopImu::velAngularCallBack, this);
```

Every time the node receives a message, it takes the data from the message, creates a new geometry_msgs/Twist message, and publishes it:

```
void TeleopImu::velAngularCallBack(const std_msgs::Float32::ConstPtr&
wz){
    vel.linear.x = -1 * wz->data;
    pub.publish(vel);
}



void TeleopImu::velLinearCallBack(const std_msgs::Float32::ConstPtr&
vx){
vel.angular .z=  vx->data;
    pub.publish(vel);
}
```

To run the example, remember to compile the code and follow the steps outlined.

Start a new session using the `roscore` command in a shell. Connect Arduino to the computer and launch the following command:

```
$ rosrun rosserial_python serial_node.py
```

Now, start `turtlesim` by typing the following command:

```
$ rosrun turtlesim turtlesim_node
```

And finally, type the following command to start the node:

```
$ rosrun chapter4_tutorials c4_example8
```

If everything is OK, you should see the `turtlesim` interface with the turtle moving. If you move the sensor, the turtle will move in a straight line or change its direction.

Using a GPS system

The **Global Positioning System (GPS)** is a space-based satellite system that provides information on the position and time for any weather and any place on the face of the earth and its vicinity. You must have an unobstructed direct path with four GPS satellites to obtain valid data.

The data received from the GPS conforms to the standards of communication set up by **National Maritime Electronics Association (NMEA)** and follows a protocol with different types of sentences. In them, we can find all the information about the position of the receiver. To read more about all the types of NMEA messages, you can visit http://www.gpsinformation.org/dale/nmea.htm.

One of the most interesting pieces of information about a GPS is contained in GGA sentences. They provide the current Fix data with the 3D location of the GPS. An example of this sentence and an explanation of each field are given here:

```
$GPGGA,123519,4807.038,N,01131.000,E,1,08,0.9,545.4,M,46.9,M,,*47
Where:
     GGA             Global Positioning System Fix Data
     123519          Fix taken at 12:35:19 UTC
     4807.038,N      Latitude 48 deg 07.038' N
     01131.000,E     Longitude 11 deg 31.000' E
     1               Fix quality: 0 = invalid
                                  1 = GPS fix (SPS)
                                  2 = DGPS fix
                                  3 = PPS fix
                                  4 = Real Time Kinematic
```

```
                        5 = Float RTK
                        6 = estimated (dead reckoning) (2.3
    feature)
                        7 = Manual input mode
                        8 = Simulation mode
    08              Number of satellites being tracked
    0.9             Horizontal dilution of position
    545.4,M         Altitude, Meters, above mean sea level
    46.9,M          Height of geoid (mean sea level) above WGS84
                        ellipsoid
    (empty field)   time in seconds since last DGPS update
    (empty field)   DGPS station ID number
    *47             the checksum data, always begins with *
```

Depending on the GPS receiver, we can find different performances and precisions. We have a simple GPS at a low cost that is commonly used in different applications, such as a UAV. They have an error that can be in the range of a few meters. Also, we can find expensive GPS devices that can be configured as differential GPS or can work in the **Real Time Kinematics** (**RTK**) mode, where a second GPS at a known location sends corrections to the first GPS. This GPS can achieve great results in terms of precision, with location errors below 10 cm.

In general, GPS uses serial protocols to transmit the data received to a computer or a microcontroller, such as Arduino. We can find devices that use TTL or RS232, and they are easy to connect to the computer with a USB adapter. In this section, we will use a low-cost GPS (EM-406a) and a really accurate system, such as GR-3 Topcon in the RTK mode. We will see that, with the same drivers, we can obtain the latitude, longitude, and altitude from both devices:

Using Sensors and Actuators with ROS

In order to control a GPS sensor with ROS, we will install the NMEA GPS driver package by using the following command line (don't forget to run the `rosstack` and `rospack` profiles after that):

```
$ sudo apt-get install ros-hydro-nmea-gps-driver
$ rosstack profile & rospack profile
```

To execute the GPS driver, we will run the `nmea_gpst_driver.py` file. To do that, we have to indicate two arguments: the port that is connected to the GPS and the baud rate:

```
$ rosrun nmea_gps_driver nmea_gps_driver.py _port:=/dev/ttyUSB0 _baud:=4800
```

In the case of the EM-406a GPS, the default baud rate is 4800 hz as indicated in the preceding command line. For Topcon GR-3, the baud rate is higher; it's about 115200 hz. If we want to use it with ROS, we will modify the `_baud` argument, as shown in the following command:

```
$ rosrun nmea_gps_driver nmea_gps_driver.py _port:=/dev/ttyUSB0 _baud:=115200
```

How GPS sends messages

If everything is OK, we will see a topic called `/fix` in the topic list by typing this:

```
$ rostopic list
```

To know which kind of data we will use, we typed the `rostopic` command. The NMEA GPS driver uses the `sensor_msgs/NavSatFix` message to send the GPS status information:

```
$ rostopic type /fix
```
`sensor_msgs/NavSatFix`

The `/fix` topic is `sensor_msg/NavSatFix`. The fields are used to indicate the latitude, longitude, altitude, status, quality of the service, and the covariance matrix. In our example, we will use the latitude and the longitude to project them to a 2D Cartesian coordinate system called **Universal Transverse Mercator** (**UTM**).

Check a message to see a real example of the data sent. You can do it with the following command:

```
$ rostopic echo /fix
```

You will see something that looks similar to the following output:

```
---
header:
  seq: 3
  stamp:
    secs: 1404993925
    nsecs: 255094051
  frame_id: /gps
status:
  status: 0
  service: 1
latitude: 28.0800916667
longitude: -15.451595
altitude: 315.3
position_covariance: [3.24, 0.0, 0.0, 0.0, 3.24, 0.0, 0.0, 0.0, 12.96]
position_covariance_type: 1
---
```

Creating an example project to use GPS

In this example, we are going to project the latitude and the longitude of a GPS to a 2D Cartesian space. For this, we will use a function written by Chuck Gantz that converts latitudes and longitudes into UTM coordinates. The node will subscribe to the /fix topic where GPS data is sent. You can find the code in chapter4_tutorials in the c4_example8.cpp file:

```
#include <ros/ros.h>
#include <tf/transform_broadcaster.h>
#include <nav_msgs/Odometry.h>
#include <stdio.h>
#include <iostream>
#include <sensor_msgs/NavSatFix.h>
geometry_msgs::Point global_position;
ros::Publisher position_pub;
void gpsCallBack(const sensor_msgs::NavSatFixConstPtr& gps)
{
   double northing, easting;
   char zone;
   LLtoUTM(gps->latitude, gps->longitude,  northing, easting , &zone);
   global_position.x = easting;
```

```
    global_position.y = northing;
    global_position.z = gps->altitude;
  }
  int main(int argc, char** argv){
    ros::init(argc,argv, "Geoposition");
    ros::NodeHandle n;
    ros::Subscriber gps_sub = n.subscribe("fix",10, gpsCallBack);
    position_pub = n.advertise<geometry_msgs::Point> ("global_position",
1);
    ros::Rate loop_rate(10);
    while(n.ok())
    {
      ros::spinOnce();
      loop_rate.sleep();
    }
  }
```

First, you should declare the NavSatFix message by using #include <sensor_msgs/NavSatFix.h>.

This way, we can subscribe to the /fix topic in the ros::Subscriber gps_sub = n.subscribe("fix",10, gpsCallBack) main function.

All the action happens in the gpsCallBack() function. We will use the LltoUTM() function to make the conversion from latitudes and longitudes to the UTM space. We will publish a geometry_msg/Point topic called /global_position with the UTM northing and easting coordinates and the altitude from the GPS.

To try this code, after running the GPS driver, you can use the following command:

```
$ rosrun chapter4_tutorials c4_example8
```

Summary

The use of sensors and actuators in robotics is very important since this is the only way to interact with the real world. In this chapter, you learned how to use, configure, and investigate further how certain common sensors and actuators work, which are used by a number of people in the world of robotics. We are sure that if you wish to use another type of sensor, you will find information on the Internet and in the ROS documentation about how to use it without problems.

In our opinion, Arduino is a very interesting device because you can add more devices and cheap sensors to your computer with it and use them within the ROS framework easily and transparently. Arduino has a large community and you can find information on many sensors, which cover the spectrum of applications you can imagine.

Finally, we must mention that the range laser will be a very useful sensor in the upcoming chapters. The reason is that it is a mandatory device to implement the navigation stack, which relies on the range readings it provides at a high frequency and with good precision. In the next chapter, you will see how to model your robot, visualize it in `rviz`, and use it by loading it on the Gazebo simulator, which is also integrated into ROS.

5
Computer Vision

ROS provides basic support for Computer Vision. First, drivers are available for different cameras and protocols, especially for FireWire (IEEE1394a or IEEE1394b) cameras. An image pipeline helps with the camera calibration process, distortion rectification, color decoding, and other low-level operations. For more complex tasks, you can use OpenCV, and the `cv_bridge` and `image_transport` libraries to interface with it and subscribe and publish images on topics. Finally, there are several packages that implement algorithms for object recognition, augmented reality, visual odometry, and so on.

Although FireWire cameras are best integrated in ROS, it is not difficult to support other protocols, such as USB and GigaEthernet. Since USB cameras are usually less expensive and easier to find, in this chapter we discuss several options, and we will also provide a driver that integrates seamlessly in the image pipeline, using the OpenCV video capture API.

The camera calibration and the result integration in the image pipeline is explained in detail. ROS provides GUIs to help with the camera calibration process, using a calibration pattern. Furthermore, we cover stereo cameras and explain how we can manage rigs of two or more cameras, with more complex setups than a binocular camera. Stereo vision will also let us obtain depth information from the world, up to an extent and depending on certain conditions. Hence, we will see how to inspect that information as point clouds and how to improve its quality to the best possible extent for our camera's quality and its setup.

Here, we explain the ROS image pipeline, which simplifies the process of converting the RAW images acquired by the camera into monochrome (grayscale) and color images; this sometimes means to "debayer" the RAW images if they are codified as a Bayer pattern. If the camera has been calibrated, the calibration information is used to rectify the images, that is, to correct the distortion. For stereo images, since we have the baseline between the left and right cameras, we can compute the disparity image that allows obtaining depth information and a 3D point cloud, once it has been fine-tuned; here, we will give tuning advice, which may be quite difficult for low-quality cameras and sometimes require good calibration results beforehand.

Finally, using OpenCV inside ROS, even though it's only version 2.x (version 3.x is not yet supported), we have the ability to implement a wide range of Computer Vision and Machine Learning algorithms or even to run some algorithms or examples already present in this library. Here, we will not see the OpenCV API, which is outside the scope of this book. On the contrary, we advise the reader to check the online documentation (http://docs.opencv.org) or any book about OpenCV and Computer Vision. Here, we simply show you how you can use OpenCV in your nodes, with an example of feature detection, descriptor extraction, and matching to compute the homography between two images. Additionally, this chapter will finish with a tutorial to set up and run a visual odometry implementation integrated into ROS: the viso2_ros wrapper of the libviso2 visual odometry library, using a stereo pair built with two cheap webcams attached to a supporting bar. Other visual odometry libraries will be mentioned, for example, fovis, along with some advice to start working with them and how to improve the results with RGBD sensors, such as Kinect, or even sensor fusion or additional information in the case of monocular vision.

Connecting and running the camera

The first few steps that we must perform are connecting the camera to the computer, running the driver, and seeing the images it acquires in ROS. Before we get into ROS, it is always a good idea to use external tools to check that the camera is actually recognized by our system, which, in our case, is an Ubuntu distribution. We will start with FireWire cameras since they are better supported in ROS, and later, we will see USB cameras.

FireWire IEEE1394 cameras

Connect your camera to the computer, which should have a FireWire IEEE1394a or IEEE1394b slot. Then, in Ubuntu, you only need coriander to check that the camera is recognized and working. If it is not already installed, just install coriander. Then, run it (in old Ubuntu distributions, you may have to run it as sudo):

```
$ coriander
```

> **Downloading the example code**
>
> You can download the example code files from your account at http://www.packtpub.com for all the Packt Publishing books you have purchased. If you purchased this book elsewhere, you can visit http://www.packtpub.com/support and register to have the files e-mailed directly to you. You can also download these code files from https://github.com/AaronMR/ROS_Book_Hydro.

It will automatically detect all your FireWire cameras, as shown in the next screenshot:

The great thing about `coriander` is that it also allows us to view the image and configure the camera. Indeed, our advice is to use the `coriander` package's camera configuration interface and then take those values into ROS, as we will see later. The advantage of this approach is that `coriander` gives us the dimensional values of some parameters, and in ROS, there are certain parameters that sometimes fail to be set, that is, gamma, and they may need to be set beforehand in `coriander` as a workaround.

Now that we know that the camera is working, we can close `coriander` and run the ROS FireWire camera driver (with `roscore` running):

```
$ rosrun camera1394 camera1394_node
```

Computer Vision

Simply run `roscore` and the preceding command. It will start the first camera on the bus, but note that you can select the camera by its GUID, which you can see in the `coriander` package's GUI.

The FireWire camera's parameters supported are listed and assigned sensible values in the `camera1394/config/firewire_camera/format7_mode0.yaml` file, as shown in the following code:

```
guid: 00b09d0100ab1324        # (defaults to first camera on bus)
iso_speed: 800  # IEEE1394b
video_mode: format7_mode0  # 1384x1036 @ 30fps bayer pattern
# Note that frame_rate is overwritten by frame_rate_feature; some useful values:
# 21fps (480)
frame_rate: 21 # max fps (Hz)
auto_frame_rate_feature: 3 # Manual (3)
frame_rate_feature: 480
format7_color_coding: raw8  # for bayer
bayer_pattern: rggb
bayer_method: HQ
auto_brightness: 3 # Manual (3)
brightness: 0
auto_exposure: 3 # Manual (3)
exposure: 350
auto_gain: 3 # Manual (3)
gain: 700
# We cannot set gamma manually in ROS, so we switch it off
auto_gamma: 0 # Off (0)
#gamma: 1024      # gamma 1
auto_saturation: 3 # Manual (3)
saturation: 1000
auto_sharpness: 3 # Manual (3)
sharpness: 1000
auto_shutter: 3 # Manual (3)
#shutter: 1000 # = 10ms
shutter: 1512 # = 20ms (1/50Hz), max. in 30fps
auto_white_balance: 3 # Manual (3)
```

```
white_balance_BU: 820
```

```
white_balance_RV: 520
```

```
frame_id: firewire_camera
```

```
camera_info_url: package://chapter5_tutorials/calibration/firewire_
camera/calibration_firewire_camera.yaml
```

The values must be tuned by watching the images acquired, for example, in `coriander`, and setting the values that give better images. The GUID parameter is used to select the camera, which is a unique value. You should usually set the shutter speed to a frequency equal to, or a multiple of, the electric light you have in the room to avoid flickering. If outside, with sun light, you only have to worry about setting a value that gives you an appropriate lightness. You can also put a high gain, but it will introduce noise. However, in general, it is better to have a salt-and-pepper noise such as that of a low shutter speed (to receive most light), because with a low shutter speed, we will have motion blur, and most algorithms perform badly with it. As you see, the configuration depends on the lighting conditions of the environment, and you may have to adapt the configuration to them. That is quite easy using `coriander` or the `rqt_reconfigure` interface (see the screenshots following the upcoming code, for instance):

```
$ rosrun rqt_reconfigure rqt_reconfigure /camera
```

```
$ coriander
```

In order to better understand how to properly set the parameters of the camera to obtain high-quality images, which are also algorithm-friendly, you are encouraged to find out more about the basic concepts of photography, such as the exposure triangle, which is a combination of shutter speed, ISO, and aperture.

Here, the camera's namespace is `/camera`. Then, we can change all the parameters that are specified in the `camera1394` dynamic reconfigure `cfg` file, as shown in *Chapter 3, Visualization and Debug Tools*. Here, for your convenience, you can create a launch file, which is also in `launch/firewire_camera.launch`:

```
<launch>
  <!-- Arguments -->
  <!-- Show video output (both RAW and rectified) -->
  <arg name="view" default="false"/>
  <!-- Camera params (config) -->
  <arg name="params" default="$(find chapter5_tutorials)/config/firewire_camera/format7_mode0.yaml"/>

  <!-- Camera driver -->
  <node pkg="camera1394" type="camera1394_node" name="camera1394_node">
      <rosparam file="$(arg params)"/>
  </node>

  <!-- Camera image processing (color + rectification) -->
```

```
        <node ns="camera" pkg="image_proc" type="image_proc" name="image_
proc"/>

        <!-- Show video output -->
        <group if="$(arg view)">
          <!-- Image viewer (non-rectified image) -->
          <node pkg="image_view" type="image_view" name="non_rectified_
image">
             <remap from="image" to="camera/image_color"/>
          </node>

          <!-- Image viewer (rectified image) -->
          <node pkg="image_view" type="image_view" name="rectified_image">
             <remap from="image" to="camera/image_rect_color"/>
          </node>
        </group>
</launch>
```

The `camera1394` driver is started with the parameters shown so far. Then, it also runs the image pipeline that we will see in the sequel in order to obtain the color-rectified images using the Debayer algorithm and the calibration parameters (once the camera has been calibrated). Finally, we have a conditional group to visualize the color and color-rectified images using `image_view` (or `rqt_image_view`).

In sum, in order to run a FireWire camera in ROS and view the images, once you have set its GUID in the parameters file, simply run the following command:

$ roslaunch chapter5_tutorials firewire_camera.launch view:=true

Then, you can also configure it dynamically with `rqt_reconfigure`.

USB cameras

Now, we are going to do the same thing with USB cameras. The only problem is that, surprisingly, they are not inherently supported by ROS. First of all, once you connect the camera to the computer, test it with a chat or video meeting program, for example, Skype or Cheese. The camera resource should appear in /dev/video?, where ? should be a number starting with 0 (that may be your internal webcam if you are using a laptop).

There are two main options that deserve to be mentioned as possible USB camera drivers for ROS. First, we have `usb_cam`. To install it, use the following command:

$ sudo apt-get install ros-hydro-usb-cam

Then, run the following command:

```
$ roslaunch chapter5_tutorials usb_cam.launch view:=true
```

It simply does `rosrun usb_cam usb_cam_node` and also shows the camera images with `image_view` (or `rqt_image_view`), so you should see something similar to the following screenshot. It has the RAW image of the USB camera, which is already in color:

Similarly, another good option is `gscam`, which is installed as follows:

```
$ sudo apt-get install ros-hydro-gscam
```

Then, run the following command:

```
$ roslaunch chapter5_tuturials gscam.launch view:=true
```

As for `usb_cam`, this launch file performs a `rosrun gscam gscam` and also sets the camera's parameters. It also visualizes the camera's images with `image_view` (or `rqt_image_view`), as shown in the following screenshot:

The parameters required by `gscam` are as follows (see `config/gscam/logitech.yaml`):

```
gscam_config: v4l2src device=/dev/video0 ! video/x-raw-
rgb,framerate=30/1 ! ffmpegcolorspace
frame_id: gscam
camera_info_url: package://chapter5_tutorials/calibration/gscam/
calibration_gscam.yaml
```

The `gscam_config` parameter invokes the `v4l2src` command with appropriate arguments to run the camera. The rest of the parameters will be useful once the camera is calibrated and used in the ROS image pipeline.

Writing your own USB camera driver with OpenCV

Although we have the preceding two options, this book comes with its own USB camera driver, implemented on top of OpenCV, using the `cv::VideoCapture` class. It runs the camera and also allows changing some of its parameters as long as they are supported by the camera's firmware. It also allows us to set the calibration information in the same way as with the FireWire cameras. With `usb_cam`, this is not possible because the `CameraInfo` message is not available. With respect to `gscam`, we will have more control; we can change the camera configuration and also see how to publish the camera's images and information in ROS. In order to implement a camera driver using OpenCV, we have two options about how we read images from the camera. First, we can poll with a target **Frames Per Second** (**FPS**); secondly, we can set a timer for the period of such FPS and, in the timer callback, we perform the actual reading. Depending on the FPS, one solution may be better than the other in terms of CPU consumption. Anyway, note that the polling is not blocking since the OpenCV reading function waits until an image is ready; meanwhile, other processes can take the CPU. In general, for fast FPS, it is better to use polling, so we do not incur the time penalty of using the timer and its callback. For low FPS, the timer should be similar to polling, and the code is in some way cleaner. We invite the reader to compare both implementations in the `src/camera_polling.cpp` and `src/camera_timer.cpp` files. For the sake of space, here we show the timer-based approach. Indeed, the final driver in `src/camera.cpp` uses a timer. Note that the final driver also includes the camera information management, which we will see in the sequel.

Computer Vision

In the package, we must set the dependency with OpenCV, the ROS image message libraries, and related. They are the following packages:

```
<depend package="sensor_msgs"/>
<depend package="opencv2"/>
<depend package="cv_bridge"/>
<depend package="image_transport"/>
```

Consequently, in `src/camera_timer.cpp`, we have the following headers:

```
#include <ros/ros.h>
#include <image_transport/image_transport.h>
#include <cv_bridge/cv_bridge.h>
#include <sensor_msgs/image_encodings.h>
#include <opencv2/highgui/highgui.hpp>
```

The `image_transport` API allows the publishing of images using several transport formats seamlessly, which can be compressed images, with different codecs, based on the plugins installed in the ROS system, for example, `compressed` and `theora`. The `cv_bridge` is used to convert from OpenCV images to ROS `Image` messages, for which we may need the image encoding of `sensor_msgs`, in the case of grayscale/color conversion. Finally, we need the `highgui` API of OpenCV (`opencv2`) in order to use `cv::VideoCapture`.

Here, we will explain the main parts of the code in `src/camera_timer.cpp`, which has a class that implements the camera driver. Its attributes are as follows:

```
ros::NodeHandle nh;
image_transport::ImageTransport it;
image_transport::Publisher pub_image_raw;

cv::VideoCapture camera;
cv::Mat image;
cv_bridge::CvImagePtr frame;

ros::Timer timer;

int camera_index;
int fps;
```

As usual, we need the node handle. Then, we need `ImageTransport` that is used to send the images in all available formats in a seamless way. In the code, we only need to use `Publisher` (only one), but note that it must be a specialization of the `image_transport` library.

Then, we have the OpenCV stuff to capture images/frames. In the case of the frame, we directly use the `cv_brigde` frame, which is `CvImagePtr`, because we can access the image field it has.

Finally, we have the timer, and the basic camera parameters for the driver to work. This is the most basic driver possible. These parameters are the camera index, that is, the number for the `/dev/video?` device, for example, 0 for `/dev/video0`; the camera index is passed to `cv::VideoCapture`. And the `fps` parameter sets the camera FPS (if possible) and the timer. Here, we use an `int` value, but it will be a double in the final version, `src/camera.cpp`.

The driver uses the class constructor for the setup or initialization of the node, the camera, and the timer:

```
nh.param<int>( "camera_index", camera_index, DEFAULT_CAMERA_INDEX );

if ( not camera.isOpened() )
{
    ROS_ERROR_STREAM( "Failed to open camera device!" );
    ros::shutdown();
}

nh.param<int>( "fps", fps, DEFAULT_FPS );
ros::Duration period = ros::Duration( 1. / fps );

pub_image_raw = it.advertise( "image_raw", 1 );

frame = boost::make_shared< cv_bridge::CvImage >();
frame->encoding = sensor_msgs::image_encodings::BGR8;

timer = nh.createTimer( period, &CameraDriver::capture, this );
```

First, we open the camera and abort it if it does not open. Note that we must do this in the attribute constructor, shown as follows, where `camera_index` is passed by the parameter:

```
camera( camera_index )
```

Then, we read the `fps` parameter and compute the timer period, which is used to create the timer and set the capture callback at the end. We advertise the image publisher using the image transport API, for `image_raw` (RAW images), and initialize the `frame` variable.

The capture callback method reads and publishes images as follows:

```
camera >> frame->image;
if( not frame->image.empty() )
{
  frame->header.stamp = ros::Time::now();
  pub_image_raw.publish( frame->toImageMsg() );
}
```

The preceding method captures the images, checks whether a frame was actually captured, and in that case, sets the timestamp and publishes the image, which is converted to a ROS `Image`.

You can run this node with the following command:

```
$ rosrun chapter5_tutorials camera_timer _camera_index:=0 _fps:=15
```

This will open the `/dev/video0` camera at 15 fps.

Then, you can use `image_view` or `rqt_image_view` to see the images. Similarly, for the polling implementation, you have the following command:

```
$ roslaunch chapter5_tutorials camera_polling.launch camera_index:=0 fps:=15 view:=true
```

With the preceding command, you will see the `/camera/image_raw` topic images.

For the timer implementation, we also have the `camera.launch` file, which runs the final version and provides more options that we will see throughout this entire chapter. The main contributions of the final version are the support for dynamic reconfiguration parameters and that it provides the camera information that includes the camera calibration. We are going to show how to do this in brief, and we advise that you see the source code for a more detailed understanding.

As with the FireWire cameras, we can give support for the dynamic reconfiguration of the camera's parameters. However, most USB cameras do not support changing certain parameters. What we do is expose all OpenCV supported parameters and warn in case of error (or disable a few of them). The configuration file is in `cfg/Camera.cfg`; check it for the details. It supports the following parameters:

- `camera_index`: This parameter is used to select the `/dev/video?` device.
- `frame_width` and `frame_height`: These parameters give the image resolution.
- `fps`: This parameter sets the camera FPS.

- `fourcc`: This parameter specifies the camera pixel format in the FOURCC format (http://www.fourcc.org). The file format is typically YUYV or MJPEG, but they fail to change in most USB cameras with OpenCV.

- `brightness, contrast, saturation, hue`: These parameters set the camera's properties. In digital cameras, this is done by software, during the acquisition process in the sensor, or simply on the resulting image.

- `gain`: This parameter sets the gain of the **Analog-Digital Converter (ADC)** of the sensor. It introduces salt-and-pepper noise into the image but increases the lightness in dark environments.

- `exposure`: This parameter sets the lightness of the images, usually by adapting the gain and shutter speed (in low-cost cameras, this is simply the integration time of the light that enters the sensor).

- `frame_id`: This parameter is the camera frame, useful if we use it for navigation, as we will see in the *Using visual odometry with viso2* section.

- `camera_info_url`: This parameter provides the path to the camera's information, which is basically its calibration.

Then, in the following line of code, in the driver, we use a dynamic reconfigure server:

```
#include <dynamic_reconfigure/server.h>
```

We set a callback in the constructor:

```
server.setCallback( boost::bind( &CameraDriver::reconfig, this, _1, _2 ) );
```

The `setCallback` constructor reconfigures the camera. We even allow changing the camera and stopping the current one when the `camera_index` is changed. Then, we use the OpenCV `cv::VideoCapture` class to set the camera's properties, which are part of the parameters shown in the preceding line. As an example, in the case of `frame_width`, we use the following commands:

```
newconfig.frame_width = setProperty( camera, CV_CAP_PROP_FRAME_WIDTH , newconfig.frame_width );
```

This relies on a private method named `setProperty`, which calls the `set` method of `cv::VideoCapture` and controls the cases in which it fails to print an ROS warning message. Note that the FPS is changed in the timer itself and usually cannot be modified in the camera. Finally, it is important to note that all this reconfiguration is done within a locked mutex to avoid acquiring any images while reconfiguring the driver.

Computer Vision

In order to set the camera's information, ROS has a `camera_info_manager` library that helps us to do so, as shown in the following line:

```
#include <camera_info_manager/camera_info_manager.h>
```

We use the library to obtain the `CameraInfo` message. Now, in the capture callback of the timer, we use `image_transport::CameraPublisher` and not only for the images. The code is as follows:

```
camera >> frame->image;
if( not frame->image.empty() )
{
  frame->header.stamp = ros::Time::now();

  *camera_info = camera_info_manager.getCameraInfo();
  camera_info->header = frame->header;

  camera_pub.publish( frame->toImageMsg(), camera_info );
}
```

This is run within the mutex mentioned previously for the reconfiguration method. Now, we do the same as for the first version of the driver but also retrieve the camera information from the manager, which is set with the node handler, the camera name, and `camera_info_url` in the reconfiguration method (which is always called once on loading). Then, we publish both the image/frame (ROS `Image`) and the `CameraImage` messages.

In order to use this driver, use the following command:

```
$ roslaunch chapter5_tutorials camera.launch view:=true
```

The command will use the `config/camera/webcam.yaml` parameter as default, which sets all the dynamic reconfiguration parameters seen so far.

You can check that the camera is working with `rostopic list` and `rostopic hz /camera/image_raw`; you can also check with `image_view` or `rqt_image_view`.

With the implementation of this driver, we have used all the resources available in ROS to work with cameras, images, and Computer Vision. In the following sections, for the sake of clarity, we explain each of them separately.

Using OpenCV and ROS images with cv_bridge

If we have an OpenCV image, that is, `cv::Mat image`, we need the `cv_bridge` library to convert it into a ROS `Image` message and publish it. We have the option to share or copy the image, with `CvShare` or `CvCopy`, respectively. However, if possible, it is easier to use the OpenCV image field inside the `CvImage` class provided by `cv_bridge`. That is exactly what we do in the camera driver as a pointer:

```
cv_bridge::CvImagePtr frame;
```

Being a pointer, we initialize it in the following way:

```
frame = boost::make_shared< cv_bridge::CvImage >();
```

If we know the image encoding beforehand, we can use the following code:

```
frame->encoding = sensor_msgs::image_encodings::BGR8;
```

Later, we set the OpenCV image at some point, for example, capturing it from a camera:

```
camera >> frame->image;
```

It is also common to set the timestamp of the message at this point:

```
frame->header.stamp = ros::Time::now();
```

Now we only have to publish it. To do so, we need a publisher and it must use the `image_transport` API of ROS. This is shown in the following section.

Publishing images with image transport

We can publish single images with `ros::Publisher`, but it is better to use an `image_transport` publisher. It can publish images with their corresponding camera information. That is exactly what we did for the camera driver previously. The `image_transport` API is useful to provide different transport formats in a seamless way. The images you publish actually appear in several topics. Apart from the basic, uncompressed one, you will see a compressed one or even more. The number of supported transports depends on the plugins installed in your system; you will usually have the `compressed` and `theora` transports. You can see this with `rostopic info`. In order to install all the plugins, use the following command:

```
$ sudo apt-get install ros-hydro-image-transport-plugins
```

Computer Vision

In your code, you need the node handle to create the image transport and then the publisher. In this example, we will use a simple image publisher; please check the final USB camera driver for the `CameraPublisher` usage:

```
ros::NodeHandle nh;
image_transport::ImageTransport it;
image_transport::Publisher pub_image_raw;
```

The node handle and the image transport are constructed with (in the attribute constructors of a class) the following code:

```
nh( "~" ),
it( nh )
```

Then, for an `image_raw` topic, the publisher is created this way within the node namespace:

```
pub_image_raw = it.advertise( "image_raw", 1 );
```

Hence, now the frame shown in the previous section can be published with the following code:

```
pub_image_raw.publish( frame->toImageMsg() );
```

Using OpenCV in ROS

ROS uses the standalone OpenCV library installed on your system. However, you must specify a build and running dependency with an `opencv2` package in the `package.xml` file:

```
<build_depend>opencv2</build_depend>
<run_depend>opencv2</run_depend>
```

In `CMakeLists.xml`, we have to insert the following lines:

```
find_package(OpenCV)
include_directories(${catkin_INCLUDE_DIRS} ${OpenCV_INCLUDE_DIRS})
```

Then, for each library or executable that uses OpenCV, we must add `${OpenCV_LIBS}` to `target_link_libraries` (see `CMakeLists.txt` provided for the `chapter5_tutorials` package).

In our node `cpp` file, we include any of the OpenCV libraries we need. For example, for `highgui.hpp`, we use the following line:

```
#include <opencv2/highgui/highgui.hpp>
```

Now, you can use any of the OpenCV API classes, functions, and so on, in your code, as usual. Simply use its `cv` namespace and follow any OpenCV tutorial if you are starting with it. Note that this book is not about OpenCV—just how we can do Computer Vision inside ROS.

Visualizing the camera input images

In *Chapter 3*, *Visualization and Debug Tools*, we explained how to visualize any image published in the ROS framework by using the `image_view` node of the `image_view` package or `rqt_image_view`. The following code encapsulates this discussion:

```
$ rosrun image_view image_view image:=/camera/image_raw
```

What is important here is the fact that using the image transport, we can select different topics to see the images using compressed formats if required. Also, in the case of stereo vision, as we will see later, we can use `rqtrviz` to see the point cloud obtained with the disparity image.

Calibrating the camera

Most cameras, especially wide-angle ones, exhibit large distortions. We can model such distortions as radial or tangential and compute the coefficients of that model using calibration algorithms. The camera calibration algorithms also obtain a calibration matrix that contains the focal distance and principle point of the lens and, hence, provide a way to measure distances in the world using the images acquired. In the case of stereo vision, it is also possible to retrieve depth information, that is, the distance of the pixels to the camera, as we will see later. Consequently, we have 3D information of the world up to an extent.

The calibration is done by showing several views of a known image named calibration pattern, which is typically a chessboard/checkerboard. It can also be an array of circles or an asymmetric pattern of circles; note that circles are seen as ellipses by the camera for skew views. A detection algorithm obtains the inner corner point of the cells in the chessboard and uses them to estimate the camera's intrinsic and extrinsic parameters. In brief, the extrinsic parameters are the pose of the camera or, in other words, the pose of the pattern with respect to the camera if we left the camera in a fixed position. What we want are the intrinsic parameters because they do not change, can be used later for the camera in any pose, allow the measuring of distances in the images, and allow correcting the image distortion, that is, rectifying the image.

Computer Vision

With our camera driver running, we can use the calibration tool of ROS to calibrate it. It is important that the camera driver provides `CameraInfo` messages and has the `camera_info_set` service, which allows the setting of the path to the calibration results file. Later, this calibration information is always loaded by the image pipeline when using the camera. One camera driver that satisfies these prerequisites is the `camera1394` driver for the FireWire cameras. In order to calibrate your FireWire camera, use the following command:

```
$ roslaunch chapter5_tutorials calibration_firewire_camera_chessboard.launch
```

This will open a GUI that automatically selects the views of our calibration pattern and provides bars to inform how each axis is covered by the views retrieved. It comprises the *x* and *y* axes, meaning how close the pattern has been shown to each extreme of these axes in the image plane, that is, the horizontal and vertical axes, respectively. Then, the scale goes from close to far (up to the distance at which the detection works). Finally, skew requires that views of the pattern tilt in both the *x* and *y* axes. The three buttons below these bars are disabled by default, as shown in the following screenshot:

You will see the points detected overlaid over the pattern every time the detector finds them. The views are automatically selected to cover a representative number of different views, so you must show views to make the bars become green from one side to the other, following the instructions given in the following section. In theory, two views are enough, but in practice, around ten are usually needed. In fact, this interface captures even more (30 to 40). You should avoid fast movements because blurry images are bad for detection. Once the tool has enough views, it will allow you to calibrate, that is, to start the optimizer that, given the points detected in the calibration pattern views, solve the system of the pinhole camera model. This is shown in the following screenshot:

Then, you can save the calibration data and commit the calibration results to the camera, that is, it uses the `camera_info_set` service to commit the calibration to the camera, so later, it is detected automatically by the ROS image pipeline.

The launch file provided for the calibration simply uses `cameracalibrator.py` of the `camera_calibration` package:

```
<node pkg="camera_calibration" type="cameracalibrator.py"
  name="cameracalibrator" args="--size 8x6 --square 0.030"
  output="screen">
    <remap from="image" to="camera/image_color" />
    <remap from="camera" to="camera" />
</node>
```

Computer Vision

The calibration tool only needs the pattern's characteristics (the number of squares and their size, `--size 8x6` and `--square 0.030` in this case), the `image` topic, and the `camera` namespace.

The launch file also runs the image pipeline, but it is not required. In fact, instead of the `image_color` topic, we could have used the `image_raw` one.

Once you have saved the calibration (save button), a file is created in your `/tmp` directory. It contains the calibration pattern views used for the calibration. You can find it at `/tmp/calibrationdata.tar.gz`; the ones used for the calibration in the book can be found in the `calibration` directory and the `firewire_camera` subfolder for the FireWire camera. Similarly, on the terminal (`stdout` output), you will see information regarding the views taken and the calibration results. The ones obtained for the book are in the same folder as the calibration data. The calibration results can also be consulted in the `ost.txt` file inside the `calibrationdata.tar.gz` ZIP file. Anyway, remember that, after the commit, the calibration file is updated with the calibration matrix and the coefficients of the distortion model. A good way to do so consists of on creating a dummy calibration file before the calibration. In our package, that file is in `calibration/firewire_camera/calibration_firewire_camera.yaml`, which is referenced by the parameters file:

```
camera_info_url: package://chapter5_tutorials/calibration/firewire_camera/calibration_firewire_camera.yaml
```

Now, we can use our camera again with the image pipeline, and the rectified images will have the distortion corrected as a clear sign that the camera is calibrated correctly. Since ROS uses the Zhang calibration method implemented in OpenCV, for more details on the calibration formulas, our advice is that you consult its documentation at http://docs.opencv.org/doc/tutorials/calib3d/camera_calibration/camera_calibration.html.

Finally, you can also play with different calibration patterns using the following launch files for circles and asymmetric circles (http://docs.opencv.org/trunk/_downloads/acircles_pattern.png), prepared for FireWire cameras, as an example:

```
roslaunch chapter5_tutorials calibration_firewire_camera_circles.launch
roslaunch chapter5_tutorials calibration_firewire_camera_acircles.launch
```

You can also use multiple chessboard patterns for a single calibration using patterns of different sizes. However, we think it is enough to use a single chessboard pattern printed with good quality. Indeed, for the USB camera driver, we only use that.

In the case of the USB camera driver, we have a more powerful launch file, which integrates the camera calibration node; there is also a standalone one for FireWire cameras, though. Hence, in order to calibrate your camera, use the following action:

```
$ roslaunch chapter5_tutorials camera.launch calibrate:=true
```

In the next screenshots, you can see the steps of the calibration process in the GUI, identical to the case of FireWire cameras. That means we have an operating `camera_info_set` service.

After pressing the calibrate button, the calibration optimization algorithm will take a while to find the best camera intrinsic and extrinsic parameters. Once it is done, the save and commit will be enabled. The following screenshot shows this:

Stereo calibration

The next step consists of working with stereo cameras. One option is to run two monocular camera nodes, but in general, it is better to consider the whole stereo pair as a single sensor because the images must be synchronized. In ROS, there is no driver for FireWire stereo cameras, but we can use an extension to stereo using the following command line:

```
$ git clone git://github.com/srv/camera1394stereo.git
```

However, FireWire stereo pairs are quite expensive. For this reason, we provide a stereo camera driver for USB cameras. We use the Logitech C120 USB webcam, which is very cheap. It is also noisy, but we will see that we can do great things with it after we calibrate them. It is important that, in the stereo pair, the cameras are similar, but you can try with different cameras as well. Our setup for the cameras is shown in the images. You only need the two cameras on the same plane and pointing in parallel directions. We have a baseline of approximately 12 cm, which will also be computed in the stereo calibration process. As you can see in the following screenshot, you only need a rod to attach the cameras to, with zip ties:

Now, connect the cameras to your USB slots. It is good practice to connect the left-hand side camera first and then the right-hand side one. This way, they are assigned to the /dev/video0 and /dev/video1 devices, or 1 and 2 if 0 was already taken. Alternatively, you can create a udev rule.

Then, you can test each camera individually as we would do for a single camera. Some tools you will find useful are the video4linux control panels for cameras:

```
$ sudo apt-get install v4l-utils qv4l2
```

You might experience the following problem:

```
In case of problems with stereo:
libv4l2: error turning on stream: No space left on device
```

Computer Vision

This happens because you must connect each camera to a different USB controller; note that certain USB slots are managed by the same controller and hence it cannot deal with the bandwidth of more than a single camera. If you only have a USB controller, there are other options you can try. First, try to use a compressed pixel format, such as MJPEG in both cameras. You can check whether it is supported by your camera or not using the following command:

```
$ v4l2-ctl -d /dev/video2 --list-formats
```

The command will generate something similar to the following output:

```
ioctl: VIDIOC_ENUM_FMT
Index          : 0
Type           : Video Capture
Pixel Format: 'YUYV'
Name           : YUV 4:2:2 (YUYV)

Index          : 1
Type           : Video Capture
Pixel Format: 'MJPG' (compressed)
Name           : MJPEG
```

If MJPEG is supported, we can use more than one camera in the same USB controller; otherwise, with uncompressed pixel formats, we must use different USB controllers or reduce the resolution to 320 x 240 or lower. Similarly, with the GUI of qv4l2, you can check this and test your camera. You can also check whether it is possible to set the desired pixel format. In fact, this does not work for our USB cameras using the OpenCV set method, so we use an USB slot managed by a different USB controller.

The USB stereo camera driver that comes with this book is based on the USB camera discussed so far. Basically, the driver extends the camera to support camera publishers, which send the left-hand side and right-hand side images and the camera information as well. You can run it and view the images by using the following command:

```
$ roslaunch chapter5_tutorials camera_stereo.launch view:=true
```

It also shows the disparity image of the left-hand side and right-hand side cameras, which will be useful once the cameras are calibrated since it is used by the ROS image pipeline. In order to calibrate the cameras, use the following command:

```
$ roslaunch chapter5_tutorials camera_stereo.launch calibrate:=true
```

Chapter 5

You will see a GUI for monocular cameras similar to the following screenshot:

At the time the preceding image was taken, we showed enough views to start the calibration. Note that the calibration pattern must be detected by both cameras simultaneously to be included for the calibration optimization step. Depending on the setup, this may be quite tricky, so you should put the pattern at the appropriate distance from the camera. You can see the setup used for the calibration of this book in the next image:

The calibration is done by the same `cameracalibrator.py` node used for monocular cameras. We pass the left-hand side and right-hand side cameras and images, so the tool knows that we are going to do stereo calibration. The following is the node in the launch file:

```
<node ns="$(arg camera)" name="cameracalibrator"
  pkg="camera_calibration" type="cameracalibrator.py"
  args="--size 8x6 --square 0.030" output="screen">
    <remap from="left" to="left/image_raw"/>
    <remap from="right" to="right/image_raw"/>
    <remap from="left_camera" to="left"/>
    <remap from="right_camera" to="right"/>
</node>
```

The result of the calibration is the same as for monocular cameras, but in this case, we have two calibration files, one for each camera. In accordance with the parameters file in `config/camera_stereo/logitech_c120.yaml`, we have the following code:

```
camera_info_url_left: package://chapter5_tutorials/calibration/camera_stereo/${NAME}.yaml
camera_info_url_right: package://chapter5_tutorials/calibration/camera_stereo/${NAME}.yaml
```

`${NAME}` is the name of the camera, which resolved to `logitech_c120_left` and `logitech_c120_right` for the left-hand side and right-hand side cameras, respectively. After the commit of the calibration, those files are updated with the calibration of each camera. They contain the calibration matrix, the distortion model coefficients, and the rectification and projection matrix, which includes the baseline, that is, the separation between each camera in the x axis of the image plane. In the parameters file, you can also see values for the camera properties that have been set for indoor environments with artificial light; the camera model used has some autocorrection, so sometimes, the images may be quite bad, but these values seem to work well in most cases.

The ROS image pipeline

The ROS image pipeline is run with the `image_proc` package. It provides all the conversion utilities to obtain monochrome and color images from the RAW images acquired from the camera. In the case of FireWire cameras, which may use a Bayer pattern to code the images (actually in the sensor itself), it debayers them to obtain the color images. Once you have calibrated the camera, the image pipeline takes the `CameraInfo` messages, which contain that information, and rectifies the images. Here, rectification means to un-distort the images, so it takes the coefficients of the distortion model to correct the radial and tangential distortion.

As a result, you will see more topics for your camera in its namespace. In the following screenshots, you can see the `image_raw`, `image_mono`, and `image_color` topics, which display the RAW, monochrome, and color images, respectively:

Computer Vision

Chapter 5

The rectified images are provided in monochrome and color in the `image_rect` and `image_rect_color` topics. In the following image, we compare the uncalibrated, distorted RAW images with the rectified ones. You can see the correction because the pattern shown in the screenshots has straight lines only in the rectified images, particularly in areas far from the center (principle point) of the image (sensor):

Computer Vision

You can see all the topics available with `rostopic list` or `rqt_graph`, which include the `image_transport` topics as well.

You can view the `image_raw` topic of a monocular camera directly with the following command:

```
$ roslaunch chapter5_tutorials camera.launch view:=true
```

It can be changed to see other topics, but for these cameras, the RAW images are already in color. However, in order to see the rectified ones, use `image_rect_color` with `image_view` or `rqt_image_view`, or change the launch file. The `image_proc` node is used to make all these topics available. The following code shows this:

```
<node ns="$(arg camera)" pkg="image_proc" type="image_proc" name="image_proc"/>
```

The image pipeline for stereo cameras

In the case of stereo cameras, we have the same for the left-hand side and right-hand side cameras. However, there are specific visualization tools for them because we can use the left-hand side and right-hand side images to compute and see the disparity image. An algorithm uses stereo calibration and the texture of both images to estimate the depth of each pixel, which is the disparity image. To obtain good results, we must tune the algorithm that computes such an image. In the next screenshot, we see the left-hand side, right-hand side, and disparity images as well as `rqt_reconfiguire` for `stereo_image_proc`, which is the node that builds the image pipeline for stereo images; in the launch file, we only need the following lines:

```
<node ns="$(arg camera)" pkg="stereo_image_proc" type="stereo_image_proc"
    name="stereo_image_proc" output="screen">
  <rosparam file="$(arg params_disparity)"/>
</node>
```

It requires the disparity parameters, which can be set with `rqt_reconfigure` as shown in the following screenshot and saved with `rosparam dump /stereo/stereo_image_proc`:

We have good values for the environment used in this book's demonstration in the `config/camera_stereo/disparity.yaml` parameters file. This is shown in the following code:

```
{correlation_window_size: 33, disparity_range: 32, min_disparity: 25,
prefilter_cap: 5,
  prefilter_size: 15, speckle_range: 15, speckle_size: 50, texture_
threshold: 1000,
  uniqueness_ratio: 5.0}
```

However, these parameters depend a lot on the calibration quality and the environment. You should adjust it to your experiments. It takes time and it is quite tricky, but you can follow the next guidelines. Basically, you start by setting a `disparity_range` value that makes enough blobs appear. You also have to set `min_disparity`, so you see areas covering the whole range of depths (from red to blue/purple). Then, you can fine-tune the result, setting `speckle_size`, to remove small, noisy blobs. Also, modify `uniqueness_ratio` and `texture_threshold` to have larger blobs. The `correlation_window_size` is also important since it affects the detection of initial blobs.

If it becomes very difficult to obtain good results, you might have to recalibrate or use better cameras for your environment and lighting conditions. You can also try it in another environment or with more light. It is important that you have texture in the environment; for example, from a flat, white wall, you cannot find any disparity. Also, depending on the baseline, you cannot retrieve depth information very close to the camera. For stereo navigation, it is better to have a large baseline, say 12 cm or more. We use it here because, later, we will try visual odometry. However, with this setup, we only have depth information one meter apart from the cameras. With a smaller baseline, on the contrary, we can obtain depth information from closer objects. This is bad for navigation because we lose resolution far away, but it is good for perception and grasping.

As far as calibration problems go, you can check your calibration results with the `cameracheck.py` node, which is integrated in both the monocular and stereo camera launch files:

```
$ roslaunch chapter5_tutorials camera.launch view:=true check:=true
$ roslaunch chapter5_tutorials camera_stereo.launch view:=true check:=true
```

For the monocular camera, our calibration yields this RMS error (see more in `calibration/camera/cameracheck-stdout.log`):

```
Linearity RMS Error: 1.319 Pixels      Reprojection RMS Error: 1.278
Pixels
Linearity RMS Error: 1.542 Pixels      Reprojection RMS Error: 1.368
Pixels
Linearity RMS Error: 1.437 Pixels      Reprojection RMS Error: 1.112
Pixels
Linearity RMS Error: 1.455 Pixels      Reprojection RMS Error: 1.035
Pixels
Linearity RMS Error: 2.210 Pixels      Reprojection RMS Error: 1.584
Pixels
Linearity RMS Error: 2.604 Pixels      Reprojection RMS Error: 2.286
Pixels
Linearity RMS Error: 0.611 Pixels      Reprojection RMS Error: 0.349
Pixels
```

For the stereo camera, we have `epipolar error` and the estimation of the cell size of the calibration pattern (see more in `calibration/camera_stereo/cameracheck-stdout.log`):

```
epipolar error: 0.738753 pixels    dimension: 0.033301 m
epipolar error: 1.145886 pixels    dimension: 0.033356 m
epipolar error: 1.810118 pixels    dimension: 0.033636 m
epipolar error: 2.071419 pixels    dimension: 0.033772 m
epipolar error: 2.193602 pixels    dimension: 0.033635 m
epipolar error: 2.822543 pixels    dimension: 0.033535 m
```

To obtain these results, you only have to show the calibration pattern to the camera/s; that is the reason why we also pass `view:=true` to the launch files. An RMS error greater than 2 pixels is quite large; we have something around it, but remember that these are very low-cost cameras. Something below a 1 pixel error is desirable. For the stereo pair, the `epipolar error` should also be lower than 1 pixel; in our case, it is still quite large (usually greater than 3 pixels), but we still can do many things. Indeed, the disparity image is just a representation of the depth of each pixel shown with the `stereo_view` node. We also have a 3D point cloud that can be visualized texturized with `rviz`. We will see this in the following demonstrations, doing visual odometry.

ROS packages useful for Computer Vision tasks

The great advantage of doing Computer Vision in ROS is the fact that we do not have to re-invent the wheel. A lot of third-party software is available, and we can also connect our vision stuff to the real robots or do some simulations. Here, we are going to enumerate interesting Computer Vision tools for the most common visual tasks, but we will only explain in detail one of them later, including all the steps to set it up. We will do it for visual odometry, but other packages are also easy to install and it is also easy to start playing with them; simply follow the tutorials or manuals in the links provided here:

- **Visual Servoing**: Also known as Vision-based Robot Control, this is a technique that uses feedback information obtained from a vision sensor to control the motion of a robot, typically an arm used for grasping. In ROS, we have a wrapper of the **Visual Servoing Platform (ViSP)** software (http://www.irisa.fr/lagadic/visp/visp.html, http://www.ros.org/wiki/vision_visp). ViSP is a complete cross-platform library that allows prototyping and developing applications in visual tracking and visual servoing. The ROS wrapper provides a tracker that can be run with the visp_tracker (moving edge tracker) node as well as visp_auto_tracker (a model-based tracker). It also helps to calibrate the camera and perform hand-to-eye calibration, which is crucial for visual servoing in grasping tasks.

- **Augmented Reality**: An **Augmented Reality (AR)** application involves overlaying virtual imagery on the real world. A well-known library for this purpose is ARToolkit (http://www.hitl.washington.edu/artoolkit/). The main problem in this application is tracking the user's viewpoint to draw the virtual imagery on the viewpoint where the user is looking in the real world. ARToolkit video tracking libraries calculate the real camera position and orientation relative to physical markers in real time. In ROS, we have a wrapper named ar_pose (http://www.ros.org/wiki/ar_pose). It allows us to track single or multiple markers where we can render our virtual imagery (for example, a 3D model).

- **Perception and object recognition**: Most basic perception and object recognition is possible with the OpenCV libraries. However, there are several packages that provide an object recognition pipeline, such as the `object_recognition` stack, which provides `tabletop_object_detector` to detect objects on a table, for example; a more general solution provided by **Object Recognition Kitchen (ORK)** can be found at http://wg-perception.github.io/object_recognition_core. It is also worth mentioning a tool called RoboEarth (http://www.roboearth.org), which allows you to detect and build 3D models of physical objects and store them in a global database accessible for any robot (or human) worldwide. The models stored can be 2D or 3D and can be used to recognize similar objects and their viewpoint, that is, to identify what the camera/robot is watching. The RoboEarth project is integrated into ROS, and many tutorials are provided to have a running system (http://www.ros.org/wiki/roboearth).

- **Visual odometry**: A visual odometer is an algorithm that uses the images of the environment to track features and estimate the robot's movement, assuming a static environment. It can solve the 6 DoF pose of the robot with a monocular or stereo system, but it may require additional information in the monocular case. There are two main libraries for visual odometry: `libviso2` (http://www.cvlibs.net/software/libviso2.html) and `libfovis` (http://www.ros.org/wiki/fovis_ros), both of which have wrappers for ROS. The wrappers just expose these libraries to ROS. They are the `viso2` and `fovis` stacks respectively. In the next section, we will see how we can do visual odometry with our homemade stereo camera using the `viso2_ros` node of `viso2`. The `libviso2` library allows us to do monocular and stereo visual odometry. However, for monocular odometry, we also need the pitch and heading for the ground plane estimation. You can try the monocular case with one camera and an IMU (see *Chapter 4, Using Sensors and Actuators with ROS*), but you will always have better results with a good stereo pair, correctly calibrated, as seen so far in this chapter. Finally, `libfovis` does not allow the monocular case, but it supports RGBD cameras, such as the Kinect sensor (see *Chapter 6, Point Clouds*). As regards the stereo case, it is possible to try both libraries and see which one works better in your case. Here, we show a step-by-step tutorial to install and run `viso2` in ROS and `fovis` with Kinect.

Using visual odometry with viso2

In order to use `viso2`, go to your `catkin` workspace (`~/dev/catkin_ws`) and use the following commands:

```
$ cd src
$ wstool init
$ wstool set viso2 --git git://github.com/srv/viso2.git
$ wstool update
```

Now, to build it, run the following command:

```
$ cd ..
$ catkin_make
```

Once it is built, we set up our environment by using the following command:

```
$ source devel/setup.bash
```

Now we can run `viso2_ros` nodes, such as `stereo_odometer`, which is the one we are going to use here. But before that, we need to publish the frame transformation between our camera and the robot or its base link. The stereo camera driver is already prepared for that, but we have explained how it is done in the next sections.

Camera pose calibration

In order to set the transformation between the different frames in our robot system, we must publish the TF message of such transforms. The most appropriate and generic way to do so consists of using the `camera_pose` stack; we use the latest version from this repository, which can be found at https://github.com/jbohren-forks/camera_pose. This stack offers a series of launch files that calibrates the camera poses with respect to each other. It comes with launch files for 2, 3, 4, or more cameras. In our case, we only have two cameras (stereo), so we proceed this way. First, we extend `camera_stereo.launch` with the `calibrate_pose` argument that calls `calibration_tf_publisher.launch` from `camera_pose`:

```
<include file="$(find camera_pose_calibration)/blocks/calibration_tf_publisher.launch">
    <arg name="cache_file" value="/tmp/camera_pose_calibration_cache.bag"/>
</include>
```

Chapter 5

Now, run the following command:

```
$ roslaunch chapter5_tutorials camera_stereo.launch calibrate_pose:=true
```

The `calibration_tf_publisher` will publish the frame transforms (`tf`) as soon as the calibration has been done correctly. The calibration is similar to the one we have seen so far but using the specific tools from `camera_pose`, which are run using the following command:

```
$ roslaunch camera_pose_calibration calibrate_2_camera.launch camera1_ns:=/stereo/left camera2_ns:=/stereo/right checker_rows:=6 checker_cols:=8 checker_size:=0.03
```

With this call, we can use the same calibration pattern we used with our previous calibration tools. However, it requires the images to be static; some bars can move from one side to another of the image and turn green when the images in all the cameras have been static for a sufficient period of time. This is shown in the following screenshot:

With our noisy cameras, we need support for the calibration pattern, such as a tripod or a panel, as shown in the following image:

Then, we can calibrate as shown in the following screenshot:

This creates `tf` from the left-hand side camera to the right-hand side camera. However, although this is the most appropriate way to perform the camera pose calibration, we are going to use a simpler approach that is enough for a stereo pair, and is also required by `viso2`, since it needs the frame of the whole stereo pair as a single unit/sensor; internally, it uses the stereo calibration results of `cameracalibrator.py` to retrieve the baseline.

We have a launch file that uses `static_transform_publisher` for the camera link to the base link (robot base) and another from the camera link to the optical camera link because the optical one requires rotation; recall that the camera frame has the z axis pointing forward from the camera's optical lens, while the other frames (world, navigation, or odometry) have the z axis pointing up. This launch file is in `launch/frames/stereo_frames.launch`:

```
<launch>
  <arg name="camera" default="stereo" />

  <arg name="baseline/2" value="0.06"/>
  <arg name="optical_translation" value="0 -$(arg baseline/2) 0"/>

  <arg name="pi/2" value="1.5707963267948966"/>
  <arg name="optical_rotation" value="-$(arg pi/2) 0 -$(arg pi/2)"/>

  <node pkg="tf" type="static_transform_publisher" name="$(arg camera)_link"
        args="0 0 0.1 0 0 0 /base_link /$(arg camera) 100"/>
  <node pkg="tf" type="static_transform_publisher" name="$(arg camera)_optical_link"
        args="$(arg optical_translation) $(arg optical_rotation) /$(arg camera) /$(arg camera)_optical 100"/>
</launch>
```

[219]

This launch file is included in our stereo camera launch file and publishes these static frame transforms. Hence, we only have to run the following command to get the launch file to publish them:

```
$ roslaunch chapter5_tutorials camera_stereo.launch tf:=true
```

Then, you can check whether they are being published in `rqt_rviz`, with the TF display, as we will see in the following running `viso2`; you can also use `rqt_tf_tree` for this (see *Chapter 3, Visualization and Debug Tools*).

Running the viso2 online demo

At this point, we are ready to run the visual odometry algorithm: our stereo pair cameras are calibrated, their frame has the appropriate name for `viso2` (ends with `_optical`), and TF for the camera and optical frames is published. However, before using our own stereo pair, we are going to test `viso2` with the bag files provided in http://srv.uib.es/public/viso2_ros/sample_bagfiles/; just run `bag/viso2_demo/download_amphoras_pool_bag_files.sh` to obtain all the bag files (this totals about 4 GB). Then, we have a launch file for both the monocular and stereo odometers in the `launch/visual_odometry` folder. In order to run the stereo demo, we have a launch file on top that plays the bag files and also allows inspecting and visualizing its contents. For instance, to calibrate the disparity image algorithm, run the following command:

```
$ roslaunch chapter5_tutorials viso2_demo.launch config_disparity:=true view:=true
```

You will see the left-hand side, right-hand side, and disparity images and the `rqt_reconfigure` interface to configure the disparity algorithm. You need to do this tuning because the bag files only have the RAW images. We have found good parameters that are in `config/viso2_demo/disparity.yaml`. In the following screenshot, you can see the results obtained using them, where you can clearly appreciate the depth of the rocks in the stereo images:

In order to run the stereo odometry and see the result in `rqt_rviz`, run the following command:

```
$ roslaunch chapter5_tutorials viso2_demo.launch odometry:=true rviz:=true
```

Note that we provide an adequate configuration for `rqt_rviz` in `config/viso2_demo/rviz.rviz`, which is automatically loaded by the launch file. The next sequence of images shows different instants of the texturized 3D point cloud and the `/odom` and `/stereo_optical` frames that show the camera pose estimate from the stereo odometer. The third image has a decay time of 3 seconds for the point cloud, so we can see how the points overlay over time. This way, with good images and odometry, we can even see a map drawn in `rqt_rviz`, but it is quite difficult and generally needs a SLAM algorithm for that (see *Chapter 8, The Navigation Stack – Robot Setups*). All this is encapsulated in the following screenshots:

Computer Vision

Chapter 5

Running viso2 with our low-cost stereo camera

Finally, we can do what `viso2_demo` does with our own stereo pair. We only have to run the following command to run the stereo odometry and see the results in `rqt_rviz` (note that the `tf` tree is published by default):

```
$ roslaunch chapter5_tutorials camera_stereo.launch odometry:=true
rviz:=true
```

Computer Vision

The next image shows an example of the visual odometry system running for our low-cost stereo camera. If you move the camera, you should see the `/odom` frame moving. If the calibration is bad or the cameras are very noisy, the odometer may get lost, which is indicated by a warning message on the terminal. In that case, you should look for better cameras or recalibrate them to see whether better results are obtained. You also might have to look for better parameters for the disparity algorithm.

Performing visual odometry with an RGBD camera

Now we are going to see how to perform visual odometry using RGBD cameras using `fovis`.

Installing fovis

Since `fovis` is not provided as a Debian package, you must build it in your catkin workspace (use the same workspace you use for `chapter5_tutorials`). Therefore, proceed with the following commands within any workspace:

```
$ cd src
$ git clone https://github.com/srv/libfovis.git
$ git clone https://github.com/srv/fovis.git
$ cd ..
$ catkin_make
```

This clones two repositories that allow us to have the `fovis` software integrated in ROS. Note that the original code is hosted on this Google Code Project at https://code.google.com/p/fovis/.

Once this has been built successfully, set up the environment for this workspace before using the software:

```
$ source devel/setup.bash
```

Using fovis with the Kinect RGBD camera

At this point, we are going to run `fovis` for the Kinect RGBD camera. This means that we are going to have 3D information to compute the visual odometry, so better results are expected than when we use stereo vision or a monocular camera (as with `viso2`).

We simply have to launch the Kinect RGBD camera driver and `fovis`. For convenience, we provide a single `launch` file that runs both:

```
$ roslaunch chapter5_tutorials fovis_demo.launch
```

Computer Vision

Move the camera around and you should be able to have a good odometry estimation of the trajectory followed by the camera. The next figure shows this on `rviz` in the initial state before moving the camera. You can see the RGBD point cloud and two arrows showing the odometry and the current position of the camera in the following screenshot:

After moving the camera, you should see the arrows showing the camera pose (as shown in the following screenshot). Take into account that you have to move it quite slowly since the software needs time to compute the odometry depending on the computer you are using:

By default, the `fovis_demo.launch` file uses the `no_registered` depth information. This means that the depth image is not registered or transformed into the RGB camera frame. Although it is better to have it registered, this drops the frame rate dramatically from the raw throughput of 30 Hz provided by the Kinect sensor to something around 2.5 Hz depending on your computing resources.

Anyway, you can use `throttle` on the RGB camera frames to still use the registered version. This is automatically done by the `launch` file provided. You can select between the following modes: `no_registered` (default), `hw_registered`, and `sw_registered`. Note that, in principle, the Kinect sensor does not support the hardware registration mode (`hw_registered`), which is expected to be the fastest one. Therefore, you can try the software registration mode (`sw_registered`), for which we throttle the RGB camera messages to 2.5 Hz; you can change this in `fovis_sw_registered.launch`, as shown here:

```
$ roslaunch chapter5_tutorials fovis_demo.launch mode:=sw_registered
```

Computer Vision

Computing the homography of two images

The homography matrix is a 3 x 3 matrix that provides transformation up to scale from a given image and a new one, which must be coplanar. In `src/homography.cpp`, there is an extensive example that takes the first image acquired by the camera and then computes the homography for every new frame with respect to the first image. In order to run the example, take something planar, such as a book cover, and run the following command:

```
$ roslaunch chapter5_tutorials homography.launch
```

This runs the camera driver that should grab frames from your camera (webcam), detect features (SURF by default), extract descriptors for each of them, and match them with the ones extracted for the first image using a Flann-based matching with a cross-check filter. Once the program has the matches, the homography matrix H is computed. With H, we can warp the new frame to obtain the original one, as shown in the next screenshot (matches on the top, warped image using H, which is shown in plain text in the terminal):

Summary

In this chapter, we have given an overview of the Computer Vision tools provided by ROS. We started by showing how we can connect and run several types of cameras, particularly FireWire and USB ones. The basic functionality to change their parameters was presented, so now you can adjust certain parameters to obtain images of good quality. Additionally, we provided a complete USB camera driver example.

Then, we showed how you can calibrate the camera. The importance of calibration is the ability to correct the distortion of wide-angle cameras, particularly cheap ones. Also, the calibration matrix allows you to perform many Computer Vision tasks, such as visual odometry and perception.

We showed how you can work with stereo vision in ROS and how you can set up an easy solution with two inexpensive webcams. We also explained the image pipeline, several APIs that work with Computer Vision in ROS, such as `cv_bridge`, `image_transport`, and the integration of OpenCV within ROS packages.

Finally, we enumerated useful tasks and topics in Computer Vision that are supported by tools developed in ROS. In particular, we illustrated the example of visual odometry using the `viso2` and `fovis` libraries. We showed an example with data recorded with a high-quality camera and also with the inexpensive stereo pair proposed. Finally, feature detection, descriptor extraction, and matching is shown to illustrate how you can obtain the homography between two images. All in all, after reading and running the code in this chapter, you will have seen the basics to perform Computer Vision in ROS.

In the next chapter, you will learn to work with point clouds using PCL, which allows you to work with RGBD cameras.

6
Point Clouds

Point clouds appeared in the robotics toolbox as a way to intuitively represent and manipulate the information provided by 3D sensors, such as time-of-flight cameras and laser scanners, in which the space is sampled in a finite set of points in a 3D frame of reference. The Point Cloud Library (PCL) provides a number of data types and data structures to easily represent not only the points of our sampled space, but also the different properties of the sampled space, such as color, normal vectors, and so on. PCL also provides a number of state-of-the-art algorithms to perform data processing on our data samples, such as filtering, model estimation, surface reconstruction, and much more.

ROS provides a message-based interface through which PCL point clouds can be efficiently communicated, and a set of conversion functions from native PCL types to ROS messages, in much the same way as it is done with OpenCV images. Aside from the standard capabilities of the ROS API, there are a number of standard packages that can be used to interact with common 3D sensors, such as the widely used Microsoft Kinect or the Hokuyo laser, and visualize the data in different reference frames with RViz.

This chapter will provide a background on the PCL library, relevant data types, and ROS interface messages that will be used throughout the rest of the sections. Later, a number of techniques will be presented on how to perform data processing using the PCL library and how to communicate the incoming and outgoing data through ROS.

Understanding the point cloud library

Before we dive into the code, it's important to understand the basic concepts of both the Point Cloud Library and the PCL interface for ROS. As mentioned before, the former provides a set of data structures and algorithms for 3D data processing, and the latter provides a set of messages and conversion functions between messages and PCL data structures. All of these software packages and libraries, in combination with the capabilities of the distributed communication layer provided by ROS, open up possibilities for many new applications in the robotics field.

In general, PCL contains one very important data structure, which is PointCloud. This data structure is designed as a template class that takes the type of point to be used as a template parameter. As a result of this, the point cloud class is not much more than a container of points that includes all of the common information required by all point clouds regardless of their point type. The following are the most important public fields in a point cloud:

- `header`: This field is of the `pcl::PCLHeader` type and specifies the acquisition time of the point cloud.
- `points`: This field is of the `std::vector<PointT, ... >` type and is the container where all of the points are stored. `PointT` in the vector definition corresponds to the class template parameter, that is, the point type.
- `width`: This field specifies the width of the point cloud when organized as an image; otherwise, it contains the number of points in the cloud.
- `height`: This field specifies the height of the point cloud when organized as an image; otherwise, it's always one.
- `is_dense`: This field specifies whether the cloud contains invalid values (infinite or NaN).
- `sensor_origin_`: This field is of the `Eigen::Vector4f` type, and it defines the sensor acquisition pose in terms of a translation from the origin.
- `sensor_orientation_`: This field is of the `Eigen::Quaternionf` type, and it defines the sensor acquisition pose as a rotation.

These fields are used by PCL algorithms to perform data processing and can be used by the user to create their own algorithms. Once the point cloud structure is understood, the next step is to understand the different point types a point cloud can contain, how PCL works, and the PCL interface for ROS.

Different point cloud types

As described earlier, `pcl::PointCloud` contains a field that serves as a container for the points; this field is of the `PointT` type, which is the template parameter of the `pcl::PointCloud` class and defines the type of point the cloud is meant to store. PCL defines many types of points, but a few of the most commonly used ones are the following:

- `pcl::PointXYZ`: This is the simplest type of point and probably one of the most used; it stores only 3D xyz information.

- `pcl::PointXYZI`: This type of point is very similar to the previous one, but it also includes a field for the intensity of the point. Intensity can be useful when obtaining points based on a certain level of return from a sensor. There are two other standard identical point types to this one: the first one is `pcl::InterestPoint`, which has a field to store strength instead of intensity, and `pcl::PointWithRange`, which has a field to store the range instead of either intensity or strength.

- `pcl::PointXYZRGBA`: This type of point stores 3D information as well as color (RGB = Red, Green, Blue) and transparency (A = Alpha).

- `pcl::PointXYZRGB`: This type is similar to the previous point type, but it differs in that it lacks the transparency field.

- `pcl::Normal`: This is one of the most used types of points; it represents the surface normal at a given point and a measure of its curvature.

- `pcl::PointNormal`: This type is exactly the same as the previous one; it contains the surface normal and curvature information at a given point, but it also includes the 3D *xyz* coordinates of the point. Variants of this point are `PointXYZRGBNormal` and the `PointXYZINormal`, which, as the names suggest, include color (former) and intensity (latter).

Aside from these common types of points, there are many more standard PCL types, such as `PointWithViewpoint`, `MomentInvariants`, `Boundary`, `PrincipalCurvatures`, `Histogram`, and many more. More importantly, the PCL algorithms are all templated so that not only the available types can be used, but also semantically valid user-defined types can be used.

Algorithms in PCL

PCL uses a very specific design pattern throughout the entire library to define point cloud processing algorithms. In general, the problem with these types of algorithms is that they can be highly configurable, and in order to deliver their full potential, the library must provide a mechanism for the user to specify all of the parameters required as well as the commonly used defaults.

In order to solve this problem, PCL developers decided to make each algorithm a class belonging to a hierarchy of classes with specific commonalities. This approach allows PCL developers to reuse existing algorithms in the hierarchy by deriving from them and adding the required parameters for the new algorithm, and it also allows the user to easily provide the parameter values it requires through accessors, leaving the rest to their default value. The following snippet shows how using a PCL algorithm usually looks:

```
pcl::PointCloud<pcl::PointXYZ>::Ptr cloud(new pcl::PointCloud<pcl::PointXYZ>);
pcl::PointCloud<pcl::PointXYZ>::Ptr result(new pcl::PointCloud<pcl::PointXYZ>);

pcl::Algorithm<pcl::PointXYZ> algorithm;
algorithm.setInputCloud(cloud);
algorithm.setParameter(1.0);
algorithm.setAnotherParameter(0.33);
algorithm.process (*result);
```

This approach is only followed when required within the library, so there might be exceptions to the rule, such as the I/O functionality, which are not bound by the same requirements.

The PCL interface for ROS

The PCL interface for ROS provides the means required to communicate PCL data structures through the message-based communication system provided by ROS. To do so, there are several message types defined to hold point clouds as well as other data products from the PCL algorithms. In combination with these message types, a set of conversion functions are also provided to convert from native PCL data types to messages. Some of the most useful message types are the following:

- `std_msgs::Header`: This is not really a message type, but it is usually part of every ROS message; it holds the information about when the message was sent as well a sequence number and the frame name. The PCL equivalent is `pcl::Header` type.

- `sensor_msgs::PointCloud2`: This is possibly the most important type; this message is used to transfer the `pcl::PointCloud` type. However, it is important to take into account that this message will be deprecated in future versions of PCL in favor of `pcl::PCLPointCloud2`.

- `pcl_msgs::PointIndices`: This type stores indices of points belonging to a point cloud; the PCL equivalent type is `pcl::PointIndices`.

- `pcl_msgs::PolygonMesh`: This holds the information required to describe meshes, that is, vertices and polygons; the PCL equivalent type is `pcl::PolygonMesh`.

- `pcl_msgs::Vertices`: This type holds a set of the vertices as indices in an array, for example, to describe a polygon. The PCL equivalent type is `pcl::Vertices`.

- `pcl_msgs::ModelCoefficients`: This stores the values of the different coefficients of a model, for example, the four coefficients required to describe a plane. The PCL equivalent type is `pcl::ModelCoefficients`.

The previous messages can be converted to and from PCL types with the conversion functions provided by the ROS PCL package. All of the functions have a similar signature, which means that once we know how to convert one type, we know how to convert them all. The following functions are provided in the `pcl_conversions` namespace:

```
void fromPCL(const <PCL Type> &, <ROS Message type> &);
void moveFromPCL(<PCL Type> &, <ROS Message type> &);
void toPCL(const <ROS Message type> &, <PCL Type> &);
void moveToPCL(<ROS Message type> &, <PCL Type> &);
```

Here, the PCL type must be replaced by one of the previously specified PCL types and the ROS message types by their message counterpart. `sensor_msgs::PointCloud2` has a specific set of functions to perform the conversions:

```
void toROSMsg(const pcl::PointCloud<T> &, sensor_msgs::PointCloud2 &);
void fromROSMsg(const sensor_msgs::PointCloud2 &, pcl::PointCloud<T> &);
void moveFromROSMsg(sensor_msgs::PointCloud2 &, pcl::PointCloud<T> &);
```

You might be wondering about what the difference between each function and its move version is. The answer is simple, the normal version performs a deep copy of the data, while the move versions perform a shallow copy and nullify the source data container. This is referred to as "move semantics".

My first PCL program

In this section, you will learn how to integrate PCL and ROS. Knowledge and understanding of how ROS packages are laid out and how to compile are required although the steps will be repeated for simplicity. The example used in this first PCL program has no use whatsoever other than serving as a valid ROS node, which will successfully compile.

The first step is to create the ROS package for this entire chapter in your workspace. This package will depend on the pcl_conversions, pcl_ros, pcl_msgs, and sensor_msgs packages:

```
$ catkin_create_pkg chapter6_tutorials pcl_conversions pcl_ros pcl_msgs sensor_msgs
```

The next step is to create the source directory in the package using the following commands:

```
$ rospack profile
$ roscd   chapter6_tutorials
$ mkdir src
```

In this new source directory, you should create a file called pcl_sample.cpp with the following code, which creates a ROS node and publishes a point cloud with 100 elements. Again, what the code does should not really be of any concern to you as it is just for the purpose of having a valid node that uses PCL and compiles without problems:

```cpp
#include <ros/ros.h>
#include <pcl/point_cloud.h>
#include <pcl_ros/point_cloud.h>
#include <pcl_conversions/pcl_conversions.h>
#include <sensor_msgs/PointCloud2.h>

main (int argc, char** argv)
{
    ros::init (argc, argv, "pcl_sample");
    ros::NodeHandle nh;
    ros::Publisher pcl_pub = nh.advertise<sensor_msgs::PointCloud2>("pcl_output", 1);

    sensor_msgs::PointCloud2 output;
    pcl::PointCloud<pcl::PointXYZ>::Ptr cloud (new pcl::PointCloud<pcl::PointXYZ>);

    // Fill in the cloud data
```

```
        cloud->width  = 100;
        cloud->height = 1;
        cloud->points.resize (cloud->width * cloud->height);

        //Convert the cloud to ROS message
        pcl::toROSMsg (*cloud, output);

        pcl_pub.publish(output);
        ros::spinOnce();

        return 0;
    }
```

The next step is to add PCL libraries to `CMakeLists.txt` so that the ROS node executable can be properly linked against the system's PCL libraries:

```
find_package(PCL REQUIRED)

include_directories(include ${PCL_INCLUDE_DIRS})
link_directories(${PCL_LIBRARY_DIRS})
```

Finally, the lines to generate the executable and link against the appropriate libraries are added:

```
add_executable(pcl_sample src/pcl_sample.cpp)
target_link_libraries(pcl_sample ${catkin_LIBRARIES} ${PCL_LIBRARIES})
```

Once the final step has been reached, the package can be compiled by calling `catkin_make` as usual from the workspace `root` directory.

Creating point clouds

In this first example, the reader will learn how to create PCL point clouds composed solely of pseudorandom points. The PCL point clouds will then be published periodically through a topic named `/pcl_output`. This example provides practical knowledge on how to generate point clouds with custom data and how to convert them to the corresponding ROS message type in order to broadcast point clouds to subscribers. The source code for this first example can be found in the `chapter6 tutorials/src` folder, and it is called `pcl_create.cpp`:

```
#include <ros/ros.h>
#include <pcl/point_cloud.h>
#include <pcl_conversions/pcl_conversions.h>
#include <sensor_msgs/PointCloud2.h>

main (int argc, char **argv)
```

```
{
    ros::init (argc, argv, "pcl_create");

    ros::NodeHandle nh;
    ros::Publisher pcl_pub = nh.advertise<sensor_msgs::PointCloud2>
("pcl_output", 1);
    pcl::PointCloud<pcl::PointXYZ> cloud;
    sensor_msgs::PointCloud2 output;

    // Fill in the cloud data
    cloud.width  = 100;
    cloud.height = 1;
    cloud.points.resize(cloud.width * cloud.height);

    for (size_t i = 0; i < cloud.points.size (); ++i)
    {
        cloud.points[i].x = 1024 * rand () / (RAND_MAX + 1.0f);
        cloud.points[i].y = 1024 * rand () / (RAND_MAX + 1.0f);
        cloud.points[i].z = 1024 * rand () / (RAND_MAX + 1.0f);
    }

    //Convert the cloud to ROS message
    pcl::toROSMsg(cloud, output);
    output.header.frame_id = "odom";

    ros::Rate loop_rate(1);
    while (ros::ok())
    {
        pcl_pub.publish(output);
        ros::spinOnce();
        loop_rate.sleep();
    }

    return 0;
}
```

The first step in this, and every other snippet, is including the appropriate header files; in this case, we'll include a few PCL-specific headers as well as the standard ROS header and the one that contains the declarations for the PointCloud2 message:

```
#include <ros/ros.h>
#include <pcl/point_cloud.h>
#include <pcl_conversions/pcl_conversions.h>
#include <sensor_msgs/PointCloud2.h>
```

After the node initialization, a `PointCloud2` ROS publisher is created and advertised; this publisher will later be used to publish the point clouds created through PCL. Once the publisher is created, two variables are defined. The first one, of the `PointCloud2` type, is the message type that will be used to store the information to be sent through the publisher. The second variable, of the `PointCloud<PointXYZ>` type, is the native PCL type that will be used to generate the point cloud in the first place:

```
ros::Publisher pcl_pub = nh.advertise<sensor_msgs::PointCloud2> ("pcl_output", 1);
pcl::PointCloud<pcl::PointXYZ> cloud;
sensor_msgs::PointCloud2 output;
```

The next step is to generate the point cloud with relevant data. In order to do so, we need to allocate the required space in the point cloud structure as well as set the appropriate field. In this case, the point cloud created will be of size 100. Since this point cloud is not meant to represent an image, the height will only be of size 1:

```
// Fill in the cloud data
cloud.width  = 100;
cloud.height = 1;
cloud.points.resize(cloud.width * cloud.height);
```

With the space allocated and the appropriate fields set, the point cloud is filled with random points between 0 and 1024:

```
for (size_t i = 0; i < cloud.points.size (); ++i)
{
  cloud.points[i].x = 1024 * rand () / (RAND_MAX + 1.0f);
  cloud.points[i].y = 1024 * rand () / (RAND_MAX + 1.0f);
  cloud.points[i].z = 1024 * rand () / (RAND_MAX + 1.0f);
}
```

At this point, the cloud has been created and filled with data. Since this node is meant to be a data source, the next and last step in this snippet is to convert the PCL point cloud type into a ROS message type and publish it. In order to perform the conversion, the `toROSMsg` function will be used, performing a deep copy of the data from the PCL point cloud type to the `PointCloud2` message.

Finally, the `PointCloud2` message is published periodically at a rate of 1 Hz in order to have a constant source of information, albeit immutable:

```
//Convert the cloud to ROS message
pcl::toROSMsg(cloud, output);
output.header.frame_id = "odom";

ros::Rate loop_rate(1);
```

Point Clouds

```
  while (ros::ok())
  {
    pcl_pub.publish(output);
    ros::spinOnce();
    loop_rate.sleep();
  }
```

Perhaps the reader has also noticed that the `frame_id` field in the message header has been set to the `odom` value; this has been done in order to be able to visualize our `PointCloud2` message on the RViz visualizer.

In order to run this example, the first step is to open a terminal and run the `roscore` command:

$ roscore

In another terminal, the following command will run the example:

rosrun chapter6_tutorials pcl_create

To visualize the point cloud, RViz must be run with the following command:

$ rosrun rviz rviz

Once `rviz` has been loaded, a `PointCloud2` object needs to be added by clicking on **Add** and adding the `pcl_output` topic. The reader must make sure to set `odom` as the fixed frame in the **Global Options** section. If everything has worked properly, a randomly spread point cloud should be shown in the 3D view, just as in the following screenshot:

[240]

Loading and saving point clouds to the disk

PCL provides a standard file format to load and store point clouds to the disk as it is a common practice among researchers to share interesting datasets for other people to experiment with. This format is called PCD, and it has been designed to support PCL-specific extensions.

The format is very simple: it starts with a header containing information about the point type and the number of elements in the point cloud, followed by a list of points conforming to the specified type. The following lines are an example of a PCD file header:

```
# .PCD v.5 - Point Cloud Data file format
FIELDS x y z intensity distance sid
SIZE 4 4 4 4 4
TYPE F F F F F
COUNT 1 1 1 1 1
WIDTH 460400
HEIGHT 1
POINTS 460400
DATA ascii
```

Reading PCD files can be done through the PCL API, which makes it a very straightforward process. The following example can be found in `chapter6_tutorials/src`, and it is called `pcl_read.cpp`. This example shows how to load a PCD file and publish the resulting point cloud as an ROS message:

```
#include <ros/ros.h>
#include <pcl/point_cloud.h>
#include <pcl_conversions/pcl_conversions.h>
#include <sensor_msgs/PointCloud2.h>
#include <pcl/io/pcd_io.h>

main(int argc, char **argv)
{
    ros::init (argc, argv, "pcl_read");

    ros::NodeHandle nh;
    ros::Publisher pcl_pub = nh.advertise<sensor_msgs::PointCloud2> ("pcl_output", 1);

    sensor_msgs::PointCloud2 output;
```

Point Clouds

```
        pcl::PointCloud<pcl::PointXYZ> cloud;

        pcl::io::loadPCDFile ("test_pcd.pcd", cloud);

        pcl::toROSMsg(cloud, output);
        output.header.frame_id = "odom";

        ros::Rate loop_rate(1);
        while (ros::ok())
        {
            pcl_pub.publish(output);
            ros::spinOnce();
            loop_rate.sleep();
        }

        return 0;
}
```

As always, the first step is to include the required header files. In this particular case, the only new header file that has been added is pcl/io/pcd_io.h, which contains the required definitions to load and store point clouds to PCD and other file formats.

The main difference between the previous example and this new one is simply the mechanism used to obtain the point cloud. While in the first example we manually filled the point cloud with random points, in this case, we just load them from the disk:

```
    pcl::io::loadPCDFile ("test_pcd.pcd", cloud);
```

As we can see, the process of loading a PCD file has no complexity whatsoever. Further versions of the PCD file format also allow reading and writing of the current origin and orientation of the point cloud.

In order to run the previous example, we need to access the data directory in the package provided, which includes an example PCD file containing a point cloud that will be used further in this chapter:

```
$ roscd chapter6_tutorials/data
$ rosrun chapter6_tutorials pcl_read
```

Chapter 6

As in the previous example, the point cloud can be easily visualized through RViz:

Obvious though it may sound, the second interesting operation when dealing with PCD files is creating them. In the following example, our goal is to subscribe to a `sensor_msgs/PointCloud2` topic and store the received point clouds into a file. The code can be found in `chapter6_tutorials`, and it is called `pcl_write.cpp`:

```
#include <ros/ros.h>
#include <pcl/point_cloud.h>
#include <pcl_conversions/pcl_conversions.h>
#include <sensor_msgs/PointCloud2.h>
#include <pcl/io/pcd_io.h>

void cloudCB(const sensor_msgs::PointCloud2 &input)
{
    pcl::PointCloud<pcl::PointXYZ> cloud;
    pcl::fromROSMsg(input, cloud);
    pcl::io::savePCDFileASCII ("write_pcd_test.pcd", cloud);
}

main (int argc, char **argv)
{
    ros::init (argc, argv, "pcl_write");

    ros::NodeHandle nh;
```

```
    ros::Subscriber bat_sub = nh.subscribe("pcl_output", 10, cloudCB);

    ros::spin();

    return 0;
}
```

The topic subscribed to is the same used in the two previous examples, namely pcl_output, so they can be linked together for testing:

```
    ros::Subscriber bat_sub = nh.subscribe("pcl_output", 10, cloudCB);
```

When a message is received, the callback function is called. The first step in this callback function is to define a PCL cloud and convert PointCloud2 that is received, using the pcl_conversions function fromROSMsg. Finally, the point cloud is saved to the disk in the ASCII format, but it could also be saved in the binary format, which will generate smaller PCD files:

```
void cloudCB(const sensor_msgs::PointCloud2 &input)
{
    pcl::PointCloud<pcl::PointXYZ> cloud;
    pcl::fromROSMsg(input, cloud);
    pcl::io::savePCDFileASCII ("write_pcd_test.pcd", cloud);
}
```

In order to be able to run this example, it is necessary to have a publisher providing point clouds through the pcl_output topic. In this particular case, we will use the pcl_read example shown earlier, which fits this requirement. In three different terminals, we will run the roscore, the pcl_read node, and the pcl_write node:

$ **roscore**

$ **roscd chapter6_tutorials/data && rosrun chapter6_tutorials pcl_read**

$ **roscd chapter6_tutorials/data && rosrun chapter6_tutorials pcl_write**

If everything worked properly, after the first (or second) message is produced, the pcl_write node should have created a file called write_pcd_test.pcd in the data directory of the chapter6_tutorials package.

Visualizing point clouds

PCL provides several ways of visualizing point clouds. The first and simplest is through the basic cloud viewer, which is capable of representing any sort of PCL point cloud in a 3D viewer, while at the same time providing a set of callbacks for user interaction. In the following example, we will create a small node that will subscribe to sensor_msgs/PointCloud2 and the node will display sensor_msgs/PointCloud2 using cloud_viewer (basic) from the library. The code for this example can be found in the chapter6_tutorials/src source directory, and it is called pcl_visualize.cpp:

```
#include <iostream>
#include <ros/ros.h>
#include <pcl/visualization/cloud_viewer.h>
#include <sensor_msgs/PointCloud2.h>
#include <pcl_conversions/pcl_conversions.h>

class cloudHandler
{
public:
    cloudHandler()
    : viewer("Cloud Viewer")
    {
        pcl_sub = nh.subscribe("pcl_output", 10, &cloudHandler::cloudCB, this);
        viewer_timer = nh.createTimer(ros::Duration(0.1), &cloudHandler::timerCB, this);
    }

    void cloudCB(const sensor_msgs::PointCloud2 &input)
    {
        pcl::PointCloud<pcl::PointXYZ> cloud;
        pcl::fromROSMsg(input, cloud);

        viewer.showCloud(cloud.makeShared());
    }

    void timerCB(const ros::TimerEvent&)
    {
        if (viewer.wasStopped())
        {
            ros::shutdown();
```

```
            }
        }

    protected:
        ros::NodeHandle nh;
        ros::Subscriber pcl_sub;
        pcl::visualization::CloudViewer viewer;
        ros::Timer viewer_timer;
};

main (int argc, char **argv)
{
    ros::init (argc, argv, "pcl_visualize");

    cloudHandler handler;

    ros::spin();

    return 0;
}
```

The code for this particular example introduces a different pattern; in this case, all of our functionality is encapsulated in a class, which provides a clean way of sharing variables with the callback functions, as opposed to using global variables.

The constructor implicitly initializes the node handle through the default constructor, which is automatically called for the missing objects in the initializer list. The cloud handle is explicitly initialized with a very simple string, which corresponds to the window name, after everything is correctly initialized. The subscriber to the `pcl_output` topic is set as well as a timer, which will trigger a callback every 100 milliseconds. This timer is used to periodically check whether the window has been closed and, if this is the case, shut down the node:

```
cloudHandler()
: viewer("Cloud Viewer")
{
  pcl_sub = nh.subscribe("pcl_output", 10, &cloudHandler::cloudCB, this);
  viewer_timer = nh.createTimer(ros::Duration(0.1), &cloudHandler::timerCB, this);
}
```

The point cloud callback function is not very different from the previous examples except that, in this particular case, the PCL point cloud is passed directly to the viewer through the `showCloud` function, which automatically updates the display:

```
void cloudCB(const sensor_msgs::PointCloud2 &input)
{
  pcl::PointCloud<pcl::PointXYZ> cloud;
  pcl::fromROSMsg(input, cloud);

  viewer.showCloud(cloud.makeShared());
}
```

Since the viewer window usually comes with a close button as well as a keyboard shortcut to close the window, it is important to take into account this event and act upon it by, for example, shutting down the node. In this particular case, we are handling the current state of the window in a callback, which is called through a ROS timer every 100 milliseconds. If the viewer has been closed, our action is to simply shut down the node:

```
void timerCB(const ros::TimerEvent&)
{
  if (viewer.wasStopped())
  {
    ros::shutdown();
  }
}
```

To execute this example, and any other for that matter, the first step is to run the `roscore` command in a terminal:

$ roscore

In a second terminal, we will run the `pcl_read` example and a source of data, such as a reminder, using the following commands:

$ roscd chapter6_tutorials/data

$ rosrun chapter6_tutorials pcl_read

Finally, in a third terminal, we will run the following command:

$ rosrun chapter6_tutorials pcl_visualize

Point Clouds

Running this code will cause a window to launch; this window will display the point cloud contained in the test PCD file provided with the examples. The following screenshot shows this:

The current example uses the simplest possible viewer, namely the PCL `cloud_viewer`, but the library also provides a much more complex and complete visualization component called PCLVisualizer. This visualizer is capable of displaying point clouds, meshes, and surfaces, as well as including multiple viewports and color spaces. An example of how to use this particular visualizer is provided in the `chapter6_tutorials` source directory called `pcl_visualize2.cpp`.

> **Downloading the example code**
>
> You can download the example code files from your account at http://www.packtpub.com for all the Packt Publishing books you have purchased. If you purchased this book elsewhere, you can visit http://www.packtpub.com/support and register to have the files e-mailed directly to you. You can also download these code files from https://github.com/AaronMR/ROS_Book_Hydro.

In general, all of the visualizers provided by PCL use the same underlying functionality and work in much the same way. The mouse can be used to move around the 3D view; in combination with the shift, it allows the you to translate the image, and in combination with the control, it allows you to rotate the image. Finally, upon pressing *h*, the help text is printed in the current terminal, which should look like the following screenshot:

```
| Help:
-------
        p, P         : switch to a point-based representation
        w, W         : switch to a wireframe-based representation (where available)
        s, S         : switch to a surface-based representation (where available)

        j, J         : take a .PNG snapshot of the current window view
        c, C         : display current camera/window parameters
        f, F         : fly to point mode

        e, E         : exit the interactor
        q, Q         : stop and call VTK's TerminateApp

         +/-         : increment/decrement overall point size
   +/- [+ ALT]       : zoom in/out

        g, G         : display scale grid (on/off)
        u, U         : display lookup table (on/off)

    r, R [+ ALT]     : reset camera [to viewpoint = {0, 0, 0} -> center_{x, y, z}]

    ALT + s, S       : turn stereo mode on/off
    ALT + f, F       : switch between maximized window mode and original size

        l, L             : list all available geometric and color handlers for the current actor map
    ALT + 0..9 [+ CTRL]  : switch between different geometric handlers (where available)
          0..9 [+ CTRL]  : switch between different color handlers (where available)

    SHIFT + left click   : select a point

        x, X         : toggle rubber band selection mode for left mouse button
```

Filtering and downsampling

The two main issues that we may face when attempting to process point clouds are excessive noise and excessive density. The former causes our algorithms to misinterpret the data and produce incorrect or inaccurate results, while the latter makes our algorithms take a long time to complete their operation. In this section, we will provide insight into how to reduce the amount of noise or outliers of our point clouds and how to reduce the point density without losing valuable information.

Point Clouds

The first part is to create a node that will take care of filtering outliers from the point clouds produced in the pcl_output topic and sending them back through the pcl_filtered topic. The example can be found in the source directory of the chapter6_tutorials package, and it is called pcl_filter.cpp:

```
#include <ros/ros.h>
#include <pcl/point_cloud.h>
#include <pcl_conversions/pcl_conversions.h>
#include <sensor_msgs/PointCloud2.h>
#include <pcl/filters/statistical_outlier_removal.h>

class cloudHandler
{
public:
    cloudHandler()
    {
        pcl_sub = nh.subscribe("pcl_output", 10, &cloudHandler::cloudCB, this);
        pcl_pub = nh.advertise<sensor_msgs::PointCloud2>("pcl_filtered", 1);
    }

    void cloudCB(const sensor_msgs::PointCloud2& input)
    {
        pcl::PointCloud<pcl::PointXYZ> cloud;
        pcl::PointCloud<pcl::PointXYZ> cloud_filtered;
        sensor_msgs::PointCloud2 output;

        pcl::fromROSMsg(input, cloud);

        pcl::StatisticalOutlierRemoval<pcl::PointXYZ> statFilter;
        statFilter.setInputCloud(cloud.makeShared());
        statFilter.setMeanK(10);
        statFilter.setStddevMulThresh(0.2);
        statFilter.filter(cloud_filtered);

        pcl::toROSMsg(cloud_filtered, output);
        pcl_pub.publish(output);
    }

protected:
    ros::NodeHandle nh;
    ros::Subscriber pcl_sub;
```

```
        ros::Publisher pcl_pub;
};

main(int argc, char** argv)
{
    ros::init(argc, argv, "pcl_filter");

    cloudHandler handler;

    ros::spin();

    return 0;
}
```

Just as with the previous example, this one uses a class that contains a publisher as a member variable that is used in the callback function. The callback function defines two PCL point clouds, one for input messages and one for the filtered point cloud. As always, the input point cloud is converted using the standard conversion functions:

```
pcl::PointCloud<pcl::PointXYZ> cloud;
pcl::PointCloud<pcl::PointXYZ> cloud_filtered;
sensor_msgs::PointCloud2 output;

pcl::fromROSMsg(input, cloud);
```

Now, this is where things start getting interesting. In order to perform filtering, we will use the statistical outlier removal algorithm provided by PCL. This algorithm performs an analysis of the point cloud and removes those points that do not satisfy a specific statistical property, which, in this case, is the average distance in a neighborhood, removing all of those points that deviate too much from the average. The number of neighbors to use for the average computation can be set by the `setMeanK` function, and the multiplier on the standard deviation threshold can also be set through `setStddevMulThresh`. The following piece of code handles the filtering and sets the `cloud_filtered` point cloud with our new *noiseless* cloud:

```
pcl::StatisticalOutlierRemoval<pcl::PointXYZ> statFilter;
statFilter.setInputCloud(cloud.makeShared());
statFilter.setMeanK(10);
statFilter.setStddevMulThresh(0.2);
statFilter.filter(cloud_filtered);
```

Point Clouds

Finally, and as always, the filtered cloud is converted to `PointCloud2` and published so that our other algorithms can make use of this new point cloud to provide more accurate results:

```
pcl::toROSMsg (cloud_filtered, output);
pcl_pub.publish(output);
```

In the following screenshot, we can see the result of the previous code when it is applied on the point cloud provided in our test PCD file. The original point cloud can be seen on the left-hand side, and the filtered one on the right-hand side. The results are not perfect, but we can observe how much of the noise has been removed, which means that we can now proceed with reducing the density of the filtered point cloud.

Reducing the density of a point cloud, or any other data set for that matter, is called downsampling. There are several techniques that can be used to downsample a point cloud, but some of them are more rigorous or provide better results than others. In general, the goal of downsampling a point cloud is to improve the performance of our algorithms; for that reason, we need our downsampling algorithms to keep the basic properties and structure of our point cloud so that the end result of our algorithms doesn't change too much.

In the following example, we are going to demonstrate how to perform downsampling on point clouds with Voxel Grid Filter. In this case, the input point clouds are going to be the filtered ones from the previous example so that we can chain both examples together to produce better results in further algorithms. The example can be found in the source directory of the `chapter6_tutorials` package, and it's called `pcl_downsampling.cpp`:

```
#include <ros/ros.h>
#include <pcl/point_cloud.h>
#include <pcl_conversions/pcl_conversions.h>
#include <sensor_msgs/PointCloud2.h>
#include <pcl/filters/voxel_grid.h>

class cloudHandler
```

```cpp
{
public:
    cloudHandler()
    {
        pcl_sub = nh.subscribe("pcl_filtered", 10, &cloudHandler::cloudCB, this);
        pcl_pub = nh.advertise<sensor_msgs::PointCloud2>("pcl_downsampled", 1);
    }

    void cloudCB(const sensor_msgs::PointCloud2 &input)
    {
        pcl::PointCloud<pcl::PointXYZ> cloud;
        pcl::PointCloud<pcl::PointXYZ> cloud_downsampled;
        sensor_msgs::PointCloud2 output;

        pcl::fromROSMsg(input, cloud);

        pcl::VoxelGrid<pcl::PointXYZ> voxelSampler;
        voxelSampler.setInputCloud(cloud.makeShared());
        voxelSampler.setLeafSize(0.01f, 0.01f, 0.01f);
        voxelSampler.filter(cloud_downsampled);

        pcl::toROSMsg(cloud_downsampled, output);
        pcl_pub.publish(output);

    }
protected:
    ros::NodeHandle nh;
    ros::Subscriber pcl_sub;
    ros::Publisher pcl_pub;
};

main(int argc, char **argv)
{
    ros::init(argc, argv, "pcl_downsampling");

    cloudHandler handler;

    ros::spin();

    return 0;
}
```

Point Clouds

This example is exactly the same as the previous one, with the only differences being the topics subscribed and published, which, in this case, are `pcl_filtered` and `pcl_downsampled`, and the algorithms used to perform the filtering on the point cloud.

As said earlier, the algorithm used is Voxel Grid Filter, which partitions the point cloud into voxels, or more accurately a 3D grid, and replaces all of the points contained in each voxel with the centroid of that subcloud. The size of each voxel can be specified through `setLeafSize` and will determine the density of our point cloud:

```
pcl::VoxelGrid<pcl::PointXYZ> voxelSampler;
voxelSampler.setInputCloud(cloud.makeShared());
voxelSampler.setLeafSize(0.01f, 0.01f, 0.01f);
voxelSampler.filter(cloud_downsampled);
```

The following image shows the results of both the filtered and downsampled images when compared to the original one. You can appreciate how the structure has been kept, the density reduced, and much of the noise completely eliminated.

To execute both examples, as always we start running `roscore`:

```
$ roscore
```

In a second terminal, we will run the `pcl_read` example and a source of data:

```
$ roscd chapter6_tutorials/data
$ rosrun chapter6_tutorials pcl_read
```

In a third terminal, we will run the filtering example, which will produce the `pcl_filtered` image for the downsampling example:

```
$ rosrun chapter6_tutorials pcl_filter
```

Finally, in the fourth terminal, we will run the downsampling example:

```
$ rosrun chapter6_tutorials pcl_downsampling
```

As always, the results can be seen on `rviz`, but in this case, the `pcl_visualizer2` example provided in the package can also be used, although you might need to tweak the subscribed topics.

Registration and matching

Registration and matching is a common technique used in several different fields that consists of finding common structures or features in two datasets and using them to stitch the datasets together. In the case of point cloud processing, this can be achieved as easily as finding where one point cloud ends and where the other one starts. These techniques are very useful when obtaining point clouds from moving sources at a high rate, and we have an estimate of the movement of the source. With this algorithm, we can stitch each of those point clouds together and reduce the uncertainty in our sensor pose estimation.

PCL provides an algorithm called Iterative Closest Point to perform registration and matching. We will use this algorithm in the following example, which can be found in the source directory of the `chapter6_tutorials` package, and it's called `pcl_matching.cpp`:

```
#include <ros/ros.h>
#include <pcl/point_cloud.h>
#include <pcl/registration/icp.h>
#include <pcl_conversions/pcl_conversions.h>
#include <sensor_msgs/PointCloud2.h>

class cloudHandler
{
public:
    cloudHandler()
    {
        pcl_sub = nh.subscribe("pcl_downsampled", 10, &cloudHandler::cloudCB, this);
        pcl_pub = nh.advertise<sensor_msgs::PointCloud2>("pcl_matched", 1);
    }

    void cloudCB(const sensor_msgs::PointCloud2 &input)
    {
        pcl::PointCloud<pcl::PointXYZ> cloud_in;
        pcl::PointCloud<pcl::PointXYZ> cloud_out;
        pcl::PointCloud<pcl::PointXYZ> cloud_aligned;
```

```cpp
            sensor_msgs::PointCloud2 output;

            pcl::fromROSMsg(input, cloud_in);

            cloud_out = cloud_in;

            for (size_t i = 0; i < cloud_in.points.size (); ++i)
            {
                cloud_out.points[i].x = cloud_in.points[i].x + 0.7f;
            }

            pcl::IterativeClosestPoint<pcl::PointXYZ, pcl::PointXYZ> icp;
            icp.setInputSource(cloud_in.makeShared());
            icp.setInputTarget(cloud_out.makeShared());

            icp.setMaxCorrespondenceDistance(5);
            icp.setMaximumIterations(100);
            icp.setTransformationEpsilon (1e-12);
            icp.setEuclideanFitnessEpsilon(0.1);

            icp.align(cloud_aligned);

            pcl::toROSMsg(cloud_aligned, output);
            pcl_pub.publish(output);
        }

    protected:
        ros::NodeHandle nh;
        ros::Subscriber pcl_sub;
        ros::Publisher pcl_pub;
};

main(int argc, char **argv)
{
    ros::init(argc, argv, "pcl_matching");

    cloudHandler handler;

    ros::spin();

    return 0;
}
```

This example uses the `pcl_downsampled` topic as the input source of point clouds in order to improve the performance of the algorithm; the end result is published in the `pcl_matched` topic. The algorithm used for registration and matching takes three point clouds: the first one is the point cloud to transform, the second one is the fixed cloud to which the first one should be aligned, and the third one is the end result point cloud:

```
pcl::PointCloud<pcl::PointXYZ> cloud_in;
pcl::PointCloud<pcl::PointXYZ> cloud_out;
pcl::PointCloud<pcl::PointXYZ> cloud_aligned;
```

To simplify matters, and since we don't have a continuous source of point clouds, we are going to use the same original point cloud as the fixed cloud but displaced on the *x* axis. The expected behavior of the algorithm would then be to align both point clouds together:

```
cloud_out = cloud_in;

for (size_t i = 0; i < cloud_in.points.size (); ++i)
{
    cloud_out.points[i].x = cloud_in.points[i].x + 0.7f;
}
```

The next step is to call the Iterative Closest Point algorithm to perform the registration and matching. This iterative algorithm uses **Singular Value Decomposition (SVD)** to calculate the transformations to be done on the input point cloud towards decreasing the gap to the fixed point cloud. The algorithm has three basic stopping conditions:

- The difference between the previous and current transformations is smaller than a certain threshold. This threshold can be set through the `setTransformationEpsilon` function.
- The number of iterations has reached the maximum set by the user. This maximum can be set through the `setMaximumIterations` function.
- Finally, the sum of the Euclidean squared errors between two consecutive steps in the loop is below a certain threshold. This specific threshold can be set through the `setEuclideanFitnessEpsilon` function.

Another interesting parameter that is used to improve the accuracy of the result is the correspondence distance, which can be set through the `setMaxCorrespondanceDistance` function. This parameter defines the minimum distance that two correspondent points need to have between them to be considered in the alignment process.

Point Clouds

With all of these parameters, the fixed point cloud, and the input point cloud, the algorithm is capable of performing the registration and matching and returning the end result point cloud after the iterative transformations:

```
pcl::IterativeClosestPoint<pcl::PointXYZ, pcl::PointXYZ> icp;
icp.setInputSource(cloud_in.makeShared());
icp.setInputTarget(cloud_out.makeShared());
icp.setMaxCorrespondenceDistance(5);
icp.setMaximumIterations(100);
icp.setTransformationEpsilon (1e-12);
icp.setEuclideanFitnessEpsilon(0.1);
icp.align(cloud_aligned);
```

Finally, the resulting point cloud is converted into `PointCloud2` and published through the corresponding topic:

```
pcl::toROSMsg(cloud_aligned, output);
pcl_pub.publish(output);
```

In order to run this example, we need to follow the same instructions as the filtering and downsampling example, starting with `roscore` in one terminal:

`$ roscore`

In a second terminal, we will run the `pcl_read` example and a source of data:

`$ roscd chapter6_tutorials/data`
`$ rosrun chapter6_tutorials pcl_read`

In a third terminal, we will run the filtering example:

`$ rosrun chapter6_tutorials pcl_filter`

In a fourth terminal, we will run the downsampling example:

`$ rosrun chapter6_tutorials pcl_downsampling`

Finally, we will run the registration and matching node that requires the `pcl_downsampled` topic, which is produced by the chain of nodes run before:

`$ rosrun chapter6_tutorials pcl_matching`

The end result can be seen in the following image, which has been obtained from `rviz`. The blue one is the original point cloud obtained from the PCD file, and the white point cloud is the aligned one obtained from the Iterative Closest Point algorithm. It has to be noted that the original point cloud was translated in the x axis, so the results are consistent with the point cloud, completely overlapping the translated image, as shown in the following screenshot:

Partitioning point clouds

Oftentimes, when processing our point clouds, we might need to perform operations that require accessing a local region of a point cloud or manipulating the neighborhood of specific points. Since point clouds store data in a one-dimensional data structure, these kinds of operations are inherently complex. In order to solve this issue, PCL provides two spatial data structures, called the kd-tree and the octree, which can provide an alternative and more structured representation of any point cloud.

Point Clouds

As the name suggests, an octree is basically a tree structure in which each node has eight children, and which can be used to partition the 3D space. In contrast, the kd-tree is a binary tree in which nodes represent k-dimensional points. Both data structures are very interesting, but, in this particular example, we are going to learn how to use the octree to search and retrieve all the points surrounding a specific point. The example can be found in the source directory of the chapter6_tutorials package, and it's called pcl_partitioning.cpp:

```cpp
#include <ros/ros.h>
#include <pcl/point_cloud.h>
#include <pcl_conversions/pcl_conversions.h>
#include <sensor_msgs/PointCloud2.h>
#include <pcl/octree/octree.h>

class cloudHandler
{
public:
    cloudHandler()
    {
        pcl_sub = nh.subscribe("pcl_downsampled", 10, &cloudHandler::cloudCB, this);
        pcl_pub = nh.advertise<sensor_msgs::PointCloud2>("pcl_partitioned", 1);
    }

    void cloudCB(const sensor_msgs::PointCloud2 &input)
    {
        pcl::PointCloud<pcl::PointXYZ> cloud;
        pcl::PointCloud<pcl::PointXYZ> cloud_partitioned;
        sensor_msgs::PointCloud2 output;

        pcl::fromROSMsg(input, cloud);

        float resolution = 128.0f;
        pcl::octree::OctreePointCloudSearch<pcl::PointXYZ> octree (resolution);

        octree.setInputCloud (cloud.makeShared());
        octree.addPointsFromInputCloud ();

        pcl::PointXYZ center_point;
        center_point.x = 0 ;
        center_point.y = 0.4;
```

```
            center_point.z = -1.4;

            float radius = 0.5;
            std::vector<int> radiusIdx;
            std::vector<float> radiusSQDist;
            if (octree.radiusSearch (center_point, radius, radiusIdx,
radiusSQDist) > 0)
            {
                for (size_t i = 0; i < radiusIdx.size (); ++i)
                {
                    cloud_partitioned.points.push_back(cloud.
points[radiusIdx[i]]);
                }
            }

            pcl::toROSMsg(cloud_partitioned, output);
            output.header.frame_id = "odom";
            pcl_pub.publish(output);
        }

protected:
    ros::NodeHandle nh;
    ros::Subscriber pcl_sub;
    ros::Publisher pcl_pub;
};

main(int argc, char **argv)
{
    ros::init(argc, argv, "pcl_partitioning");

    cloudHandler handler;

    ros::spin();

    return 0;
}
```

Point Clouds

As usual, this example uses the `pcl_downsampled` topic as an input source of point clouds and publishes the resulting partitioned point cloud to the `pcl_partitioned` topic. The handler function starts by converting the input point cloud to a PCL point cloud. The next step is to create an octree-searching algorithm, which requires passing a resolution value that will determine the size of the voxels at the lowest level of the tree and, consequently, other properties such as the tree's depth. The algorithm also requires to be given the point cloud to explicitly load the points:

```
float resolution = 128.0f;
pcl::octree::OctreePointCloudSearch<pcl::PointXYZ> octree
(resolution);

octree.setInputCloud (cloud.makeShared());
octree.addPointsFromInputCloud ();
```

The next step is to define the center point of the partition; in this case, it has been handpicked to be close to the top of the point cloud:

```
pcl::PointXYZ center_point;
center_point.x = 0 ;
center_point.y = 0.4;
center_point.z = -1.4;
```

We can now perform a search in a radius around that specific point using the `radiusSearch` function from the octree search algorithm. This particular function is used to output arguments that return the indices of the points that fall in that radius and the squared distance from those points to the center point provided. With those indices, we can then create a new point cloud containing only the points belonging to the partition:

```
float radius = 0.5;
std::vector<int> radiusIdx;
std::vector<float> radiusSQDist;
if (octree.radiusSearch (center_point, radius, radiusIdx,
radiusSQDist) > 0)
{
  for (size_t i = 0; i < radiusIdx.size (); ++i)
  {
    cloud_partitioned.points.push_back(cloud.points[radiusIdx[i]]);
  }
}
```

Finally, the point cloud is converted to the `PointCloud2` message type and published in the output topic:

```
pcl::toROSMsg(cloud_partitioned, output);
output.header.frame_id = "odom";
pcl_pub.publish(output);
```

In order to run this example, we need to run the usual chain of nodes, starting with `roscore`:

```
$ roscore
```

In a second terminal, we can run the `pcl_read` example and a source of data:

```
$ roscd chapter6_tutorials/data
$ rosrun chapter6_tutorials pcl_read
```

In a third terminal, we will run the filtering example:

```
$ rosrun chapter6_tutorials pcl_filter
```

In a fourth terminal, we will run the downsampling example:

```
$ rosrun chapter6_tutorials pcl_downsampling
```

Finally, we will run this example:

```
$ rosrun chapter6_tutorials pcl_partitioning
```

In the following image, we can see the end result of the partitioning process. Since we handpicked the point to be close to the top of the point cloud, we managed to extract part of the cup and the table. This example only shows a tiny fraction of the potential of the octree data structure, but it's a good starting point to further your understanding.

Segmentation

Segmentation is the process of partitioning a dataset into different blocks of data satisfying certain criteria. The segmentation process can be done in many different ways and with varied criteria; sometimes, it may involve extracting structured information from a point cloud based on a statistical property, and in other cases, it can simply require extracting points in a specific color range.

In many cases, our data might fit a specific mathematical model, such as a plane, line, or sphere, amongst others. When this is the case, it is possible to use a model estimation algorithm to calculate the parameters for the model that fits our data. With those parameters, it is then possible to extract the points belonging to that model and evaluate how well they fit it.

In this example, we are going to show how to perform model-based segmentation of a point cloud. We are going to constrain ourselves to a planar model, which is one of the most common mathematical models you can usually fit to a point cloud. For this example, we will also perform the model estimation using a widespread algorithm called **RANdom SAmple Consensus (RANSAC)**, which is an iterative algorithm capable of performing accurate estimations even in the presence of outliers.

The example code can be found in the `chapter6_tutorials` package, and it's called `pcl_planar_segmentation.cpp`:

```cpp
#include <ros/ros.h>
#include <pcl/point_cloud.h>
#include <pcl_conversions/pcl_conversions.h>
#include <pcl/ModelCoefficients.h>
#include <pcl/sample_consensus/method_types.h>
#include <pcl/sample_consensus/model_types.h>
#include <pcl/segmentation/sac_segmentation.h>
#include <pcl/filters/extract_indices.h>
#include <sensor_msgs/PointCloud2.h>

class cloudHandler
{
public:
    cloudHandler()
    {
        pcl_sub = nh.subscribe("pcl_downsampled", 10, &cloudHandler::cloudCB, this);
        pcl_pub = nh.advertise<sensor_msgs::PointCloud2>("pcl_segmented", 1);
        ind_pub = nh.advertise<pcl_msgs::PointIndices>("point_indices", 1);
```

```cpp
                coef_pub = nh.advertise<pcl_msgs::ModelCoefficients>("plana
r_coef", 1);
        }

    void cloudCB(const sensor_msgs::PointCloud2 &input)
    {
        pcl::PointCloud<pcl::PointXYZ> cloud;
        pcl::PointCloud<pcl::PointXYZ> cloud_segmented;

        pcl::fromROSMsg(input, cloud);

        pcl::ModelCoefficients coefficients;
        pcl::PointIndices::Ptr inliers(new pcl::PointIndices());

        pcl::SACSegmentation<pcl::PointXYZ> segmentation;
        segmentation.setModelType(pcl::SACMODEL_PLANE);
        segmentation.setMethodType(pcl::SAC_RANSAC);
        segmentation.setMaxIterations(1000);
        segmentation.setDistanceThreshold(0.01);
        segmentation.setInputCloud(cloud.makeShared());
        segmentation.segment(*inliers, coefficients);

        pcl_msgs::ModelCoefficients ros_coefficients;
        pcl_conversions::fromPCL(coefficients, ros_coefficients);
        ros_coefficients.header.stamp = input.header.stamp;
        coef_pub.publish(ros_coefficients);

        pcl_msgs::PointIndices ros_inliers;
        pcl_conversions::fromPCL(*inliers, ros_inliers);
        ros_inliers.header.stamp = input.header.stamp;
        ind_pub.publish(ros_inliers);

        pcl::ExtractIndices<pcl::PointXYZ> extract;
        extract.setInputCloud(cloud.makeShared());
        extract.setIndices(inliers);
        extract.setNegative(false);
        extract.filter(cloud_segmented);

        sensor_msgs::PointCloud2 output;
        pcl::toROSMsg(cloud_segmented, output);
        pcl_pub.publish(output);
    }

protected:
```

```
        ros::NodeHandle nh;
        ros::Subscriber pcl_sub;
        ros::Publisher pcl_pub, ind_pub, coef_pub;
};

main(int argc, char **argv)
{
        ros::init(argc, argv, "pcl_planar_segmentation");

        cloudHandler handler;

        ros::spin();

        return 0;
}
```

As the reader might have noticed, two new message types are being used in the advertised topics. As their names suggest, the ModelCoefficients messages store the coefficients of a mathematical model, and PointIndices stores the indices of the points of a point cloud. We will publish these as an alternative way of representing the extracted information, which could then be used in combination with the original point cloud (pcl_downsampled) to extract the correct point. As a hint, this can be done by setting the timestamp of the published objects to the same timestamp of the original point cloud message and using ROS message filters:

```
pcl_pub = nh.advertise<sensor_msgs::PointCloud2>("pcl_segmented", 1);
ind_pub = nh.advertise<pcl_msgs::PointIndices>("point_indices", 1);
coef_pub = nh.advertise<pcl_msgs::ModelCoefficients>("planar_coef",
1);
```

As always, in the callback function, we perform the conversion from the PointCloud2 message to the point cloud type. In this case, we also define two new objects that correspond to the native ModelCoefficients and PointIndices types, which will be used by the segmentation algorithm:

```
        pcl::PointCloud<pcl::PointXYZ> cloud;
        pcl::PointCloud<pcl::PointXYZ> cloud_segmented;

        pcl::fromROSMsg(input, cloud);

        pcl::ModelCoefficients coefficients;
        pcl::PointIndices::Ptr inliers(new pcl::PointIndices());
```

The segmentation algorithm lets us define `ModelType` and `MethodType`, with the former being the mathematical model we are looking to fit and the latter being the algorithm to use. As we explained before, we are using RANSAC due to its robustness against outliers. The algorithm also lets us define the two stopping criteria: the maximum number of iterations (`setMaxIterations`) and the maximum distance to the model (`setDistanceThreshold`). With those parameters set, plus the input point cloud, the algorithm can then be performed, returning the inliers (points which fall in the model) and the coefficients of the model:

```
pcl::SACSegmentation<pcl::PointXYZ> segmentation;
segmentation.setModelType(pcl::SACMODEL_PLANE);
segmentation.setMethodType(pcl::SAC_RANSAC);
segmentation.setMaxIterations(1000);
segmentation.setDistanceThreshold(0.01);
segmentation.setInputCloud(cloud.makeShared());
segmentation.segment(*inliers, coefficients);
```

Our next step is to convert and publish the inliers and the model coefficients. As usual, conversions are performed with the standard functions, but you might notice that the namespace and signature of the conversion function is different from the one being used for point cloud conversions. To further improve this example, these messages also include the timestamp of the original point cloud in order to link them together. This also allows the use of the ROS message filters on other nodes to create callbacks containing objects that are linked together:

```
pcl_msgs::ModelCoefficients ros_coefficients;
pcl_conversions::fromPCL(coefficients, ros_coefficients);
ros_coefficients.header.stamp = input.header.stamp;
coef_pub.publish(ros_coefficients);

pcl_msgs::PointIndices ros_inliers;
pcl_conversions::fromPCL(*inliers, ros_inliers);
ros_inliers.header.stamp = input.header.stamp;
ind_pub.publish(ros_inliers);
```

Point Clouds

In order to create the segmented point cloud, we extract the inliers from the point cloud. The easiest way to do this is with the `ExtractIndices` object, but it could be easily done by simply looping through the indices and pushing the corresponding points into a new point cloud:

```
pcl::ExtractIndices<pcl::PointXYZ> extract;
extract.setInputCloud(cloud.makeShared());
extract.setIndices(inliers);
extract.setNegative(false);
extract.filter(cloud_segmented);
```

Finally, we convert the segmented point cloud into a `PointCloud2` message type and we publish it:

```
sensor_msgs::PointCloud2 output;
pcl::toROSMsg (cloud_segmented, output);
pcl_pub.publish(output)
```

The result can be seen in the following image; the original point cloud is represented in white and the segmented inliers are represented in blueish. In this particular case, the floor was extracted as it's the biggest flat surface. This is quite convenient as it is probably one of the main elements we will usually want to extract from our point clouds.

Summary

In this chapter we have explored the different tools, algorithms and interfaces which can be used to work with point clouds in ROS. The reader might have noticed that we have tried to link the examples together to provide more insight into how these kinds of nodes might be used in a reusable manner. In any case, given the computational price of point cloud processing, any kind of architectural design will be inextricably linked to the computational capabilities of the system at hand.

The data flow of our examples should start with all of the data producers, which are the `pcl_create` and the `pcl_read`. It should continue to the data filters which are the `pcl_filter` and the `pcl_downsampling`. After the filtering is performed, more complex information can be extracted through the `pcl_planar_segmentation`, `pcl_partitioning` and `pcl_matching`. Finally, the data can be written to disk through the `pcl_write` or visualized through the `pcl_visualize`.

The main objective of this particular chapter was to provide clear and concise examples of how to integrate the basic capabilities of the PCL library with ROS, something which can be limited to messages and conversion functions. In order to accomplish this goal, we have taken the liberty of also explaining the basic techniques and common algorithms used to perform data processing on point clouds as we are aware of the growing importance of this kind of knowledge.

3D Modeling and Simulation

Programming directly on a real robot gives us a good feedback and is more impressive than simulations, but not everybody has access to real robots. For this reason, we have programs that simulate the physical world.

In this chapter, we are going to learn how to:

- Create a 3D model of our robot
- Provide movements, physical limits, inertia, and other physical aspects to our robot
- Add simulated sensors to our 3D model
- Use the model on the simulator

A 3D model of our robot in ROS

The way ROS uses the 3D model of a robot or its parts, to simulate them or to simply help the developers in their daily work, is by means of the URDF files.

Unified Robot Description Format (**URDF**) is an XML format that describes a robot, its parts, its joints, dimensions, and so on. Every time you see a 3D robot on ROS, for example, the **PR2 (Willow Garage)** or the **Robonaut (NASA)**, a URDF file is associated with it. In the next few sections, we will learn how to create this file, and the format for defining different values.

Creating our first URDF file

The robot that we are going to build in the following sections, is a mobile robot with four wheels and an arm with a gripper.

3D Modeling and Simulation

To start with, we create the base of the robot with four wheels. Create a new file in the `chapter7_tutorials/robot1_description/urdf` folder with the name `robot1.urdf`, and enter the following code; this URDF code is based on XML, and the indentation is not mandatory but advisable. So, use an editor that supports it or an adequate plugin or configuration (for example, an appropriate `.vimrc` file in Vim):

```xml
<?xml version="1.0"?>
<robot name="Robot1">
  <link name="base_link">
    <visual>
      <geometry>
        <box size="0.2 .3 .1"/>
      </geometry>
      <origin rpy="0 0 0" xyz="0 0 0.05"/>
      <material name="white">
        <color rgba="1 1 1 1"/>
      </material>
    </visual>
  </link>

  <link name="wheel_1">
    <visual>
      <geometry>
        <cylinder length="0.05" radius="0.05"/>
      </geometry>
      <origin rpy="0 1.5 0" xyz="0.1 0.1 0"/>
        <material name="black">
          <color rgba="0 0 0 1"/>
        </material>
    </visual>
  </link>

  <link name="wheel_2">
    <visual>
      <geometry>
        <cylinder length="0.05" radius="0.05"/>
      </geometry>
      <origin rpy="0 1.5 0" xyz="-0.1 0.1 0"/>
      <material name="black"/>
    </visual>
  </link>
  <link name="wheel_3">
    <visual>
      <geometry>
```

```
        <cylinder length="0.05" radius="0.05"/>
      </geometry>
      <origin rpy="0 1.5 0" xyz="0.1 -0.1 0"/>
      <material name="black"/>
    </visual>
  </link>

  <link name="wheel_4">
    <visual>
      <geometry>
        <cylinder length="0.05" radius="0.05"/>
      </geometry>
      <origin rpy="0 1.5 0" xyz="-0.1 -0.1 0"/>
      <material name="black"/>
    </visual>
  </link>

  <joint name="base_to_wheel1" type="fixed">
    <parent link="base_link"/>
    <child link="wheel_1"/>
    <origin xyz="0 0 0"/>
  </joint>

  <joint name="base_to_wheel2" type="fixed">
    <parent link="base_link"/>
    <child link="wheel_2"/>
    <origin xyz="0 0 0"/>
  </joint>

  <joint name="base_to_wheel3" type="fixed">
    <parent link="base_link"/>
    <child link="wheel_3"/>
    <origin xyz="0 0 0"/>
  </joint>

  <joint name="base_to_wheel4" type="fixed">
    <parent link="base_link"/>
    <child link="wheel_4"/>
    <origin xyz="0 0 0"/>
  </joint>
</robot>
```

Explaining the file format

As you can see in the code, there are two principal fields that describe the geometry of a robot: `links` and `joints`.

The first link has the name `base_link`; this name must be unique to the file:

```
<link name="base_link">
  <visual>
    <geometry>
      <box size="0.2 .3 .1" />
    </geometry>
    <origin rpy="0 0 0" xyz="0 0 0.05" />
    <material name="white">
      <color rgba="1 1 1 1" />
    </material>
  </visual>
</link>
```

> **Downloading the example code**
>
> You can download the example code files from your account at http://www.packtpub.com for all the Packt Publishing books you have purchased. If you purchased this book elsewhere, you can visit http://www.packtpub.com/support and register to have the files e-mailed directly to you. You can also download these code files from https://github.com/AaronMR/ROS_Book_Hydro.

In order to define what we will see on the simulator, we use the visual field in the preceding code. Inside the code, you can define the geometry (cylinder, box, sphere, or mesh), the material (color or texture), and the origin. We then have the code for the joint, shown as follows:

```
<joint name="base_to_wheel1" type="fixed">
  <parent link="base_link"/>
  <child link="wheel_1"/>
  <origin xyz="0 0 0"/>
</joint>
```

In the `joint` field, we define the name, which must be unique as well. Also, we define the type of joint (`fixed`, `revolute`, `continuous`, `floating`, or `planar`), the parent, and the child. In our case, `wheel_1` is a child of `base_link`. It is fixed, but as it is a wheel we can set it to `revolute`, for example.

To check whether the syntax is fine or whether we have errors, we can use the `check_urdf` command tool:

```
$ check_urdf robot1.urdf
```

The output of the command will be as follows:

```
robot name is: Robot1
---------- Successfully Parsed XML ---------------

root Link: base_link has 4 child(ren)
    child(1):  wheel_1
    child(2):  wheel_2
    child(3):  wheel_3
    child(4):  wheel_4
```

If you want to see it graphically, you can use the `urdf_to_graphiz` command tool:

```
$ urdf_to_graphiz robot1.urdf
```

This command generates two files: `origins.pdf` and `origins.gv`. You can open the file using `evince`:

```
$ evince origins.pdf
```

The following image is what you will receive as an output:

Watching the 3D model on rviz

Now that we have the model of our robot, we can use it on `rviz` to watch it in 3D and see the movements of the joints.

3D Modeling and Simulation

We will create the `display.launch` file in the `robot1_description/launch` folder, and put the following code in it:

```xml
<?xml version="1.0"?>

<launch>
  <arg name="model" />
  <arg name="gui" default="False" />
  <param name="robot_description" textfile="$(arg model)" />
  <param name="use_gui" value="$(arg gui)" />
  <node name="joint_state_publisher" pkg="joint_state_publisher" type="joint_state_publisher" />
  <node name="robot_state_publisher" pkg="robot_state_publisher" type="state_publisher" />
</launch>
```

We will launch it with the following command:

```
$ roslaunch robot1_description display.launch model:="`rospack find robot1_description`/urdf/robot1.urdf"
```

If everything is fine, you will see the following window with the 3D model on it:

Let's finish the design by adding some parts: a base arm, an articulated arm, and a gripper. Try to finish the design yourself; you can find the final model in the `chapter7_tutorials/robot1_description/urdf/robot1.urdf` file. You can see the final design in the following screenshot as well:

Loading meshes to our models

Sometimes, we want to give more realistic elements to our model or make a more elaborate design, rather than using basic geometric objects/blocks. It is possible to load meshes generated by us or to use meshes of other models. URDF models support `.stl` and `.dae` meshes. For our model, we used the PR2's gripper. In the following code, you can see an example of how to use it:

```
<link name="left_gripper">
  <visual>
    <origin rpy="0 0 0" xyz="0 0 0" />
    <geometry>
      <mesh filename="package://pr2_description/meshes/gripper_v0/l_finger.dae" />
    </geometry>
  </visual>
</link>
```

3D Modeling and Simulation

This looks like the sample link that we used before, but in the geometry section, we added the mesh that we are going to use. You can see the result in the following screenshot:

Making our robot model movable

To convert the model into a robot that can actually move, the only thing you have to do is take care of the type of joints it uses. If you check the URDF model file, you will see the different types of joints used in this model.

The most used type of joint is the revolute joint. For example, the one used on arm_1_to_arm_base is shown in the following code:

```
<joint name="arm_1_to_arm_base" type="revolute">
  <parent link="arm_base"/>
  <child link="arm_1"/>
  <axis xyz="1 0 0"/>
  <origin xyz="0 0 0.15"/>
  <limit effort ="1000.0" lower="-1.0" upper="1.0" velocity="0.5"/>
</joint>
```

This means that they rotate in the same way that the continuous joints do, but they have strict limits. The limits are fixed using the `<limit effort ="1000.0" lower="-1.0" upper="1.0" velocity="0.5"/>` line, and you can select the axis to move with `axis xyz="1 0 0"`. The `<limit>` tag is used to set the following attributes: effort (maximum force supported by the joint), lower to assign the lower limit of a joint (radian per revolute joints, meters for prismatic joints), upper for the upper limit, and velocity for enforcing the maximum joint velocity.

A good way of testing whether or not the axis and limits of the joints are fine is by running `rviz` with the `Join_State_Publisher` GUI:

```
$ roslaunch robot1_description display.launch model:="`rospack find robot1_description`/urdf/robot1.urdf" gui:=true
```

You will see the `rviz` interface in another window with some sliders, each one controlling one joint:

Physical and collision properties

If you want to simulate the robot on Gazebo or any other simulation software, it is necessary to add physical and collision properties. This means that we need to set the dimension of the geometry to calculate the possible collisions, for example, the weight that will give us the inertia, and so on.

It is necessary that all links on the model file have these parameters; if not, the robot will not be simulated.

For the mesh models, it is easier to calculate collisions by using simplified geometry rather than the actual mesh. Calculating the collision between two meshes is more computationally complex than it is to calculate a simple geometry.

In the following code, you will see the new parameters added on the link with the name `wheel_1`:

```
<link name="wheel_1">
  ...
  <collision>
    <geometry>
      <cylinder length="0.05" radius="0.05"/>
    </geometry>
  </collision>
  <inertial>
    <mass value="10"/>
    <inertia ixx="1.0" ixy="0.0" ixz="0.0" iyy="1.0" iyz="0.0" izz="1.0"/>
  </inertial>
</link>
```

It is the same for the other links. Remember to put `collision` and `inertial` elements in all the links, because if you do not, Gazebo will not take the model.

You can find a complete file with all the parameters at `robot1_description/urdf/robot1_physics.urdf`.

Xacro – a better way to write our robot models

Notice the size of the `robot1_physics.urdf` file. It has 314 lines of code to define our robot. Imagine adding cameras, legs, and other geometries—the file will start increasing, and the maintenance of the code will become more complicated.

Xacro helps in reducing the overall size of the URDF file and makes it easier to read and maintain. It also allows us to create modules and reutilize them to create repeated structures such as several arms or legs.

To start using `xacro`, we need to specify a namespace so that the file is parsed properly. For example, these are the first two lines of a valid `xacro` file:

```
<?xml version="1.0"?>
<robot xmlns:xacro="http://www.ros.org/wiki/xacro" name="robot1_xacro">
```

In the preceding lines, we define the name of the model, which in this case is `robot1_xacro`. Remember that the file extension will be `.xacro` instead of `.urdf`.

Using constants

We can use `xacro` to declare constant values; hence, we can avoid putting the same value in a lot of lines. Without the use of `xacro`, it would be almost impossible to maintain the changes if we had to change some values.

For example, the four wheels have the same values for length and radius. If we want to change the value, we will need to change it in each line, but if we use the next lines, we can change all the values easily:

```
<xacro:property name="length_wheel" value="0.05" />
<xacro:property name="radius_wheel" value="0.05" />
```

And now, to use these variables, you only have to change the old value with the following new value:

`${name_of_variable}`:
`<cylinder length="${length_wheel}" radius="${radius_wheel}"/>`

Using math

You can build up arbitrarily complex expressions in the `${}` construct using the four basic operations (+, -, *, /), the unary minus, and the parenthesis. Exponentiation and modulus are, however, not supported:

```
<cylinder radius="${wheeldiam/2}" length=".1"/>
<origin xyz="${reflect*(width+.02)} 0 .25" />
```

By using mathematics, we can resize the model by only changing a value. To do this, we need a parameterized design.

Using macros

Macros are the most useful component of the `xacro` package. To reduce the file size even more, we are going to use the following macro for `inertial`:

```
<xacro:macro name="default_inertial" params="mass">
  <inertial>
    <mass value="${mass}" />
    <inertia ixx="1.0" ixy="0.0" ixz="0.0"
      iyy="1.0" iyz="0.0"
      izz="1.0" />
```

```
        </inertial>
    </xacro:macro>
    <xacro:default_inertial mass="100"/>
```

If we compare the robot1.urdf file with robot1.xacro, we will have eliminated 30 duplicate lines without effort. It is possible to reduce it further using more macros and variables.

To use the xacro file with rviz and Gazebo, you need to convert it to .urdf. To do this, we execute the following command inside the robot1_description/urdf folder:

```
$ rosrun xacro xacro.py robot1.xacro > robot1_processed.urdf
```

You can also execute the following command everywhere and it should give the same result as the other command:

```
$ rosrun xacro xacro.py "`rospack find robot1_description`/urdf/robot1.xacro" > "`rospack find robot1_description`/urdf/robot1_processed.urdf"
```

So, in order to make the commands easier to write, we recommend you to continue working in the same folder.

Moving the robot with code

Okay, we have the 3D model of our robot and we can see it on rviz, but how do we move the robot using a node?

We are going to create a simple node to move the robot; if you want to learn more, ROS offers great tools to control robots, such as the ros_control package. Create a new file in the robot1_description/src folder with the name state_publisher.cpp and copy the following code:

```cpp
#include <string>
#include <ros/ros.h>
#include <sensor_msgs/JointState.h>
#include <tf/transform_broadcaster.h>

int main(int argc, char** argv) {
  ros::init(argc, argv, "state_publisher");
  ros::NodeHandle n;
  ros::Publisher joint_pub = n.advertise<sensor_msgs::JointState>("joint_states", 1);
  tf::TransformBroadcaster broadcaster;
```

```cpp
    ros::Rate loop_rate(30);

    const double degree = M_PI/180;

    // robot state
    double inc= 0.005, base_arm_inc= 0.005, arm1_armbase_inc= 0.005,
arm2_arm1_inc= 0.005, gripper_inc= 0.005, tip_inc= 0.005;
    double angle= 0 ,base_arm = 0, arm1_armbase = 0, arm2_arm1 = 0,
gripper = 0, tip = 0;
    // message declarations
    geometry_msgs::TransformStamped odom_trans;
    sensor_msgs::JointState joint_state;
    odom_trans.header.frame_id = "odom";
    odom_trans.child_frame_id = "base_link";

    while (ros::ok()) {
        //update joint_state
        joint_state.header.stamp = ros::Time::now();
        joint_state.name.resize(7);
        joint_state.position.resize(7);
        joint_state.name[0] ="base_to_arm_base";
        joint_state.position[0] = base_arm;
        joint_state.name[1] ="arm_1_to_arm_base";
        joint_state.position[1] = arm1_armbase;
        joint_state.name[2] ="arm_2_to_arm_1";
        joint_state.position[2] = arm2_arm1;
        joint_state.name[3] ="left_gripper_joint";
        joint_state.position[3] = gripper;
        joint_state.name[4] ="left_tip_joint";
        joint_state.position[4] = tip;
        joint_state.name[5] ="right_gripper_joint";
        joint_state.position[5] = gripper;
        joint_state.name[6] ="right_tip_joint";
        joint_state.position[6] = tip;

        // update transform
        // (moving in a circle with radius 1)
        odom_trans.header.stamp = ros::Time::now();
        odom_trans.transform.translation.x = cos(angle);
        odom_trans.transform.translation.y = sin(angle);
        odom_trans.transform.translation.z = 0.0;
```

```
                odom_trans.transform.rotation = tf::createQuaternionMsgFromYaw(
angle);

          //send the joint state and transform
          joint_pub.publish(joint_state);
          broadcaster.sendTransform(odom_trans);

          // Create new robot state
          arm2_arm1 += arm2_arm1_inc;
          if (arm2_arm1<-1.5 || arm2_arm1>1.5) arm2_arm1_inc *= -1;
            arm1_armbase += arm1_armbase_inc;
    if (arm1_armbase>1.2 || arm1_armbase<-1.0) arm1_armbase_inc *= -1;
          base_arm += base_arm_inc;
          if (base_arm>1. || base_arm<-1.0) base_arm_inc *= -1;
          gripper += gripper_inc;
          if (gripper<0 || gripper>1) gripper_inc *= -1;
           angle += degree/4;

          // This will adjust as needed per iteration
          loop_rate.sleep();
    }
    return 0;
}
```

We are going to see what we can do to the code to get these movements.

For moving the model, first we have to know some `tf` frames that are generally used in ROS, such as map, odom, and base_link. The `tf` frame map is a world fixed frame that is useful as a long-term global reference. The odom frame is useful as an accurate, short-term local reference. The coordinate frame called base_link is rigidly attached to the mobile robot base. Normally, these frames are attached and their relationship can be illustrated as map | odom | base_link.

First, we create a new frame called odom, and all the transforms will be referred to this new frame. As you might remember, all the links are children of base_link and all the frames will be linked to the odom frame:

```
...
geometry_msgs::TransformStamped odom_trans;
odom_trans.header.frame_id = "odom";
odom_trans.child_frame_id = "base_link";
...
```

Now, we are going to create a new topic to control all the joints of the model. `Joint_state` is a message that holds data to describe the state of a set of torque-controlled joints. As our model has seven joints, we create a message with seven elements:

```
sensor_msgs::JointState joint_state;

joint_state.header.stamp = ros::Time::now();
joint_state.name.resize(7);
joint_state.position.resize(7);
joint_state.name[0] ="base_to_arm_base";
joint_state.position[0] = base_arm;
...
```

In our example, the robot will move in circles. We calculate the coordinates and the movement in the next portion of our code:

```
odom_trans.header.stamp = ros::Time::now();
odom_trans.transform.translation.x = cos(angle)*1;
odom_trans.transform.translation.y = sin(angle)*1;
odom_trans.transform.translation.z = 0.0;
odom_trans.transform.rotation = tf::createQuaternionMsgFromYaw(angle);
```

Finally, we publish the new state of our robot:

```
joint_pub.publish(joint_state);
broadcaster.sendTransform(odom_trans);
```

We are also going to create a launch file to launch the node, the model, and all the necessary elements. Create a new file with the name `display_xacro.launch` (content given as follows), and put it in the `robot1_description/launch` folder:

```
<?xml version="1.0"?>

<launch>
  <arg name="model" />
  <arg name="gui" default="False" />
  <param name="robot_description" command="$(find xacro)/xacro.py $(arg model)" />
  <param name="use_gui" value="$(arg gui)"/>
  <node name="state_publisher tutorials" pkg="robot1_description" type="state_publisher_tutorials" />
  <node name="robot_state_publisher" pkg="robot_state_publisher" type="state_publisher" />
  <node name="rviz" pkg="rviz" type="rviz" args="-d $(find robot1_description)/urdf.rviz" />
</launch>
```

3D Modeling and Simulation

Before starting our node, we have to install the following packages:

```
$ sudo apt-get instal ros-hydro-map-server
$ sudo apt-get install ros-hydro-fake-localization
$ cd ~/dev/catkin_ws && catkin_make
```

Using the following command, we will start our new node with the complete model. We will see the 3D model on `rviz`, moving all the articulations:

```
$ roslaunch robot1_description state_xacro.launch model:="`rospack find robot1_description`/urdf/robot1.xacro"
```

In the following screenshot, you can see a mix of four screens captured to show you the movements that we obtained with the node. If you see it fine, you will see the trajectory through a circle and the arms moving:

3D modeling with SketchUp

It is possible to generate the model using 3D programs such as **SketchUp**. In this section, we will show you how to make a simple model, export it, generate a `urdf`, and watch the model on `rviz`. Notice that SketchUp works on Windows and Mac, and that this model was developed using Mac and not Linux.

First, you need to have SketchUp installed on your computer. When you have it, make a model similar to the following:

The model was exported only to one file, so the wheels and chassis are the same object. If you want to make a robot model with mobile parts, you must export each part in a separate file.

To export the model, navigate to **Export | 3D Model | Save As COLLADA File** (*.dae).

We named the file bot.dae and saved it in the robot1_description/meshes folder.

Now, to use the 3D model, we are going to create a new file in the robot1_description/urdf folder with the name dae.urdf and type in the following code:

```
<?xml version="1.0"?>
<robot name="robot1">
  <link name="base_link">
    <visual>
      <geometry>
        <mesh scale="0.025 0.025 0.025" filename="package://robot1_description/meshes/bot.dae"/>
```

```
            </geometry>
            <origin xyz="0 0 0.226"/>
        </visual>
    </link>
</robot>
```

As you can notice, when we load the mesh, we can choose the scale of the model with the command line `<mesh scale="0.025 0.025 0.025" filename="package://robot1_description/meshes/bot.dae"/>`. Test the model with the following command:

```
$ roslaunch robot1_description display.launch model:="`rospack find robot1_description`/urdf/dae.urdf"
```

You will see the following output:

Simulation in ROS

In order to make simulations with our robots on ROS, we are going to use Gazebo.

Gazebo (http://gazebosim.org/) is a multirobot simulator for complex indoor and outdoor environments. It is capable of simulating a population of robots, sensors, and objects in a three-dimensional world. It generates both realistic sensor feedback and physically plausible interactions between objects.

Gazebo is now independent from ROS and is installed as a standalone package in Ubuntu. In this section, we will see how to interface Gazebo and ROS. You will learn how to use the model created before, how to include a laser sensor and a camera, and how to move it as a real robot.

Using our URDF 3D model in Gazebo

We are going to use the model that we designed in the last section, but without the arm to make it simple.

Make sure that you have Gazebo installed by typing the following command in a terminal:

```
$ gazebo
```

Before starting to work with Gazebo, we will install ROS packages to interface Gazebo:

```
$ sudo apt-get install ros-hydro-gazebo-ros-pkgs ros-hydro-gazebo-ros-control
```

The Gazebo GUI will open after this command. If all is working well, we are going to prepare our robot model to be used on Gazebo. You can test the integration of Gazebo with ROS using the following commands and checking that the GUI is open.

```
$ roscore & rosrun gazebo_ros gazebo
```

To introduce the robot model in Gazebo, it is necessary to complete the URDF model. In order to use it in Gazebo, we need to declare more elements. We will also use the .xacro file; although this may be more complex, it is more powerful for the development of the code. You have a file with all the modifications at `chapter7_tutorials/robot1_description/urdf/robot1_base_01.xacro`:

```
    <link name="base_link">
      <visual>
        <geometry>
          <box size="0.2 .3 .1"/>
        </geometry>
        <origin rpy="0 0 1.54" xyz="0 0 0.05"/>
        <material name="white">
          <color rgba="1 1 1 1"/>
        </material>
      </visual>
      <collision>
        <geometry>
          <box size="0.2 .3 0.1"/>
        </geometry>
```

```
    </collision>
    <xacro:default_inertial mass="10"/>
  </link>
```

This is the new code for the chassis of the robot `base_link`. Notice that the `collision` and `inertial` sections are necessary to run the model on Gazebo in order to calculate the physics of the robot.

To launch everything, we are going to create a new `.launch` file. Create a new file with the name `gazebo.launch` in the `chapter7_tutorials/robot1_gazebo/launch` folder, and put in the following code:

```
<?xml version="1.0"?>

<launch>
  <!-- these are the arguments you can pass this launch file, for example paused:=true -->
  <arg name="paused" default="true" />
  <arg name="use_sim_time" default="false" />
  <arg name="gui" default="true" />
  <arg name="headless" default="false" />
  <arg name="debug" default="true" />
  <!-- We resume the logic in empty_world.launch, changing only the name of the world to be launched -->
  <include file="$(find gazebo_ros)/launch/empty_world.launch">
    <arg name="world_name" value="$(find robot1_gazebo)/worlds/robot.world" />
    <arg name="debug" value="$(arg debug)" />
    <arg name="gui" value="$(arg gui)" />
    <arg name="paused" value="$(arg paused)" />
    <arg name="use_sim_time" value="$(arg use_sim_time)" />
    <arg name="headless" value="$(arg headless)" />
  </include>
  <!-- Load the URDF into the ROS Parameter Server -->
  <arg name="model" />
  <param name="robot_description" command="$(find xacro)/xacro.py $(arg model)" />
  <!-- Run a python script to the send a service call to gazebo_ros to spawn a URDF robot -->
  <node name="urdf_spawner" pkg="gazebo_ros" type="spawn_model" respawn="false" output="screen" args="-urdf -model robot1 -param robot_description -z 0.05" />
</launch>
```

To launch the file, use the following command:

```
$ roslaunch robot1_gazebo gazebo.launch  model:="`rospack find robot1_description`/urdf/robot1_base_01.xacro"
```

You will now see the robot in Gazebo. The simulation is initially paused; you can click on play to start it. Congratulations! This is your first step in the virtual world:

As you can see, the model has no texture. In `rviz`, you observed the textures that were declared in the URDF file. But in Gazebo, you cannot see them.

To add visible textures in Gazebo, use the following code on your model `.gazebo` file. In `robot1_description/urdf`, create a file `robot.gazebo`:

```
<gazebo reference="base_link">
  <material>Gazebo/Orange</material>
</gazebo>

<gazebo reference="wheel_1">
  <material>Gazebo/Black</material>
</gazebo>

<gazebo reference="wheel_2">
```

```
    <material>Gazebo/Black</material>
  </gazebo>

  <gazebo reference="wheel_3">
    <material>Gazebo/Black</material>
  </gazebo>

  <gazebo reference="wheel_4">
    <material>Gazebo/Black</material>
  </gazebo>
```

Copy the `robot1_description/urdf/robot1_base_01.xacro` file, save it with the name `robot1_base_02.xacro`, and add the following code inside:

```
<xacro:include filename="$(find robot1_description)/urdf/robot.gazebo" />
```

Launch the new file and you will see the same robot, but with the added textures:

```
$ roslaunch robot1_gazebo gazebo.launch  model:="`rospack find robot1_description`/urdf/robot1_base_02.xacro"
```

You will see the following output:

Adding sensors to Gazebo

In Gazebo, you can simulate the physics of the robot and its movement, and you can also simulate sensors.

Normally, when you want to add a new sensor you need to implement the behavior. Fortunately, some sensors are already developed for Gazebo and ROS.

In this section, we are going to add a camera and a laser sensor to our model. These sensors will be a new part on the robot. Therefore, you need to select where to put them. In Gazebo, you will see a new 3D object that looks like a Hokuyo laser and a red cube that will be the camera. We talked about these sensors in the previous chapters.

We are going to take the laser from the `gazebo_ros_demos` package. This is the magic of ROS — you can re-use code from other packages for your development.

It is necessary to add the following lines in our `.xacro` file for adding the 3D model of a Hokuyo laser to our robot:

```xml
<?xml version="1.0" encoding="UTF-8"?>
<link name="hokuyo_link">
  <collision>
    <origin xyz="0 0 0" rpy="0 0 0" />
    <geometry>
      <box size="0.1 0.1 0.1" />
    </geometry>
  </collision>
  <visual>
    <origin xyz="0 0 0" rpy="0 0 0" />
    <geometry>
      <mesh filename="package://robot1_description/meshes/hokuyo.dae" />
    </geometry>
  </visual>
  <inertial>
    <mass value="1e-5" />
    <origin xyz="0 0 0" rpy="0 0 0" />
    <inertia ixx="1e-6" ixy="0" ixz="0" iyy="1e-6" iyz="0" izz="1e-6" />
  </inertial>
</link>
```

3D Modeling and Simulation

In our .gazebo file, we are going to add the plugin libgazebo_ros_laser.so that will simulate the behavior of a Hokuyo range laser:

```
<gazebo reference="hokuyo_link">
  <sensor type="ray" name="head_hokuyo_sensor">
    <pose>0 0 0 0 0 0</pose>
    <visualize>false</visualize>
    <update_rate>40</update_rate>
    <ray>
      <scan>
        <horizontal>
          <samples>720</samples>
          <resolution>1</resolution>
          <min_angle>-1.570796</min_angle>
          <max_angle>1.570796</max_angle>
        </horizontal>
      </scan>
      <range>
        <min>0.10</min>
        <max>30.0</max>
        <resolution>0.01</resolution>
      </range>
      <noise>
        <type>gaussian</type>
        <!-- Noise parameters based on published spec for Hokuyo laser
             achieving "+-30mm" accuracy at range < 10m.  A mean of 0.0m and
             stddev of 0.01m will put 99.7% of samples within 0.03m of the true
             reading. -->
        <mean>0.0</mean>
        <stddev>0.01</stddev>
      </noise>
    </ray>
    <plugin name="gazebo_ros_head_hokuyo_controller" filename="libgazebo_ros_laser.so">
      <topicName>/robot/laser/scan</topicName>
      <frameName>hokuyo_link</frameName>
    </plugin>
  </sensor>
</gazebo>
```

Launch the new model with the following command:

```
$ roslaunch robot1_gazebo gazebo.launch model:="`rospack find robot1_description`/urdf/robot1_base_03.xacro"
```

You will see the robot with the laser module attached to it.

In a similar way, we have added lines to `robot.gazebo` and `robot1_base_03.xacro` to add another sensor: a camera. Check these files!

In the following screenshot, you can see the robot model with the Hokuyo laser and a red cube that simulates the camera model:

Notice that this laser is generating "real" data as a real laser. You can see the data generated using the `rostopic echo` command:

```
$ rostopic echo /robot/laser/scan
```

We can say the same about the camera. If you want to see the gazebo simulation of the images taken, you can write the following command in a terminal:

```
$ rosrun image_view image_view image:=/robot/camera1/image_raw
```

3D Modeling and Simulation

Gazebo allows us to add objects to the world using the right menu. We have added some elements like a traffic cone, a table, and a can to check how the sensors react to them. You can see three screenshots showing this. The first image is that of Gazebo and our simulated world, then we have a top-down view of Rviz with the laser data, and finally, an image visualization of the camera.

Loading and using a map in Gazebo

In Gazebo, you can use virtual worlds as offices, mountains, and so on.

In this section, we are going to use a map of the office of Willow Garage that is installed by default with the ROS installation.

This 3D model is in the `gazebo_worlds` package. If you do not have the package, install it before you continue.

To check the model, you will only have to start the `.launch` file using the following command:

```
$ roslaunch gazebo_ros willowgarage_world.launch
```

You will see the 3D office in Gazebo. The office has walls only. You can add tables, chairs, and much more, if you want. By inserting and placing objects, you can create your own worlds in Gazebo to simulate your robots. You have the option of saving your world by selecting **Menu | Save as**.

Please note that Gazebo requires a good machine, with a relatively recent GPU. You can check whether your graphics are supported at the Gazebo home page. Also, note that sometimes this software crashes, but great effort is being taken by the community to make it more stable. Usually, it is enough to run it again (probably several times) if it crashes. If the problem persists, our advice is to try with a newer version, which will be installed by default with more recent distributions of ROS.

What we are going to do now is create a new `.launch` file to load the map and the robot together. To do that, create a new file in the `robot1_gazebo/launch` folder with the name `gazebo_wg.launch`, and add the following code:

```
<?xml version="1.0"?>
<launch>
  <include file="$(find gazebo_ros)/launch/willowgarage_world.launch">
  </include>

  <!-- Load the URDF into the ROS Parameter Server -->
  <param name="robot_description"
         command="$(find xacro)/xacro.py '$(find robot1_description)/urdf/robot1_base_03.xacro'" />

  <!-- Run a python script to the send a service call to gazebo_ros to spawn a URDF robot -->
  <node name="urdf_spawner" pkg="gazebo_ros" type="spawn_model"
    respawn="false" output="screen"
```

```
                    args="-urdf -model robot1 -param robot_description -z 0.05"/>
</launch>
```

Now, launch the file of the model with the laser:

```
$ roslaunch robot1_gazebo gazebo_wg.launch
```

You will see the robot and the map on the Gazebo GUI. The next step is to command the robot to move and receive the simulated readings of its sensors as it evolves around the virtual world loaded in the simulator.

Moving the robot in Gazebo

A skid-steer robot is a mobile robot whose movement is based on separately driven wheels placed on either side of the robot body. It can thus change its direction by varying the relative rate of rotation of its wheels, and it does not require an additional steering motion.

As we said before, in Gazebo you need to program the behaviors of the robot, joints, sensors, and so on. As for the laser, Gazebo already has a skid drive implemented and we can use it to move our robot.

To use this controller, you only have to add the following code to the model file:

```
<gazebo>
  <plugin name="skid_steer_drive_controller" filename="libgazebo_ros_skid_steer_drive.so">
    <updateRate>100.0</updateRate>
    <robotNamespace>/</robotNamespace>
    <leftFrontJoint>base_to_wheel1</leftFrontJoint>
```

```
                <rightFrontJoint>base_to_wheel3</rightFrontJoint>
                <leftRearJoint>base_to_wheel2</leftRearJoint>
                <rightRearJoint>base_to_wheel4</rightRearJoint>
                <wheelSeparation>4</wheelSeparation>
                <wheelDiameter>0.1</wheelDiameter>
                <robotBaseFrame>base_link</robotBaseFrame>
                <torque>1</torque>
                <topicName>cmd_vel</topicName>
                <broadcastTF>0</broadcastTF>
            </plugin>
        </gazebo>
```

The parameters that you can see in the code are simply the configuration set up to make the controller work with our four-wheeled robot.

For example, we selected the `base_to_wheel1`, `base_to_wheel2`, `base_to_wheel3`, and `base_to_wheel4` joints as wheels to move the robot.

Another interesting parameter is `topicName`. We need to publish commands with this name in order to control the robot. In this case, when you publish a `sensor_msgs/Twist` topic call `/cmd_vel`, the robot will move. It is important to have a well-configured orientation of the wheels joint. With the current orientation on the `xacro` file, the robot will move upside-down. So, it is necessary to change the origin `rpy` for the four wheels, as shown in the following lines for the joint of the base link and the `wheel1` joint:

```
    <joint name="base_to_wheel1" type="continuous">
        <parent link="base_link"/>
        <child link="wheel_1"/>
        <origin rpy="-1.5707 0 0" xyz="0.1 0.15 0"/>
        <axis xyz="0 0 1" />
    </joint>
```

All these changes are in the `chapter7_tutorials/robot1_description/urfd/robot1_base_04.xacro` file. In `gazebo_wg.launch`, we have to update the robot model for using the new file `robot1_base_04.xacro`.

Now, to launch the model with the controller and the map, we use the following command:

$ roslaunch robot1_gazebo gazebo_wg.launch

You will see the map with the robot on the Gazebo screen. We are going to move the robot using the keyboard. This node is in the `teleop_twist_keyboard` package that publishes the `/cmd_vel` topic.

3D Modeling and Simulation

Run the following commands in a terminal to install the package:

```
$ sudo apt-get install ros-hydro-teleop-twist-keyboard
$ rosstack profile
$ rospack profile
```

Then, you can run the node as follows:

```
$ rosrun teleop_twist_keyboard teleop_twist_keyboard.py
```

You will see a new shell with some instructions and the keys to move the robot (*u*, *i* ,*o* , *j* , *k* , *l* , *m* , "," , ".") and adjust maximum speeds.

If everything has gone well, you can drive the robot across the Willow Garage office. You can see the laser data or visualize images from the camera.

Summary

For people learning robotics, the ability to have access to real robots is fun and useful, but not everyone has access to a real robot. Simulators are a great tool when we have limited access to a real robot. They were created for testing the behavior of algorithms before trying them on a real robot. This is why simulators exist.

In this chapter, you have learned how to create a 3D model of your own robot. This includes a detailed explanation that guides you in the tasks of adding textures and creating joints, and also describes how to move the robot with a node.

Then, we introduced Gazebo, a simulator where you can load the 3D model of your robot, and simulate it moving and sensing a virtual world. This simulator is widely used by the ROS community and it already supports many real robots in simulation.

Indeed, in a nutshell, we have seen how to reuse parts of other robots to design ours. In particular, we have included a gripper and added sensors, such as a laser range finder and a camera.

Hence, it is not mandatory to create a robot from scratch to start using the simulator. The community has developed a lot of robots and you can download the code, execute them in ROS and Gazebo, and modify them if it turns out to be necessary.

You can find a list of the robots supported on ROS on `http://www.ros.org/wiki/Robots`. Also, you can find tutorials about Gazebo on `http://gazebosim.org/tutorials`.

In the next chapter, we will learn about `abond` packages, such as SLAM, to perform navigation with lasers.

8
The Navigation Stack – Robot Setups

In the previous chapters, we have seen how to create our robot, mount some sensors and actuators, and move it through the virtual world using a joystick or the keyboard. Now, in this chapter, you will learn what is probably one of the most powerful features in ROS, something that will let you move your robot autonomously.

Thanks to the community and the shared code, ROS has many algorithms that can be used for navigation.

First of all, in this chapter, you will learn all the necessary ways to configure the navigation stack with your robot. In the next chapter, you will learn how to configure and launch the navigation stack on the simulated robot, giving goals and configuring some parameters to get the best results. In particular, we will cover the following topics in this chapter:

- Introduction to the navigation stacks and their powerful capabilities—clearly one of the greatest pieces of software that comes with ROS.
- The tf—showing the transformation of one physical element to the other from the frame; for example, the data received using a sensor or the command for the desired position of an actuator. tf is a library for keeping track of the coordinate frames.
- Creating a laser driver or simulating it.
- Computing and publishing the odometry and how this is provided by Gazebo.

- Base controllers and creating one for your robot.
- Executing **SLAM (Simultaneous Localization And Mapping)** with ROS—building a map from the environment with your robot as it moves through it. Localizing your robot in the map using the AMCL algorithm of the navigation stack. AMCL is a probabilistic localization system for a robot moving in 2D. It implements the adaptive Monte Carlo localization approach, which uses a particle filter to track the pose of a robot against a known map.

The navigation stack in ROS

In order to understand the navigation stack, you should think of it as a set of algorithms that use the sensors of the robot and the odometry so that you can control the robot using a standard message. It can move your robot without any problems, such as crashing, getting stuck in a location, or getting lost to another position.

You would assume that this stack can be easily used with any robot. This is almost true, but it is necessary to tune some configuration files and write some nodes to use the stack.

The robot must satisfy some requirements before it uses the navigation stack:

- The navigation stack can only handle a differential drive and holonomic-wheeled robots. The shape of the robot must either be a square or a rectangle. However, it can also do certain things with biped robots, such as robot localization, as long as the robot does not move sideways.
- It requires that the robot publishes information about the relationships between the positions of all the joints and sensors.
- The robot must send messages with linear and angular velocities.
- A planar laser must be on the robot to create the map and localization. Alternatively, you can generate something equivalent to several lasers or a sonar, or you can project the values to the ground if they are mounted at another place on the robot.

The following diagram shows you how the navigation stacks are organized. You can see three groups of boxes with colors (gray and white) and dotted lines. The plain white boxes indicate the stacks that are provided by ROS, and they have all the nodes to make your robot really autonomous:

In the following sections, we will see how to create the parts marked in gray in the diagram. These parts depend on the platform used; this means that it is necessary to write code to adapt the platform to be used in ROS and to be used by the navigation stack.

Creating transforms

The navigation stack needs to know the position of the sensors, wheels, and joints.

To do that, we use the **tf** (**Transform Frames**) software library. It manages a transform tree. You could do this with mathematics, but if you have a lot of frames to calculate, it will be a bit complicated and messy.

Thanks to the tf, we can add more sensors and parts to the robot, and tf will handle all the relations for us.

If we put the laser 10 cm backwards and 20 cm above with reference to the origin of the base_link coordinates, we would need to add a new frame to the transformation tree with these offsets.

Once inserted and created, we could easily know the position of the laser with reference to the `base_link` value or the wheels. The only thing we need to do is call the `tf` library and get the transformation.

Creating a broadcaster

Let's test this with a simple code. Create a new file in `chapter8_tutorials/src` with the name `tf_broadcaster.cpp`, and put the following code inside it:

```cpp
#include <ros/ros.h>
#include <tf/transform_broadcaster.h>

int main(int argc, char** argv){
  ros::init(argc, argv, "robot_tf_publisher");
  ros::NodeHandle n;

  ros::Rate r(100);

  tf::TransformBroadcaster broadcaster;

  while(n.ok()){
    broadcaster.sendTransform(
      tf::StampedTransform(
        tf::Transform(tf::Quaternion(0, 0, 0, 1), tf::Vector3(0.1, 0.0, 0.2)),
        ros::Time::now(),"base_link", "base_laser"));
    r.sleep();
  }
}
```

> **Downloading the example code**
>
> You can download the example code files from your account at http://www.packtpub.com for all the Packt Publishing books you have purchased. If you purchased this book elsewhere, you can visit http://www.packtpub.com/support and register to have the files e-mailed directly to you. You can also download these code files from https://github.com/AaronMR/ROS_Book_Hydro.

Remember to add the following line in your `CMakelist.txt` file to create the new executable:

```
add_executable(tf_broadcaster src/tf_broadcaster.cpp)
target_link_libraries(tf_broadcaster ${catkin_LIBRARIES})
```

We also create another node that will use the transform, and which will give us the position of a point on the sensor with reference to the center of base_link (our robot).

Creating a listener

Create a new file in chapter8_tutorials/src with the name tf_listener.cpp and input the following code:

```
#include <ros/ros.h>
#include <geometry_msgs/PointStamped.h>
#include <tf/transform_listener.h>

void transformPoint(const tf::TransformListener& listener){
  //we'll create a point in the base_laser frame that we'd like to transform to the base_link frame
  geometry_msgs::PointStamped laser_point;
  laser_point.header.frame_id = "base_laser";

  //we'll just use the most recent transform available for our simple example
  laser_point.header.stamp = ros::Time();

  //just an arbitrary point in space
  laser_point.point.x = 1.0;
  laser_point.point.y = 2.0;
  laser_point.point.z = 0.0;

    geometry_msgs::PointStamped base_point;
    listener.transformPoint("base_link", laser_point, base_point);

    ROS_INFO("base_laser: (%.2f, %.2f. %.2f) -----> base_link: (%.2f, %.2f, %.2f) at time %.2f",
        laser_point.point.x, laser_point.point.y, laser_point.point.z,
        base_point.point.x, base_point.point.y, base_point.point.z,
    base_point.header.stamp.toSec());

    ROS_ERROR("Received an exception trying to transform a point from \"base_laser\" to \"base_link\": %s", ex.what());

}

int main(int argc, char** argv){
  ros::init(argc, argv, "robot_tf_listener");
```

```
    ros::NodeHandle n;

    tf::TransformListener listener(ros::Duration(10));

    //we'll transform a point once every second
    ros::Timer timer = n.createTimer(ros::Duration(1.0),
 boost::bind(&transformPoint, boost::ref(listener)));

    ros::spin();
}
```

Remember to add the line in the `CMakeList.txt` file to create the executable. Compile the package and run both the nodes using the following commands in each terminal:

```
$ catkin_make
$ rosrun chapter8_tutorials tf_broadcaster
$ rosrun chapter8_tutorials tf_listener
```

Remember, always run `roscore` before starting with the examples. You will see the following message:

```
[ INFO] [1368521854.336910465]: base_laser: (1.00, 2.00. 0.00) ----->
base_link: (1.10, 2.00, 0.20) at time 1368521854.33
[ INFO] [1368521855.336347545]: base_laser: (1.00, 2.00. 0.00) ----->
base_link: (1.10, 2.00, 0.20) at time 1368521855.33
```

This means that the point that you published on the node, with the position (1.00, 2.00, 0.00) relative to `base_laser`, has the position (1.10, 2.00, 0.20) relative to `base_link`.

As you can see, the `tf` library performs all the mathematics for you to get the coordinates of a point or the position of a joint relative to another point.

A transform tree defines offsets in terms of both translation and rotation between different coordinate frames. Let us see an example to help you understand this.

In our robot model used in *Chapter 7, 3D Modeling and Simulation*, we are going to add another laser, say, on the back of the robot (`base_link`):

The system in our robot had to know the position of the new laser to detect collisions, such as the one between the wheels and walls. With the `tf` tree, this is very simple to do and maintain, apart from being scalable. Thanks to `tf`, we can add more sensors and parts, and the `tf` library will handle all the relations for us. All the sensors and joints must be correctly configured on `tf` to permit the navigation stack to move the robot without problems, and to know exactly where each one of their components is.

Before starting to write the code to configure each component, keep in mind that you have the geometry of the robot specified in the URDF file. So, for this reason, it is not necessary to configure the robot again. Perhaps you do not know it, but you have been using the `robot_state_publisher` package to publish the transform tree of your robot. In *Chapter 7, 3D Modeling and Simulation*, we used it for the first time; therefore, you do have the robot configured to be used with the navigation stack.

Watching the transformation tree

If you want to see the transformation tree of your robot, use the following command:

```
$ roslaunch chapter8_tutorials gazebo_map_robot.launch model:="`rospack find chapter8_tutorials`/urdf/robot1_base_01.xacro"
$ rosrun tf view_frames
```

The resultant frame is depicted as follows:

And now, if you run `tf_broadcaster` and run the `rosrun tf view_frames` command again, you will see the frame that you have created using code:

```
$ rosrun chapter8_tutorials tf_broadcaster
$ rosrun tf view_frames
```

The resultant frame is depicted as follows:

Publishing sensor information

Your robot can have a lot of sensors to see the world; you can program a lot of nodes to take this data and do something, but the navigation stack is prepared only to use the planar laser's sensor. So, your sensor must publish the data with one of these types: `sensor_msgs/LaserScan` or `sensor_msgs/PointCloud2`.

We are going to use the laser located in front of the robot to navigate in Gazebo. Remember that this laser is simulated on Gazebo, and it publishes data on the `hokuyo_link` frame with the topic name `/robot/laser/scan`.

In our case, we do not need to configure anything in our laser to use it on the navigation stack. This is because we have `tf` configured in the `.urdf` file, and the laser is publishing data with the correct type.

If you use a real laser, ROS might have a driver for it. Indeed, in *Chapter 4, Using Sensors and Actuators with ROS*, you learned how to connect the Hokuyo laser to ROS. Anyway, if you are using a laser that has no driver on ROS and want to write a node to publish the data with the `sensor_msgs/LaserScan` sensor, you have an example template to do it, which is shown in the following section.

But first, remember the structure of the message `sensor_msgs/LaserScan`. Use the following command:

```
$ rosmsg show sensor_msgs/LaserScan
```

The preceding command will generate the following output:

```
std_msgs/Header header
  uint32 seq
  time stamp
  string frame_id
float32 angle_min
float32 angle_max
float32 angle_increment
float32 time_increment
float32 scan_time
float32 range_min
float32 range_max
float32[] ranges
float32[] intensities
```

Creating the laser node

Now we will create a new file in chapter8_tutorials/src with the name laser.cpp and put the following code in it:

```
#include <ros/ros.h>
#include <sensor_msgs/LaserScan.h>

int main(int argc, char** argv){
  ros::init(argc, argv, "laser_scan_publisher");

  ros::NodeHandle n;
  ros::Publisher scan_pub = n.advertise<sensor_msgs::LaserScan>("scan", 50);

  unsigned int num_readings = 100;
  double laser_frequency = 40;
  double ranges[num_readings];
  double intensities[num_readings];

  int count = 0;
  ros::Rate r(1.0);
  while(n.ok()){
    //generate some fake data for our laser scan
    for(unsigned int i = 0; i < num_readings; ++i){
      ranges[i] = count;
      intensities[i] = 100 + count;
    }
    ros::Time scan_time = ros::Time::now();
    //populate the LaserScan message
    sensor_msgs::LaserScan scan;
    scan.header.stamp = scan_time;
    scan.header.frame_id = "base_link";
    scan.angle_min = -1.57;
    scan.angle_max = 1.57;
    scan.angle_increment = 3.14 / num_readings;
    scan.time_increment = (1 / laser_frequency) / (num_readings);
    scan.range_min = 0.0;
    scan.range_max = 100.0;

    scan.ranges.resize(num_readings);
    scan.intensities.resize(num_readings);
    for(unsigned int i = 0; i < num_readings; ++i){
      scan.ranges[i] = ranges[i];
      scan.intensities[i] = intensities[i];
    }

    scan_pub.publish(scan);
    ++count;
    r.sleep();
  }
}
```

As you can see, we are going to create a new topic with the name `scan` and the message type `sensor_msgs/LaserScan`. You must be familiar with this message type from *Chapter 4, Using Sensors and Actuators with ROS*. The name of the topic must be unique. When you configure the navigation stack, you will select this topic to be used for navigation. The following command line shows how to create the topic with the correct name:

```
ros::Publisher scan_pub = n.advertise<sensor_msgs::LaserScan>("scan",
50);
```

It is important to publish data with `header`, `stamp`, `frame_id`, and many more elements because, if not, the navigation stack could fail with such data:

```
scan.header.stamp = scan_time;
scan.header.frame_id = "base_link";
```

Other important data on `header` is `frame_id`. It must be one of the frames created in the `.urdf` file and must have a frame published on the `tf` frame transforms. The navigation stack will use this information to know the real position of the sensor and make transforms, such as the one between the data sensor and obstacles.

With this template, you can use any laser, even if it has no driver for ROS. You only have to change the fake data with the right data from your laser.

This template can also be used to create something that looks like a laser but is not. For example, you could simulate a laser using stereoscopy or using a sensor such as a sonar.

Publishing odometry information

The navigation stack also needs to receive data from the robot odometry. The odometry is the distance of something relative to a point. In our case, it is the distance between base_link and a fixed point in the frame odom.

The type of message used by the navigation stack is nav_msgs/Odometry. We can see its structure using the following command:

```
$ rosmsg show nav_msgs/Odometry
```

The output of the preceding command is shown as follows:

```
std_msgs/Header header
  uint32 seq
  time stamp
  string frame_id
string child_frame_id
geometry_msgs/PoseWithCovariance pose
  geometry_msgs/Pose pose
    geometry_msgs/Point position
      float64 x
      float64 y
      float64 z
    geometry_msgs/Quaternion orientation
      float64 x
      float64 y
      float64 z
      float64 w
```

```
    float64[36] covariance
geometry_msgs/TwistWithCovariance twist
  geometry_msgs/Twist twist
    geometry_msgs/Vector3 linear
      float64 x
      float64 y
      float64 z
    geometry_msgs/Vector3 angular
      float64 x
      float64 y
      float64 z
  float64[36] covariance
```

As you can see in the message structure, `nav_msgs/Odometry` gives the position of the robot between `frame_id` and `child_frame_id`. It also gives us the pose of the robot using the `geometry_msgs/Pose` message, and the velocity with the `geometry_msgs/Twist` message.

The pose has two structures that show the position in Euler coordinates and the orientation of the robot using a quaternion. The orientation is the angular displacement of the robot.

The velocity has two structures that show the linear velocity and the angular velocity. For our robot, we will use only the linear *x* velocity and the angular *z* velocity. We will use the linear *x* velocity to know whether the robot is moving forward or backward. The angular *z* velocity is used to check whether the robot is rotating towards the left or right.

As the odometry is the displacement between two frames, it is necessary to publish its transform. We did it in the last section, but later on in this section, I will show you an example for publishing the odometry and the transform of our robot.

Now, let me show you how Gazebo works with the odometry.

How Gazebo creates the odometry

As you have seen in other examples with Gazebo, our robot moves in the simulated world just like a robot in the real world. We use a driver for our robot, `diffdrive_plugin`. We configured this plugin in *Chapter 7, 3D Modeling and Simulation*, when you created the robot to use it in Gazebo.

This driver publishes the odometry generated in the simulated world, so we do not need to write anything for Gazebo.

Execute the robot sample in Gazebo to see the odometry working. Type the following commands in the shell:

```
$ roslaunch chapter8_tutorials gazebo_xacro.launch model:="`rospack find robot1_description`/urdf/robot1_base_04.xacro"
$ rosrun teleop_twist_keyboard teleop_twist_keyboard.py
```

Then, with the `teleop` node, move the robot for a few seconds to generate new data on the odometry topic.

On the screen of the Gazebo simulator, if you click on `robot_model1`, you will see some properties of the object. One of these properties is the pose of the robot. Click on the pose, and you will see some fields with data. What you are watching is the position of the robot in the virtual world. If you move the robot, the data changes:

Gazebo continuously publishes the odometry data. Check the topic and see what data it is sending. Type the following command in a shell:

```
$ rostopic echo /odom/pose/pose
```

The following is the output that you will receive:

```
---
position:
  x: 1.36988769868
  y: 0.620282427846
  z: 0.0
orientation:
  x: 0.0
  y: 0.0
  z: 0.28708429626
  w: 0.957905322477
---
```

As you can observe, Gazebo is creating the odometry as the robot moves. We are going to see how Gazebo creates it by looking inside the plugin's source code.

The plugin file is located in the gazebo_plugins package, and the file is gazebo_ros_skid_steer_drive.cpp. You can find the code at https://github.com/ros-simulation/gazebo_ros_pkgs/blob/hydro-devel/gazebo_plugins/src/gazebo_ros_skid_steer_drive.cpp.

The file has a lot of code, but the important part for us now is the following function, publishOdometry():

```
void GazeboRosSkidSteerDrive::publishOdometry(double step_time)
{
  ros::Time current_time = ros::Time::now();
  std::string odom_frame =
  tf::resolve(tf_prefix_, odometry_frame_);
  std::string base_footprint_frame =
  tf::resolve(tf_prefix_, robot_base_frame_);
  // TODO create some non-perfect odometry!
  // getting data for base_footprint to odom transform
  math::Pose pose = this->parent->GetWorldPose();
  tf::Quaternion qt(pose.rot.x, pose.rot.y, pose.rot.z, pose.rot.w);
  tf::Vector3 vt(pose.pos.x, pose.pos.y, pose.pos.z);
  tf::Transform base_footprint_to_odom(qt, vt);
  if (this->broadcast_tf_)
```

```
{
  transform_broadcaster_->sendTransform(
  tf::StampedTransform(base_footprint_to_odom, current_time,
  odom_frame, base_footprint_frame));
}
// publish odom topic
odom_.pose.pose.position.x = pose.pos.x;
odom_.pose.pose.position.y = pose.pos.y;
odom_.pose.pose.orientation.x = pose.rot.x;
odom_.pose.pose.orientation.y = pose.rot.y;
odom_.pose.pose.orientation.z = pose.rot.z;
odom_.pose.pose.orientation.w = pose.rot.w;
odom_.pose.covariance[0] = 0.00001;
odom_.pose.covariance[7] = 0.00001;
odom_.pose.covariance[14] = 1000000000000.0;
odom_.pose.covariance[21] = 1000000000000.0;
odom_.pose.covariance[28] = 1000000000000.0;
odom_.pose.covariance[35] = 0.01;
// get velocity in /odom frame
math::Vector3 linear;
linear = this->parent->GetWorldLinearVel();
odom_.twist.twist.angular.z = this->parent->GetWorldAngularVel().z;
// convert velocity to child_frame_id (aka base_footprint)
float yaw = pose.rot.GetYaw();
  odom_.twist.twist.linear.x = cosf(yaw) * linear.x + sinf(yaw) * linear.y;
  odom_.twist.twist.linear.y = cosf(yaw) * linear.y - sinf(yaw) * linear.x;
  odom_.header.stamp = current_time;
  odom_.header.frame_id = odom_frame;
  odom_.child_frame_id = base_footprint_frame;
  odometry_publisher_.publish(odom_);
}
```

The publishOdometry() function is where the odometry is published. You can see how the fields of the structure are filled and the name of the topic for the odometry is set (in this case, it is odom). The pose is generated in the other part of the code that we will see in the following section.

Once you have learned how and where Gazebo creates the odometry, you will be ready to learn how to publish the odometry and the transform for a real robot. The following code will show a robot doing circles continuously. The final outcome does not really matter; the important thing to know here is how to publish the correct data for our robot.

Chapter 8

Creating our own odometry

Create a new file in `chapter8_tutorials/src` with the name `odometry.cpp`, and put the following code in it:

```
#include <string>
#include <ros/ros.h>
#include <sensor_msgs/JointState.h>
#include <tf/transform_broadcaster.h>
#include <nav_msgs/Odometry.h>

int main(int argc, char** argv) {

ros::init(argc, argv, "state_publisher");
    ros::NodeHandle n;
    ros::Publisher odom_pub = n.advertise<nav_msgs::Odometry>("odom", 10);

    // initial position
    double x = 0.0;
    double y = 0.0;
    double th = 0;

    // velocity
    double vx = 0.4;
    double vy = 0.0;
    double vth = 0.4;
    ros::Time current_time;
    ros::Time last_time;
    current_time = ros::Time::now();
    last_time = ros::Time::now();

    tf::TransformBroadcaster broadcaster;
    ros::Rate loop_rate(20);

    const double degree = M_PI/180;

    // message declarations
    geometry_msgs::TransformStamped odom_trans;
    odom_trans.header.frame_id = "odom";
    odom_trans.child_frame_id = "base_footprint";

    while (ros::ok()) {
```

[319]

```cpp
            current_time = ros::Time::now();

            double dt = (current_time - last_time).toSec();
            double delta_x = (vx * cos(th) - vy * sin(th)) * dt;
            double delta_y = (vx * sin(th) + vy * cos(th)) * dt;
            double delta_th = vth * dt;

            x += delta_x;
            y += delta_y;
            th += delta_th;

            geometry_msgs::Quaternion odom_quat;
            odom_quat = tf::createQuaternionMsgFromRollPitchYaw(0,0,th);

            // update transform
            odom_trans.header.stamp = current_time;
            odom_trans.transform.translation.x = x;
            odom_trans.transform.translation.y = y;
            odom_trans.transform.translation.z = 0.0;
            odom_trans.transform.rotation = tf::createQuaternionMsgFromYaw(th);

            //filling the odometry
            nav_msgs::Odometry odom;
            odom.header.stamp = current_time;
            odom.header.frame_id = "odom";
            odom.child_frame_id = "base_footprint";
            // position
            odom.pose.pose.position.x = x;
            odom.pose.pose.position.y = y;
            odom.pose.pose.position.z = 0.0;
            odom.pose.pose.orientation = odom_quat;

            // velocity
            odom.twist.twist.linear.x = vx;
            odom.twist.twist.linear.y = vy;
            odom.twist.twist.linear.z = 0.0;
            odom.twist.twist.angular.x = 0.0;
            odom.twist.twist.angular.y = 0.0;
            odom.twist.twist.angular.z = vth;

        last_time = current_time;

            // publishing the odometry and the new tf
```

```
            broadcaster.sendTransform(odom_trans);
            odom_pub.publish(odom);

       loop_rate.sleep();
    }
    return 0;
}
```

First, create the transformation variable and fill it with `frame_id` and the `child_frame_id` values in order to know when the frames have to move. In our case, the base `base_footprint` will move relatively towards the frame `odom`:

```
geometry_msgs::TransformStamped odom_trans;
    odom_trans.header.frame_id = "odom";
    odom_trans.child_frame_id = "base_footprint";
```

In this part, we generate the pose of the robot. With the linear velocity and the angular velocity, we can calculate the theoretical position of the robot after a while:

```
double dt = (current_time - last_time).toSec();
double delta_x = (vx * cos(th) - vy * sin(th)) * dt;
double delta_y = (vx * sin(th) + vy * cos(th)) * dt;
double delta_th = vth * dt;

x += delta_x;
y += delta_y;
th += delta_th;

geometry_msgs::Quaternion odom_quat;
odom_quat = tf::createQuaternionMsgFromRollPitchYaw(0,0,th);
```

In the transformation, we will only fill in the `x` and `rotation` fields, as our robot can only move forward and backward and can turn:

```
odom_trans.header.stamp = current_time;
odom_trans.transform.translation.x = x;
odom_trans.transform.translation.y = 0.0;
odom_trans.transform.translation.z = 0.0;
odom_trans.transform.rotation = tf::createQuaternionMsgFromYaw(th);
```

With the odometry, we will do the same. Fill the `frame_id` and `child_frame_id` fields with `odom` and `base_footprint`.

The Navigation Stack – Robot Setups

As the odometry has two structures, we will fill in the x, y, and `orientation` of the pose. In the twist structure, we will fill in the linear velocity x and the angular velocity z:

```
// position
odom.pose.pose.position.x = x;
odom.pose.pose.position.y = y;
odom.pose.pose.orientation = odom_quat;

// velocity
odom.twist.twist.linear.x = vx;
odom.twist.twist.angular.z = vth;
```

Once all the necessary fields are filled in, publish the data:

```
// publishing the odometry and the new tf
broadcaster.sendTransform(odom_trans);
odom_pub.publish(odom);
```

Remember to create the following line in the `CMakeLists.txt` file before compiling it:

```
add_executable(odometry src/odometry.cpp)
target_link_libraries(odometry ${catkin_LIBRARIES})
```

Compile the package and launch the robot without using Gazebo, using only `rviz` to visualize the model and the movement of the robot. Use the following command to do this:

```
$ roslaunch chapter8_tutorials display_xacro.launch model:="`rospack find chapter8_tutorials`/urdf/robot1_base_04.xacro"
```

Now, run the odometry node with the following command:

```
$ rosrun chapter8_tutorials odometry
```

The following output is what you will get:

On the `rviz` screen, you can see the robot moving over some red arrows (grid). The robot moves over the grid because you published a new tf frame transform for the robot. The red arrows are the graphical representation for the odometry message. You will see the robot moving in circles continuously as we programmed in the code.

Creating a base controller

A base controller is an important element in the navigation stack because it is the only way to effectively control your robot. It communicates directly with the electronics of your robot.

ROS does not provide a standard base controller, so you must write a base controller for your mobile platform.

Your robot has to be controlled with the message type `geometry_msgs/Twist`. This message was used on the `Odometry` message that we saw before.

So, your base controller must subscribe to a topic with the name `cmd_vel`, and must generate the correct commands to move the platform with the correct linear and angular velocities.

We are now going to recall the structure of this message. Type the following command in a shell to see the structure:

```
$ rosmsg show geometry_msgs/Twist
```

The output of this command is as follows:

```
geometry_msgs/Vector3 linear
    float64 x
    float64 y
    float64 z
geometry_msgs/Vector3 angular
    float64 x
    float64 y
    float64 z
```

The vector with the name `linear` indicates the linear velocity for the axes x, y, and z. The vector with the name `angular` is for the angular velocity on the axes.

For our robot, we will only use the linear velocity x and the angular velocity z. This is because our robot is on a differential-wheeled platform; it has two motors to move the robot forward and backward and to turn.

We are working with a simulated robot on Gazebo, and the base controller is implemented on the driver used to move/simulate the platform. This means that we will not have to create the base controller for this robot.

Anyway, in this chapter, you will see an example to implement the base controller on your physical robot. Before that, let's execute our robot on Gazebo to see how the base controller works. Run the following commands on different shells:

```
$ roslaunch chapter8_tutorials gazebo_xacro.launch model:="`rospack find robot1_description`/urdf/robot1_base_04.xacro"
$ rosrun teleop_twist_keyboard teleop_twist_keyboard.py
```

When all the nodes are launched and working, open rxgraph to see the relation between all the nodes:

```
$ rqt_graph
```

You can see that Gazebo subscribes automatically to the cmd_vel topic that is generated by the teleoperation node.

Inside the Gazebo simulator, the plugin of our robot is running and is getting the data from the cmd_vel topic. Also, this plugin moves the robot in the virtual world and generates the odometry.

Using Gazebo to create the odometry

To obtain some insight of how Gazebo does that, we are going to take a sneak peek inside the `diffdrive_plugin.cpp` file. You can find it at https://github.com/ros-simulation/gazebo_ros_pkgs/blob/hydro-devel/gazebo_plugins/src/gazebo_ros_skid_steer_drive.cpp.

The load function performs the function of registering the subscriber of the topic, and when a `cmd_vel` topic is received, the `cmdVelCallback()` function is executed to handle the message:

```
void GazeboRosSkidSteerDrive::Load(physics::ModelPtr _parent,
sdf::ElementPtr _sdf)
{
  ...
  ...
  // ROS: Subscribe to the velocity command topic (usually "cmd_vel")
  ros::SubscribeOptions so =
  ros::SubscribeOptions::create<geometry_msgs::Twist>(command_topic_,
1,
  boost::bind(&GazeboRosSkidSteerDrive::cmdVelCallback, this, _1),
  ros::VoidPtr(), &queue_);
  ...
  ...
}
```

When a message arrives, the linear and angular velocities are stored in the internal variables to run operations later:

```
void GazeboRosSkidSteerDrive::cmdVelCallback(
const geometry_msgs::Twist::ConstPtr& cmd_msg)
{
  boost::mutex::scoped_lock scoped_lock(lock);
  x_ = cmd_msg->linear.x;
  rot_ = cmd_msg->angular.z;
}
```

The plugin estimates the velocity for each motor, using the formulas from the kinematic model of the robot, in the following manner:

```
void GazeboRosSkidSteerDrive::getWheelVelocities() {
  boost::mutex::scoped_lock scoped_lock(lock);
  double vr = x_;
  double va = rot_;
  wheel_speed_[RIGHT_FRONT] = vr + va * wheel_separation_ / 2.0;
  wheel_speed_[RIGHT_REAR] = vr + va * wheel_separation_ / 2.0;
```

```
    wheel_speed_[LEFT_FRONT] = vr - va * wheel_separation_ / 2.0;
    wheel_speed_[LEFT_REAR] = vr - va * wheel_separation_ / 2.0;
}
```

And finally, it estimates the distance traversed by the robot using more formulas from the kinematic motion model of the robot. As you can see in the code, you must know the wheel diameter and the wheel separation of your robot:

```
// Update the controller
void GazeboRosSkidSteerDrive::UpdateChild()
{
  common::Time current_time = this->world->GetSimTime();
  double seconds_since_last_update =
  (current_time - last_update_time_).Double();
  if (seconds_since_last_update > update_period_)
  {
    publishOdometry(seconds_since_last_update);
    // Update robot in case new velocities have been requested
    getWheelVelocities();
    joints[LEFT_FRONT]->SetVelocity(0, wheel_speed_[LEFT_FRONT] / wheel_diameter_);
    joints[RIGHT_FRONT]->SetVelocity(0, wheel_speed_[RIGHT_FRONT] / wheel_diameter_);
    joints[LEFT_REAR]->SetVelocity(0, wheel_speed_[LEFT_REAR] / wheel_diameter_);
    joints[RIGHT_REAR]->SetVelocity(0, wheel_speed_[RIGHT_REAR] / wheel_diameter_);
    last_update_time_+= common::Time(update_period_);
  }
}
```

This is the way `gazebo_ros_skid_steer_drive` controls our simulated robot in Gazebo.

Creating our base controller

Now, we are going to do something similar, that is, prepare a code to be used with a real robot with two wheels and encoders.

Create a new file in `chapter8_tutorials/src` with the name `base_controller.cpp` and put in the following code:

```
#include <ros/ros.h>
#include <sensor_msgs/JointState.h>
#include <tf/transform_broadcaster.h>
#include <nav_msgs/Odometry.h>
```

```cpp
#include <iostream>

using namespace std;

double width_robot = 0.1;
double vl = 0.0;
double vr = 0.0;
ros::Time last_time;
double right_enc = 0.0;
double left_enc = 0.0;
double right_enc_old = 0.0;
double left_enc_old = 0.0;
double distance_left = 0.0;
double distance_right = 0.0;
double ticks_per_meter = 100;
double x = 0.0;
double y = 0.0;
double th = 0.0;
geometry_msgs::Quaternion odom_quat;

void cmd_velCallback(const geometry_msgs::Twist &twist_aux)
{
    geometry_msgs::Twist twist = twist_aux;
    double vel_x = twist_aux.linear.x;
    double vel_th = twist_aux.angular.z;
    double right_vel = 0.0;
    double left_vel = 0.0;

    if(vel_x == 0){
// turning
        right_vel = vel_th * width_robot / 2.0;
        left_vel = (-1) * right_vel;
    }else if(vel_th == 0){
// forward / backward
        left_vel = right_vel = vel_x;
    }else{
// moving doing arcs
        left_vel = vel_x - vel_th * width_robot / 2.0;
        right_vel = vel_x + vel_th * width_robot / 2.0;
    }
    vl = left_vel;
    vr = right_vel;
}
int main(int argc, char** argv){
```

```
    ros::init(argc, argv, "base_controller");
    ros::NodeHandle n;
    ros::Subscriber cmd_vel_sub = n.subscribe("cmd_vel", 10, cmd_
velCallback);
    ros::Rate loop_rate(10);

    while(ros::ok())
    {

        double dxy = 0.0;
        double dth = 0.0;
        ros::Time current_time = ros::Time::now();
        double dt;
        double velxy = dxy / dt;
        double velth = dth / dt;

      ros::spinOnce();
        dt =  (current_time - last_time).toSec();;
        last_time = current_time;

        // calculate odomety
        if(right_enc == 0.0){
          distance_left = 0.0;
          distance_right = 0.0;
        }else{
          distance_left = (left_enc - left_enc_old) / ticks_per_meter;
          distance_right = (right_enc - right_enc_old) / ticks_per_
meter;
        }

        left_enc_old = left_enc;
        right_enc_old = right_enc;

         dxy = (distance_left + distance_right) / 2.0;
         dth = (distance_right - distance_left) / width_robot;

        if(dxy != 0){
          x += dxy * cosf(dth);
          y += dxy * sinf(dth);
        }

        if(dth != 0){
          th += dth;
        }
```

```
            odom_quat = tf::createQuaternionMsgFromRollPitchYaw(0,0,th);
            loop_rate.sleep();
        }
    }
```

Do not forget to insert the following in your `CMakeLists.txt` file to create the executable of this file:

```
add_executable(base_controller src/base_controller.cpp)
target_link_libraries(base_controller ${catkin_LIBRARIES})
```

This code is only a common example and must be extended with more code to make it work with a specific robot. It depends on the controller used, the encoders, and so on. We assume that you have the right background to add the necessary code in order to make the example work fine.

Creating a map with ROS

Getting a map can sometimes be a complicated task if you do not have the correct tools. ROS has a tool that will help you build a map using the odometry and a laser sensor. This tool is the `map_server` (http://wiki.ros.org/map_server). In this example, you will learn how to use the robot that we created in Gazebo, as we did in the previous chapters, to create a map, save it, and load it again.

We are going to use a `.launch` file to make it easy. Create a new file in `chapter8_tutorials/launch` with the name `gazebo_mapping_robot.launch` and put in the following code:

```
<?xml version="1.0"?>
<launch>
  <param name="/use_sim_time" value="true" />
  <include file="$(find gazebo_ros)/launch/willowgarage_world.launch"/>
  <arg name="model" />
  <param name="robot_description" command="$(find xacro)/xacro.py $(arg model)" />
  <node name="joint_state_publisher" pkg="joint_state_publisher" type="joint_state_publisher" ></node>
  <!-- start robot state publisher -->
  <node pkg="robot_state_publisher" type="robot_state_publisher" name="robot_state_publisher" output="screen" >
    <param name="publish_frequency" type="double" value="50.0" />
  </node>
```

```xml
  <node name="spawn_robot" pkg="gazebo_ros" type="spawn_model"
args="-urdf -param robot_description -z 0.1 -model robot_model"
respawn="false" output="screen" />
  <node name="rviz" pkg="rviz" type="rviz" args="-d $(find chapter8_
tutorials)/launch/mapping.rviz"/>
  <node name="slam_gmapping" pkg="gmapping" type="slam_gmapping">
    <remap from="scan" to="/robot/laser/scan"/>
    <param name="base_link" value="base_footprint"/>
  </node>
</launch>
```

With this .launch file, you can launch the Gazebo simulator with the 3D model, the rviz program with the correct configuration file, and slam_mapping to build a map in real time. Launch the file in a shell, and in the other shell, run the teleoperation node to move the robot:

```
$ roslaunch chapter8_tutorials gazebo_mapping_robot.launch model:="`rospack find robot1_description`/urdf/robot1_base_04.xacro"
$ rosrun teleop_twist_keyboard teleop_twist_keyboard.py
```

When you start to move the robot with the keyboard, you will see the free and unknown space on the rviz screen, as well as the map with the occupied space; this is known as an **Occupancy Grid Map (OGM)**. The slam_mapping node updates the map state when the robot moves, or more specifically, when (after some motion) it has a good estimate of the robot's location and how the map is. It takes the laser scans and the odometry to build the OGM for you.

Saving the map using map_server

Once you have a complete map or something acceptable, you can save it to use it later in the navigation stack. To save it, use the following command:

```
$ rosrun map_server map_saver -f map
```

```
[ INFO] [1418594807.613374681]: Waiting for the map
[ INFO] [1418594807.958979924, 126.530000000]: Received a 4000 X 4000 map @ 0.050 m/pix
[ INFO] [1418594807.959452501, 126.530000000]: Writing map occupancy data to map.pgm
[ INFO] [1418594808.997886519, 127.085000000]: Writing map occupancy data to map.yaml
[ INFO] [1418594808.998301431, 127.085000000]: Done
```

This command will create two files, map.pgm and map.yaml. The first one is the map in the .pgm format (the **portable gray map** format). The other is the configuration file for the map. If you open it, you will see the following output:

```
image: map.pgm
resolution: 0.050000
origin: [-100.000000, -100.000000, 0.000000]
negate: 0
occupied_thresh: 0.65
free_thresh: 0.196
```

Now, open the .pgm image file with your favorite viewer, and you will see the map being built before you:

Loading the map using map_server

When you want to use the map built with your robot, it is necessary to load it with the `map_server` package. The following command will load the map:

```
$ rosrun map_server map_server map.yaml
```

But to make it easy, create another `.launch` file in `chapter8_tutorials/launch` with the name `gazebo_map_robot.launch`, and put in the following code:

```
<?xml version="1.0"?>
<launch>
    <param name="/use_sim_time" value="true" />
    <!-- start up wg world -->
    <include file="$(find gazebo_ros)/launch/willowgarage_world.launch"/>
    <arg name="model" />
    <param name="robot_description" command="$(find xacro)/xacro.py $(arg model)" />
    <node name="joint_state_publisher" pkg="joint_state_publisher" type="joint_state_publisher" ></node>
    <!-- start robot state publisher -->
  <node pkg="robot_state_publisher" type="robot_state_publisher" name="robot_state_publisher" output="screen" >
    <param name="publish_frequency" type="double" value="50.0" />
  </node>
    <node name="spawn_robot" pkg="gazebo_ros" type="spawn_model" args="-urdf -param robot_description -z 0.1 -model robot_model" respawn="false" output="screen" />
    <node name="map_server" pkg="map_server" type="map_server" args="$(find chapter8_tutorials)/maps/map.yaml" />
    <node name="rviz" pkg="rviz" type="rviz" args="-d $(find chapter8_tutorials)/launch/mapping.rviz" />
</launch>
```

Now, launch the file using the following command and remember to put the model of the robot that will be used:

```
$ roslaunch chapter8_tutorials gazebo_map_robot.launch model:="`rospack find chapter8_tutorials`/urdf/robot1_base_04.xacro"
```

Then, you will see rviz with the robot and the map. The navigation stack, in order to know the localization of the robot, will use the map published by the map server and the laser readings. This will help it perform a scan matching algorithm that helps in estimating the robot's location using a particle filter implemented in the `amcl` **(Adaptive Monte Carlo Localization)** node.

We will see more about maps as well as more useful tools, in the next chapter.

Summary

In this chapter, you worked on the steps required to configure your robot in order to use it with the navigation stack. Now you know that the robot must have a planar laser, must be a differential-wheeled robot, and it should satisfy some requirements for the base control and the geometry.

Keep in mind that we are working with Gazebo to demonstrate the examples and to explain how the navigation stack works with different configurations. It is more complex to explain all of this directly on a real, robotic platform because we do not know whether you have one or have access to one. In any case, depending on the platform, the instructions may vary and the hardware may fail, so it is safer and useful to run these algorithms in simulations; later, we can test them on a real robot, as long as it satisfies the requirements described thus far.

In the next chapter, you will learn how to configure the navigation stack, create the .launch files, and navigate autonomously in Gazebo with the robot that you created in the previous chapters.

In brief, what you will learn after this chapter will be extremely useful because it shows you how to configure everything correctly so you know how to use the navigation stack with other robots, either simulated or real.

9
The Navigation Stack – Beyond Setups

We are now getting close to the end of the book, and this is when we will use all the knowledge acquired through it. We have created packages, nodes, 3D models of robots, and more. In *Chapter 8, The Navigation Stack – Robot Setups*, you configured your robot in order to be used with the navigation stack, and in this chapter, we will finish the configuration for the navigation stack so that you learn how to use it with your robot.

All the work done in the previous chapters has been a preamble for this precise moment. This is when the fun begins and when the robots come alive.

In this chapter, we are going to learn how to do the following:

- Apply the knowledge of *Chapter 8, The Navigation Stack – Robot Setups* and the programs developed therein
- Understand the navigation stack and how it works
- Configure all the necessary files
- Create launch files to start the navigation stack

Let's begin!

Creating a package

The correct way to create a package is by adding the dependencies with the other packages created for your robot. For example, you could use the next command to create the package:

```
$ roscreate-pkg my_robot_name_2dnav move_base my_tf_configuration_dep my_odom_configuration_dep my_sensor_configuration_dep
```

But in our case, as we have everything in the same package, so it is only necessary to execute the following:

```
$ catkin_create_pkg chapter9_tutorials roscpp tf
```

Remember that in the repository, you may find all the necessary files for the chapter.

Creating a robot configuration

To launch the entire robot, we are going to create a launch file with all the necessary files to activate all the systems. Anyway, here you have a launch file for a real robot that you can use as a template. The following script is present in `configuration_template.launch`:

```xml
<launch>
   <node pkg="sensor_node_pkg" type="sensor_node_type" name="sensor_node_name" output="screen">
      <param name="sensor_param" value="param_value" />
   </node>

   <node pkg="odom_node_pkg" type="odom_node_type" name="odom_node" output="screen">
      <param name="odom_param" value="param_value" />
   </node>

   <node pkg="transform_configuration_pkg" type="transform_configuration_type" name="transform_configuration_name" output="screen">
      <param name="transform_configuration_param" value="param_value" />
   </node>
</launch>
```

This launch file will launch three nodes that will start up the robot.

> **Downloading the example code**
>
> You can download the example code files from your account at `http://www.packtpub.com` for all the Packt Publishing books you have purchased. If you purchased this book elsewhere, you can visit `http://www.packtpub.com/support` and register to have the files e-mailed directly to you. You can also download these code files from `https://github.com/AaronMR/ROS_Book_Hydro`.

The first one is the node responsible for activating the sensors, for example, the **Laser Imaging, Detection, and Ranging** (**LIDAR**) system. The parameter `sensor_param` can be used to configure the sensor's port, for example, if the sensor uses a USB connection. If your sensor needs more parameters, you need to duplicate the line and add the necessary parameters. Some robots have more than one sensor to help in the navigation. In this case, you can add more nodes or create a launch file for the sensors, and include it in this launch file. This could be a good option for easily managing all the nodes in the same file.

The second node is to start the odometry, the base control, and all the necessary files to move the base and calculate the robot's position. Remember that in *Chapter 8, The Navigation Stack – Robot Setups*, we looked at these nodes in some detail. As in the other section, you can use the parameters to configure something in the `odometry`, or replicate the line to add more nodes.

The third part is meant to launch the node responsible for publishing and calculating the geometry of the robot, and the transform between the arms, sensors, and so on.

The previous file is for your real robot, but for our example, the next launch file is all we need.

Create a new file in `chapter9_tutorials/launch` with the name `chapter9_configuration_gazebo.launch`, and add the following code:

```
<?xml version="1.0"?>
<launch>
        <param name="/use_sim_time" value="true" />
        <remap from="robot/laser/scan" to="/scan" />
        <!-- start up wg world -->
        <include file="$(find gazebo_ros)/launch/willowgarage_world.launch"/>
        <arg name="model" default="$(find robot1_description)/urdf/robot1_base_04.xacro"/>
        <param name="robot_description" command="$(find xacro)/xacro.py $(arg model)" />
```

```xml
        <node name="joint_state_publisher" pkg="joint_state_publisher"
type="joint_state_publisher" ></node>
        <!-- start robot state publisher -->
        <node pkg="robot_state_publisher" type="robot_state_publisher"
name="robot_state_publisher" output="screen" />
        <node name="spawn_robot" pkg="gazebo_ros" type="spawn_model"
args="-urdf -param robot_description -z 0.1 -model robot_model"
respawn="false" output="screen" />
        <node name="rviz" pkg="rviz" type="rviz" args="-d $(find
chapter9_tutorials)/launch/navigation.rviz" />
</launch>
```

This launch file is the same that we used in the previous chapters, so it does not need any additional explanation.

Now to launch this file, use the following command:

```
$ roslaunch chapter9_tutorials chapter9_configuration_gazebo.launch
```

You will see the following window:

Notice that in the previous screenshot, there are some fields in red, blue, and yellow, without you having configured anything before. This is because in the launch file, a configuration file for the `rviz` layout is loaded along with `rviz`, and this file was configured in the previous chapter of this book.

In the upcoming sections, you will learn how to configure `rviz` to use it with the navigation stack and view all the topics.

Configuring the costmaps – global_costmap and local_costmap

Okay, now we are going to start configuring the navigation stack and all the necessary files to start it. To start with the configuration, first we will learn what costmaps are and what they are used for. Our robot will move through the map using two types of navigation—`global` and `local`.

- The global navigation is used to create paths for a goal in the map or at a far-off distance
- The local navigation is used to create paths in the nearby distances and avoid obstacles, for example, a square window of 4 x 4 meters around the robot

These modules use costmaps to keep all the information of our map. The `global` costmap is used for `global` navigation and the `local` costmap for `local` navigation.

The costmaps have parameters to configure the behaviors, and they have common parameters as well, which are configured in a shared file.

The configuration basically consists of three files where we can set up different parameters. The files are as follows:

- `costmap_common_params.yaml`
- `global_costmap_params.yaml`
- `local_costmap_params.yaml`

Just by reading the names of these configuration files, you can instantly guess what they are used for. Now that you have a basic idea about the usage of costmaps, we are going to create the configuration files and explain the parameters that are configured in them.

Configuring the common parameters

Let's start with the common parameters. Create a new file in `chapter9_tutorials/launch` with the name `costmap_common_params.yaml`, and add the following code.

The following script is present in `costmap_common_params.yaml`:

```
obstacle_range: 2.5
raytrace_range: 3.0
footprint: [[-0.2,-0.2],[-0.2,0.2], [0.2, 0.2], [0.2,-0.2]]
inflation_radius: 0.5
cost_scaling_factor: 10.0
observation_sources: scan
scan: {sensor_frame: base_link,  observation_persistence: 0.0, max_obstacle_height: 0.4, min_obstacle_height: 0.0, data_type: LaserScan, topic: /scan, marking: true, clearing: true}
```

This file is used to configure common parameters. The parameters are used in `local_costmap` and `global_costmap`. Let's break the code and understand it.

The `obstacle_range` and `raytrace_range` attributes are used to indicate the maximum distance that the sensor will read and introduce new information in the costmaps. The first one is used for the obstacles. If the robot detects an obstacle closer than 2.5 meters in our case, it will put the obstacle in the costmap. The other one is used to clean/clear the costmap and update the free space in it when the robot moves. Note that we can only detect the echo of the laser or sonar with the obstacle; we cannot perceive the whole obstacle or object itself, but this simple approach will be enough to deal with these kinds of measurements, and we will be able to build a map and localize within it.

The `footprint` attribute is used to indicate the geometry of the robot to the navigation stack. It is used to keep the right distance between the obstacles and the robot, or to find out if the robot can go through a door. The `inflation_radius` attribute is the value given to keep a minimal distance between the geometry of the robot and the obstacles.

The `cost_scaling_factor` attribute modifies the behavior of the robot around the obstacles. You can make a behavior aggressive or conservative by changing the parameter.

With the `observation_sources` attribute, you can set the sensors used by the navigation stack to get the data from the real world and calculate the path.

In our case, we are using a simulated LIDAR in Gazebo, but we can use a point cloud to do the same.

The next line will configure the sensor's frame and the uses of the data:

```
scan: {sensor_frame: base_link, data_type: LaserScan, topic: /scan,
marking: true, clearing: true}
```

The laser configured in the previous line is used to add and clear obstacles in the costmap. For example, you could add a sensor with a wide range to find obstacles and another sensor to navigate and clear the obstacles. The topic's name is configured in this line. It is important to configure it well, because the navigation stack could wait for another topic and all this while, the robot is moving and could crash into a wall or an obstacle.

Configuring the global costmap

The next file to be configured is the `global costmap` configuration file. Create a new file in `chapter9_tutorials/launch` with the name `global_costmap_params.yaml`, and add the following code:

```
global_costmap:
  global_frame: /map
  robot_base_frame: /base_footprint
  update_frequency: 1.0
  static_map: true
```

The `global_frame` and the `robot_base_frame` attributes define the transformation between the map and the robot. This transformation is for the global costmap.

You can configure the frequency of updates for the costmap. In this case, it is 1 Hz. The `static_map` attribute is used for the global costmap to see whether a map or the map server is used to initialize the costmap. If you aren't using a static map, set this parameter to `false`.

Configuring the local costmap

The next file is for configuring the local costmap. Create a new file in `chapter9_tutorials/launch` with the name `local_costmap_params.yaml`, and add the following code:

```
local_costmap:
  global_frame: /map
  robot_base_frame: /base_footprint
  update_frequency: 5.0
  publish_frequency: 2.0
  static_map: false
  rolling_window: true
```

```
width: 5.0
height: 5.0
resolution: 0.02
tranform_tolerance: 0.5
planner_frequency: 1.0
planner_patiente: 5.0
```

The `global_frame`, `robot_base_frame`, `update_frequency` and `static_map` parameters are the same as described in the previous section, configuring the global costmap. The `publish_frequency` parameter determines the frequency for publishing information. The `rolling_window` parameter is used to keep the costmap centered on the robot when it is moving around the world.

The `transform_tolerance parameter` configures the maximum latency for the transforms, in our case 0.5 seconds. With the `planner_frequency parameter`, we can configure the rate in Hz at which to run the planning loop. And the `planner_patiente` parameter configures how long the planner will wait in seconds in an attempt to find a valid plan, before space-clearing operations are performed.

You can configure the dimensions and the resolution of the costmap with the `width`, `height`, and `resolution` parameters. The values are given in meters.

Base local planner configuration

Once we have the costmaps configured, it is necessary to configure the base planner. The base planner is used to generate the velocity commands to move our robot. Create a new file in `chapter9_tutorials/launch` with the name `base_local_planner_params.yaml`, and add the following code:

```
TrajectoryPlannerROS:
  max_vel_x: 0.2
  min_vel_x: 0.05
  max_rotational_vel: 0.15
  min_in_place_rotational_vel: 0.01
  min_in_place_vel_theta: 0.01
  max_vel_theta: 0.15
  min_vel_theta: -0.15
  acc_lim_th: 3.2
  acc_lim_x: 2.5
  acc_lim_y: 2.5
  holonomic_robot: false
```

The `config` file will set the maximum and minimum velocities for your robot. The acceleration is also set.

The `holonomic_robot` parameter is `true` if you are using a holonomic platform. In our case, our robot is based on a non-holonomic platform and the parameter is set to `false`. A **holonomic vehicle** is one that can move in all the configured space from any position. In other words, if the places where the robot can go are defined by any x and y values in the environment, this means that the robot can move there from any position. For example, if the robot can move forward, backward, and laterally, it is holonomic. A typical case of a non-holonomic vehicle is a car, as it cannot move laterally, and from a given position, there are many other positions (or poses) that are not reachable. Also, a differential platform is non-holonomic.

Creating a launch file for the navigation stack

Now we have all the files created and the navigation stack is configured. To run everything, we are going to create a launch file. Create a new file in the `chapter9_tutorials/launch` folder, and put the following code in a file with the name `move_base.launch`:

```xml
<launch>

  <!-- Run the map server -->

  <node name="map_server" pkg="map_server" type="map_server" args="$(find chapter9_tutorials)/maps/map.yaml" output="screen"/>

  <include file="$(find amcl)/examples/amcl_diff.launch" />

  <node pkg="move_base" type="move_base" respawn="false" name="move_base" output="screen">

    <rosparam file="$(find chapter9_tutorials)/launch/costmap_common_params.yaml" command="load" ns="global_costmap" />

    <rosparam file="$(find chapter9_tutorials)/launch/costmap_common_params.yaml" command="load" ns="local_costmap" />

    <rosparam file="$(find chapter9_tutorials)/launch/local_costmap_params.yaml" command="load" />

    <rosparam file="$(find chapter9_tutorials)/launch/global_costmap_params.yaml" command="load" />

    <rosparam file="$(find chapter9_tutorials)/launch/base_local_planner_params.yaml" command="load" />

  </node>
</launch>
```

Notice that in this file, we are launching all the files created earlier. We will launch a map server as well with a map that we created in *Chapter 8, The Navigation Stack – Robot Setups* and the `amcl` node.

The `amcl` node that we are going to use is for differential robots because our robot is also a differential robot. If you want to use `amcl` with holonomic robots, you will need to use the `amcl_omni.launch` file. If you want to use another map, go to *Chapter 8, The Navigation Stack – Robot Setups*, and create a new one.

Now launch the file and type the next command in a new shell. Recall that before you launch this file, you must launch the `chapter9_configuration_gazebo.launch` file.

```
$ roslaunch chapter9_tutorials move_base.launch
```

You will see the following window:

If you compare this image with the image that you saw when you launched the `chapter9_configuration_gazebo.launch` file, you will see that all the options are in blue; this is a good signal and it means that everything is OK.

As we said before, in the next section you will learn which options are necessary to visualize all the topics used in a navigation stack.

Setting up rviz for the navigation stack

It is good practice to visualize all possible data which what the navigation stack does. In this section, we will show you the visualization topic that you must add to `rviz` to see the correct data sent by the navigation stack. Discussions on each visualization topic that the navigation stack publishes are given next.

The 2D pose estimate

The 2D pose estimate (P shortcut) allows the user to initialize the localization system used by the navigation stack by setting the pose of the robot in the world.

The navigation stack waits for the new pose of a new topic with the name `initialpose`. This topic is sent using the `rviz` windows where we previously changed the name of the topic.

The Navigation Stack – Beyond Setups

You can see in the following screenshot how you can use `initialpose`. Click on the **2D Pose Estimate** button, and click on the map to indicate the initial position of your robot. If you don't do this at the beginning, the robot will start the auto-localization process and try to set an initial pose.

- **Topic**: `initialpose`
- **Type**: `geometry_msgs/PoseWithCovarianceStamped`

The 2D nav goal

The 2D nav goal (G shortcut) allows the user to send a goal to the navigation by setting a desired pose for the robot to achieve. The navigation stack waits for a new goal with `/move_base_simple/goal as the topic name`; for this reason, you must change the topic's name in the `rviz` windows in **Tool Properties** in the **2D Nav Goal** menu. The new name that you must put in this textbox is `/move_base_simple/goal`. In the next window, you can see how to use it. Click on the **2D Nav Goal** button, and select the map and the goal for your robot. You can select the *x* and *y* position and the end orientation for the robot.

- **Topic**: move_base_simple/goal
- **Type**: geometry_msgs/PoseStamped

[347]

The static map

This displays the static map that is being served by the `map_server`, if one exists. When you add this visualization, you will see the map we captured in *Chapter 8*, *The Navigation Stack – Robot Setups*, in the *Creating a map with ROS* section.

In the next window, you can see the display type that you need to select and the name that you must put in the display name.

- **Topic**: `map`
- **Type**: `nav_msgs/GetMap`

The particle cloud

This displays the particle cloud used by the robot's localization system. The spread of the cloud represents the localization system's uncertainty about the robot's pose. A cloud that spreads out a lot reflects high uncertainty, while a condensed cloud represents low uncertainty. In our case, you will obtain the following cloud for the robot:

- **Topic**: `particlecloud`
- **Type**: `geometry_msgs/PoseArray`

The robot's footprint

This shows the footprint of the robot; in our case, the robot has a footprint, which has a width of 0.4 meters and a height of 0.4 meters. Remember that this parameter is configured in the `costmap_common_params` file. This dimension is important because the navigation stack will move the robot in a safe mode using the values configured before.

- **Topic**: `local_costmap/robot_footprint`
- **Type**: `geometry_msgs/Polygon`

The local costmap

This shows the local costmap that the navigation stack uses for navigation. The yellow line is the detected obstacle. For the robot to avoid collision, the robot's footprint should never intersect with a cell that contains an obstacle. The blue zone is the inflated obstacle. To avoid collisions, the center point of the robot should never overlap with a cell that contains an inflated obstacle.

- **Topic**: `/move_base/local_costmap/costmap`
- **Type**: `nav_msgs/OccupancyGrid`

The global costmap

This shows the global costmap that the navigation stack uses for navigation. The yellow line is the detected obstacle. For the robot to avoid collision, the robot's footprint should never intersect with a cell that contains an obstacle. The blue zone is the inflated obstacle. To avoid collisions, the center point of the robot should never overlap with a cell that contains an inflated obstacle.

- **Topic**: /move_base/global_costmap/costmap
- **Type**: nav_msgs/OccupancyGrid

The global plan

This shows the portion of the global plan that the local planner is currently pursuing. You can see it in green in the next image. Perhaps the robot will find obstacles during its movement, and the navigation stack will recalculate a new path to avoid collisions and try to follow the global plan.

- **Topic**: `TrajectoryPlannerROS/global_plan`
- **Type**: `nav_msgs/Path`

The local plan

This shows the trajectory associated with the velocity commands currently being commanded to the base by the local planner. You can see the trajectory in blue in front of the robot in the next image. You can use this display to see whether the robot is moving, and the approximate velocity from the length of the blue line.

- **Topic**: TrajectoryPlannerROS/local_plan
- **Type**: nav_msgs/Path

The planner plan

This displays the full plan for the robot computed by the global planner. You will see that it is similar to the global plan.

- **Topic**: NavfnROS/plan
- **Type**: nav_msgs/Path

The current goal

This shows the goal pose that the navigation stack is attempting to achieve. You can see it as a red arrow, and it is displayed after you put a new 2D nav goal. It can be used to find out the final position of the robot.

- **Topic**: `current_goal`
- **Type**: `geometry_msgs/PoseStamped`

These visualizations are all you need to see the navigation stack in `rviz`. With this, you can notice whether the robot is doing something strange. Now we are going to see a general image of the system. Run `rqt_graph` to see whether all the nodes are running and to see the relations between them.

Adaptive Monte Carlo Localization

In this chapter, we are using the `amcl` (**Adaptive Monte Carlo Localization**) algorithm for the localization. The `amcl algorithm` is a probabilistic localization system for a robot moving in 2D. This system implements the adaptive Monte Carlo localization approach, which uses a particle filter to track the pose of a robot against a known map.

The `amcl` algorithm has many configuration options that will affect the performance of localization. For more information on `amcl`, please refer to the AMCL documentation at http://wiki.ros.org/amcl and also at http://www.probabilistic-robotics.org/.

The `amcl` node works mainly with laser scans and laser maps, but it could be extended to work with other sensor data, such as a sonar or stereo vision. So for this chapter, it takes a laser-based map and laser scans, transforms messages, and generates a probabilistic pose. On startup, `amcl` initializes its particle filter according to the parameters provided in the setup. If you don't set the initial position, `amcl` will start at the origin of the coordinates. Anyway, you can set the initial position in rviz using the **2D Pose Estimate** button.

When we include the `amcl_diff.launch` file, we are starting the node with a series of configured parameters. This configuration is the default configuration and the minimum setting needed to make it work.

Next, we are going to see the content of the `amcl_diff.launch` launch file to explain some parameters:

```
<launch>
<node pkg="amcl" type="amcl" name="amcl" output="screen">
  <!-- Publish scans from best pose at a max of 10 Hz -->
  <param name="odom_model_type" value="diff"/>
  <param name="odom_alpha5" value="0.1"/>
  <param name="transform_tolerance" value="0.2" />
  <param name="gui_publish_rate" value="10.0"/>
  <param name="laser_max_beams" value="30"/>
  <param name="min_particles" value="500"/>
  <param name="max_particles" value="5000"/>
  <param name="kld_err" value="0.05"/>
  <param name="kld_z" value="0.99"/>
  <param name="odom_alpha1" value="0.2"/>
  <param name="odom_alpha2" value="0.2"/>
  <!-- translation std dev, m -->
  <param name="odom_alpha3" value="0.8"/>
  <param name="odom_alpha4" value="0.2"/>
  <param name="laser_z_hit" value="0.5"/>
  <param name="laser_z_short" value="0.05"/>
  <param name="laser_z_max" value="0.05"/>
  <param name="laser_z_rand" value="0.5"/>
  <param name="laser_sigma_hit" value="0.2"/>
  <param name="laser_lambda_short" value="0.1"/>
  <param name="laser_lambda_short" value="0.1"/>
  <param name="laser_model_type" value="likelihood_field"/>
  <!-- <param name="laser_model_type" value="beam"/> -->
  <param name="laser_likelihood_max_dist" value="2.0"/>
  <param name="update_min_d" value="0.2"/>
  <param name="update_min_a" value="0.5"/>
  <param name="odom_frame_id" value="odom"/>
  <param name="resample_interval" value="1"/>
  <param name="transform_tolerance" value="0.1"/>
  <param name="recovery_alpha_slow" value="0.0"/>
  <param name="recovery_alpha_fast" value="0.0"/>
</node>
</launch>
```

The `min_particles` and `max_particles` parameters set the minimum and maximum number of particles that are allowed for the algorithm. With more particles, you get more accuracy, but this increases the use of the CPU.

Chapter 9

The `laser_model_type` parameter is used to configure the laser type. In our case, we are using a `likelihood_field` parameter but the algorithm can also use beam lasers.

The `laser_likelihood_max_dist` parameter is used to set the maximum distance for obstacle inflation on the map, which is used in the `likelihood_field` model.

The `initial_pose_x`, `initial_pose_y`, and `initial_pose_a` parameters are not in the launch file, but they are interesting because they set the initial position of the robot when the `amcl` starts, for example, if your robot always starts in the dock station and you want to set the position in the launch file.

Perhaps you should change some parameters to tune your robot and make it work fine. On http://wiki.ros.org/amcl, you have a lot of information about the configuration and the parameters that you could change.

Modifying parameters with rqt_reconfigure

A good option for understanding all the parameters configured in this chapter, is by using `rqt_reconfigure` to change the values without restarting the simulation.

To launch `rqt_reconfigure`, use the following command:

```
$ rosrun rqt_reconfigure rqt_reconfigure
```

You will see the screen as follows:

The Navigation Stack – Beyond Setups

As an example, we are going to change the parameter `max_vel_x` configured in the file, `base_local_planner_params.yaml`. Click over the `move_base` menu and expand it. Then select `TrajectoryPlannerROS` in the menu tree. You will see a list of parameters. As you can see, the parameter `max_vel_x` has the same value that we assigned in the configuration file.

You can see a brief description for the parameter by hovering the mouse over the name for a few seconds. This is very useful for understanding the function of each parameter.

Avoiding obstacles

A great functionality of the navigation stack is the recalculation of the path if it finds obstacles during the movement. You can easily see this feature by adding an object in front of the robot in Gazebo. For example, in our simulation we added a big box in the middle of the path. The navigation stack detects the new obstacle, and automatically creates an alternative path.

In the next image, you can see the object that we added. Gazebo has some predefined 3D objects that you can use in the simulations with mobile robots, arms, humanoids, and so on.

To see the list, go to the **Insert model** section. Select one of the objects and then click at the location where you want to put it, as shown in the following screenshot:

If you go to the `rviz` windows now, you will see a new global plan to avoid the obstacle. This feature is very interesting when you use the robot in real environments with people walking around the robot. If the robot detects a possible collision, it will change the direction, and it will try to arrive at the goal. Recall that the detection of such obstacles is reduced to the area covered by the local planner costmap (for example, 4 x 4 meters around the robot). You can see this feature in the next screenshot:

Sending goals

We are sure that you have been playing with the robot by moving it around the map a lot. This is funny but a little tedious, and it is not very functional.

Perhaps you were thinking that it would be a great idea to program a list of movements and send the robot to different positions with only a button, even when we are not in front of a computer with `rviz`.

Okay, now you are going to learn how to do it using `actionlib`.

The `actionlib` package provides a standardized interface for interfacing with tasks. For example, you can use it to send goals for the robot to detect something at a place, make scans with the laser, and so on. In this section, we will send a goal to the robot, and we will wait for this task to end.

It could look similar to services, but if you are doing a task that has a long duration, you might want the ability to cancel the request during the execution, or get periodic feedback about how the request is progressing. You cannot do this with services. Furthermore, `actionlib` creates messages (not services), and it also creates topics, so we can still send the goals through a topic without taking care of the feedback and the result, if we do not want to.

The following code is a simple example for sending a goal to move the robot. Create a new file in the `chapter9_tutorials/src` folder, and add the following code in a file with the name `sendGoals.cpp`:

```cpp
#include <ros/ros.h>
#include <move_base_msgs/MoveBaseAction.h>
#include <actionlib/client/simple_action_client.h>
#include <tf/transform_broadcaster.h>
#include <sstream>

typedef actionlib::SimpleActionClient<move_base_msgs::MoveBaseAction> MoveBaseClient;

int main(int argc, char** argv){
  ros::init(argc, argv, "navigation_goals");

  MoveBaseClient ac("move_base", true);

  while(!ac.waitForServer(ros::Duration(5.0))){
```

```
      ROS_INFO("Waiting for the move_base action server");
    }

    move_base_msgs::MoveBaseGoal goal;

    goal.target_pose.header.frame_id = "map";
    goal.target_pose.header.stamp = ros::Time::now();

    goal.target_pose.pose.position.x = 1.0;
    goal.target_pose.pose.position.y = 1.0;
    goal.target_pose.pose.orientation.w = 1.0;

    ROS_INFO("Sending goal");
    ac.sendGoal(goal);

    ac.waitForResult();

    if(ac.getState() == actionlib::SimpleClientGoalState::SUCCEEDED)
      ROS_INFO("You have arrived to the goal position");
    else{
      ROS_INFO("The base failed for some reason");
    }
      return 0;
}
```

Add the next file in the CMakeList.txt file to generate the executable for our program:

```
add_executable(sendGoals src/sendGoals.cpp)
target_link_libraries(sendGoals ${catkin_LIBRARIES})
```

Now, compile the package with the following command:

`$ catkin_make`

Now launch everything to test the new program. Use the next command to launch all the nodes and the configurations:

`$ roslaunch chapter9_tutorials chapter9_configuration_gazebo.launch`

`$ roslaunch chapter9_tutorials move_base.launch`

Once you have configured the 2D pose estimate, run the sendGoal node with the next command in a new shell:

`$ rosrun chapter9_tutorials sendGoals`

The Navigation Stack – Beyond Setups

If you go to the `rviz` screen, you will see a new global plan (green line) over the map. This means that the navigation stack has accepted the new goal and it will start to execute it.

When the robot arrives at the goal, you will see the next message in the shell where you ran the node:

`[ INFO ] [...,...]: You have arrived to the goal position`

You can make a list of goals or waypoints, and create a route for the robot. This way you can program missions, guardian robots, or collect things from other rooms with your robot.

Summary

At the end of this chapter, you should have a robot—simulated or real—moving autonomously through the map (which models the environment), using the navigation stack. You can program the control and the localization of the robot by following the ROS philosophy of code reusability, so that you can have the robot completely configured without much effort. The most difficult part of this chapter is to understand all the parameters and learn how to use each one of them appropriately. The correct use of them will determine whether your robot works fine or not; for this reason, you must practice changing the parameters and look for the reaction of the robot.

In the next chapter, you will learn how to use MoveIt! with some tutorials and examples. If you don't know what MoveIt! is, it is a software for building mobile manipulation applications. With it, you can move your articulated robot in an easy way.

10
Manipulation with MoveIt!

MoveIt! is a set of tools for mobile manipulation in ROS. The main web page (`http://moveit.ros.org`) contains documentation, tutorials, and installation instructions as well as example demonstrations with several robotic arms (or robots) that use MoveIt! for manipulation tasks, such as grasping, picking and placing, or simple motion planning with inverse kinematics.

The library incorporates a fast inverse kinematics solver (as part of the motion planning primitives), state-of-the-art algorithms for manipulation, grasping 3D perception (usually in the form of point clouds), kinematics, control, and navigation. Apart from the backend, it provides an easy-to-use GUI to configure new robotic arms with the MoveIt! and RViz plugins to develop motion planning tasks in an intuitive way.

In this chapter, we will see how we can create a simple robotic arm in the URDF format and how we can define motion planning groups with the MoveIt! configuration tool. For a single arm, we will have a single group, so that later we can use the inverse kinematics solvers to perform manipulation tasks specified from the RViz interface. A pick and place task is used to illustrate the capabilities and tools of MoveIt!.

The first section explains the MoveIt! architecture, explaining the basic concepts used in the framework, such as joint groups and planning scene, and general concepts such as trajectory planning, (inverse) kinematics, and collision checking concerns. Then, we will show how you can integrate an arm into MoveIt!, creating the planning groups and scene. Next, we will show you how you can perform motion planning with collisions and how you can incorporate point clouds, which will allow you to avoid collisions with dynamic obstacles.

Finally, perception and object recognition tools will be explained and later used in a pick and place demonstration. For this demonstration, we will use the MoveIt! plugin for RViz.

The MoveIt! architecture

The architecture of MoveIt! is depicted in the following diagram taken from the concepts sections of its official documentation at http://moveit.ros.org/documentation/concepts/. Here, we describe the main concepts in brief.
In order to install MoveIt!, you only have to run this command:

```
$ sudo apt-get install ros-hydro-moveit-full
```

Alternatively, you can install all the dependencies of the code that comes with this chapter by running the following command from a workspace that contains it:

```
$ rosdep install --from-paths src -iy
```

The following diagram (Figure 1) shows the architecture of MoveIt!:

Figure 1: MoveIt! architecture diagram

In the center of the architecture, we have the move_group element. The main idea is that we have to define groups of joints and other elements to perform moving actions using motion planning algorithms. These algorithms consider a scene with objects to interact with and the joints characteristics of the group.

A group is defined using standard ROS tools and definition languages, such as YAML, URDF, and SDF. In brief, we have to define the joints that are part of a group with their joint limits. Similarly, we define the end effector tools, such as a gripper and perception sensors. The robot must expose `JointTrajectoryAction` controllers so that the output of the motion planning can be planned and executed on the robot hardware (or simulator). In order to monitor the execution, `/joint_states` is also needed by means of the robot state publisher. All this is provided by the ROS control as well as specific sensor drivers. Note that MoveIt! provides a GUI wizard to define the joint groups for a given robot, which can be called directly as follows:

```
$ roslaunch moveit_setup_assistant setup_assistant.launch
```

> **Downloading the example code**
> You can download the example code files from your account at http://www.packtpub.com for all the Packt Publishing books you have purchased. If you purchased this book elsewhere, you can visit http://www.packtpub.com/support and register to have the files e-mailed directly to you. You can also download these code files from https://github.com/AaronMR/ROS_Book_Hydro.

Once `move_group` is configured properly, we can interface with it. MoveIt! provides a C++ and a Python API to do so and also an RViz plugin that integrates seamlessly and allows us to send motion goals, plan them, and send (execute) them on the robot, as shown in *Figure 2*:

Figure 2: MoveIt! integration for simulated manipulator in Gazebo

Motion planning

Motion planning deals with the problem of moving the arm to a configuration, allowing you to reach a pose with the end effector without crashing the move group with any obstacle, that is, the links themselves or other objects perceived by sensors (usually as point clouds) or violating the joint limits. The MoveIt! user interface allows you to use different libraries for motion planning, such as OMPL (http://ompl.kavrakilab.org), using ROS actions or services.

A motion plan request is sent to the motion planning, which takes care of avoiding collisions (including self-collisions) and finds a trajectory for all the joints in the groups that move the arm so that it reaches the goal requested. Such a goal consists of a location in joint space or an end effector pose, which could include an object (for example, if the gripper picks up something) as well as kinematic constraints:

- **Position constraints**: These restrict the position of a link
- **Orientation constraints**: These restrict the orientation of a link
- **Visibility constraints**: These restrict a point on a link to be visible in a particular zone (it falls inside the sensor visibility cone)
- **User-specified constraints**: These are provided with a user-defined callback

The result of the motion plan is a trajectory that moves the arm to the target goal location. This trajectory also avoids collisions and satisfies the velocity and acceleration constraints at the joint level.

Finally, MoveIt! has a motion planning pipeline made of motion planners and plan request adapters. The latter are components that allow the preprocessing and postprocessing of the motion plan request. For example, preprocessing is useful when the initial state of the arm is outside joint limits; postprocessing is useful to convert paths into time-parameterized trajectories. Some of the default motion planning adapters provided by MoveIt! are as follows:

- `FixStartStateBounds`: This fixes the initial/start state to be inside the joint limits specified in the URDF. Without this adapter, when the joints are outside the joint limits, the motion planner would not be able to find any plan since the arm is already violating the joint limits. The adapter will move the joints into the joint limits but only when the joint state is not outside by a large amount since, in such cases, it is not necessarily the best solution.
- `FixWorkspaceBounds`: This defines a default workspace to plan a 10 x 10 x 10 m3 cube.
- `FixStartStateCollision`: This will attempt to sample a collision-free configuration near a given configuration in collision. It will do that by disturbing the joint states only by a small amount.

- `FixStartStatePathConstraints`: This is applied when the initial state does not obey the given path constraints. It will attempt to find a plan from the initial configuration to a new one that satisfies the path constraints, which will then be used as the initial state for motion planning.
- `AddTimeParameterization`: This will time-parameterize the kinematic path typically generated by the motion planner (a path that does not obey any velocity or acceleration constraints) by applying velocity and acceleration constraints given in the `joint_limits.yaml` file of the robot.

The planning scene

The planning scene represents the world around the robot as well as the robot state. This is maintained by the planning scene monitor shown in the next diagram, taken from the concepts section of its official documentation at http://moveit.ros.org/documentation/concepts/. It is a subpart of move_group, which listens to `joint_states`, the sensor information (usually point clouds), and the world geometry, which is provided by the user input on the `planning_scene` topic. This is shown in *Figure 3*:

Figure 3: MoveIt! planning scene diagram

The world geometry monitor uses an occupancy map monitor to build a 3D representation of the environment around the robot and augments it with the `planning_scene` topic information, such as objects (for example, grasping objects); an octomap is used to register all this information. In order to generate the 3D representation, MoveIt! supports different sensors to perceive the environment by means of plugins supplying two kinds of inputs:

- **Point Clouds**: This is handled by a point cloud occupancy map updater plugin.
- **Depth images**: This is handled by the depth image occupancy map updater plugin, including a self-filter that removes visible parts of the robot from the depth map using the robot state information to that end.

Kinematics

Forward kinematics and its Jacobians are integrated in the `RobotState` class. On the other hand, for inverse kinematics, MoveIt! provides a default plugin that uses a numerical Jacobian-based solver that is automatically configured by the setup assistant. As with other components of MoveIt!, the users can write their own inverse kinematics plugins, such as IKFast.

Collision checking

The `CollisionWorld` object of the planning scene is used to configure collision checking using the **Flexible Collision Library** (**FCL**) package. The collision objects supported are meshes, primitive shapes, for example, boxes, cylinders, cones, spheres, and planes, and an octomap.

Collision checking is a very expensive operation that usually accounts for 90 percent of motion planning. For that reason, an **Allowed Collision Matrix** (**ACM**) is used to encode a Boolean value that indicates whether collision checking is needed for two pairs of bodies (on the robot or in the world); a value of 1 indicates that collision checking is not needed for a pair of objects. This is the case for bodies that are very far from each other, so they would never collide.

Integrating an arm in MoveIt!

In this section, we will go through the different steps required to get a robotic arm working with MoveIt! There are several elements that need to be provided beforehand, such as the arm description file (URDF), as well as the components required to make it work in Gazebo, although some of these will be covered in this chapter.

What's in the box?

In order to make it easier to understand how we can integrate a robotic arm with MoveIt!, we have provided a set of packages containing all of the necessary configurations, robot descriptions, launch scripts, and modules to integrate MoveIt! with ROS, Gazebo, and RViz. We will not cover the details of how to integrate a robot with Gazebo as that has been covered in other chapters, but an explanation on how to integrate MoveIt! with Gazebo will be provided. The following packages are provided in the repository for this chapter, in the `chapter10_tutorials` directory:

- `chapter10_tutorials`: This repository acts as a container for the rest of the packages that will be used in this chapter. This sort of structure usually requires a metapackage to let catkin know that the packages are loosely related; hence, this package is the metapackage of the repository.

- `rosbook_arm_bringup`: This package centralizes the launching of both the controllers and MoveIt! as well as the `play_motion` utility, which can be used to request predefined arm configurations. It brings up the robot—either the real one or in simulation.

- `rosbook_arm_controller_configuration`: This package contains the launch files to load the controllers required to move the arm. These are trajectory (`JointTrajectoryController`) controllers used to support the MoveIt! motion planning.

- `rosbook_arm_controller_configuration_gazebo`: This package contains the configuration for the joint trajectory controllers. This configuration also includes the PID values required to control the arm in Gazebo.

- `rosbook_arm_description`: This package contains all of the required elements to describe the robotic arm, including URDF files (actually xacro), meshes, and configuration files.

- `rosbook_arm_gazebo`: This package is one of the most important packages, containing the launch files for Gazebo, which will take care of launching the simulation environment as well as MoveIt!, and the controllers, as well as taking care of running the launch files required (mainly calling the launch file in `rosbook_arm_bringup` but also all the previous packages). It also contains the world's descriptions in order to include objects to interact with.

- `rosbook_arm_hardware_gazebo`: This package uses the ROS Control plugin used to simulate the joints in Gazebo. This package uses the robot description to register the different joints and actuators, in order to be able to control their position. This package is completely independent of MoveIt!, but it is required for the integration with Gazebo.

- `rosbook_arm_moveit_config`: This package is generated through the MoveIt! setup assistant. This contains most of the launch files required for both MoveIt! and the RViz plugins as well as several configuration files for MoveIt!.
- `rosbook_arm_snippets`: Except for the pick and place example, this package contains all of the snippets used throughout the chapter.
- `rosbook_arm_pick_and_place`: This package is the biggest and most complex example in the book, containing a demonstration of how you can perform object picking and placing with MoveIt!.

Generating a MoveIt! package with the setup assistant

MoveIt! provides a user-friendly graphical interface for the purpose of integrating a new robotics arm into it. The setup assistant takes care of generating all of the configuration files and launch scripts based on the information provided by the user. In general, it is the easiest way to start using MoveIt! as it also generates several demonstration launch scripts, which can be used to run the system without a physical arm or simulation in place.

In order to launch the setup assistant, the following command needs to be executed in a terminal:

```
$ roslaunch moveit_setup_assistant setup_assistant.launch
```

Figure 4: Initial screen of MoveIt! setup assistant

Once the command has been executed, a window similar to the one shown in *Figure 4* should appear; in this particular case, the goal is to generate a new configuration, so that's the button we should aim for. Once the button has been pressed, the assistant will request a URDF or COLLADA model of the robotic arm, which, for our example arm, can be found in the following location inside the repository package:

```
rosbook_arm_description/robots/rosbook_arm_base.urdf.xacro
```

Please note that the robot description provided is in the **XML Macros** (**Xacro**) format, which makes it easier to generate complex URDF files. Once the robot description has been loaded, the reader needs to go through each tab, adding the required information. The first tab, as seen in *Figure 5*, is used to generate the self-collision matrix. Fortunately for the user, this process is performed automatically by simply setting the sampling density (or using the default value), and clicking on the **Regenerate Default Collision Matrix** button. The collision matrix contains information about how and when links collide in order to improve the performance of the motion planner. *Figure 5* shows this in detail:

Figure 5: Self-collision tab of MoveIt! Setup Assistant

The second tab, as seen in *Figure 6*, is used to assign virtual joints to the robot. A virtual joint is used to attach the robotic arm to the world as the pose of a robot can vary with respect to it, but in this particular case, we won't need a virtual joint because the base of the arm does not move. We need virtual joints when the manipulator is not fixed in one place. In that case, for example, if the arm is on top of a mobile platform, we need a virtual joint for the odometry since `base_link` (base frame) moves with respect to the `odom` frame.

Figure 6: Virtual joints tab of MoveIt! Setup Assistant

Chapter 10

In the third tab, which can be seen in *Figure 7*, we need to define the planning groups of the robotic arm. Planning groups, as the name suggests, are sets of joints that need to be planned together in order to achieve a given goal on a specific link or end effector. In this particular case, we need to define two planning groups: one for the arm itself and another for the gripper. The planning will then be performed separately for the arm positioning and the gripper action.

Figure 7: Planning Groups tab of MoveIt! Setup Assistant

Manipulation with MoveIt!

The fourth tab, as shown on *Figure 8*, gives us the ability to define known robot poses in order to be able to reference them later; these predefined poses are also referred to as group states. As we can see, we have set up two different poses: the home position, which corresponds to the "stored" position of the arm, and the grasping position, which, as the name suggests, should allow the robot to grasp elements in the scene. Setting known poses can have multiple benefits in a real-life situation; for example, it is common to have an initial position from which planning happens, a position where the arm is safe to be stored in a container, or even a set of known positions with which to compare the position accuracy over time.

Figure 8:Robot Poses tab of MoveIt! Setup Assistant

The fifth tab, used to define the robotic arm's end effector, can be seen in *Figure 9*. As we discussed earlier, the robotic arm usually has an end effector, which is used to perform an action, such as a gripper or some other tool. In our case, the end effector is a gripper, which allows us to pick objects from the scene. In this tab, we need to define the gripper's end effector by assigning it a name, a planning group, and the parent link containing the end effector.

Figure 9: End effectors tab of MoveIt! Setup Assistant

Manipulation with MoveIt!

The sixth tab, shown in *Figure 10*, is an optional configuration step, which allows us to define joints that cannot be actuated. An important feature of these joints is that MoveIt! doesn't need to plan for them and our modules don't need to publish information about them. An example of a passive joint in a robot could be a caster, but in this case, we'll skip this step as all of our passive joints have been defined as fixed joints, which will eventually produce the same effect on motion planning.

Figure 10: Passive Joints tab of MoveIt! Setup Assistant

Chapter 10

Finally, as seen in *Figure 11*, the last step in the setup assistant is generating the configuration files. The only thing required in this step is to provide the path of the configuration package, which will be created by MoveIt!, and which will contain most of the launch and configuration files required to properly start controlling our robotic arm from MoveIt!

Figure 11: Generate Configuration Files tab of MoveIt! Setup Assistant

It is important to take into account that the configuration generated by the setup assistant has already been provided in the repository and that even though it is recommended that you go through the process, the result can be discarded in favor of the provided package, which is already being referenced by the rest of the launch scripts and configuration files in the repository.

[381]

Integration into RViz

MoveIt! provides a very useful and complete RViz plugin that gives the user the ability to perform several actions, such as plan different goals, add and remove objects to the scene, and so on. The setup assistant usually creates a number of launch files, among which there is one called demo, which takes care of launching MoveIt! as well as the fake controllers, RViz and the plugin. In order to start the demonstration, run the following command:

```
$ roslaunch rosbook_arm_moveit_config demo.launch
```

Once RViz launches, a motion planning panel should appear as well as the visualization of the robotic arm. The important tabs we need to consider are the Planning tab and the Scene objects tab. In the Planning tab, the user will be able to plan different goal positions, execute them, and set some of the common planning options. In the latter, objects can be inserted and removed from the planning scene.

Figure 12 shows the planning tab as well as a visualization of the robotic arm in both white and orange. The former is the current state of the arm, and the latter is the goal position defined by the user. In this particular case, the goal position has been generated using the tools in the Query panel. Once the user is happy with the goal state, the next step can be to either plan to visualize how the arm is going to move or plan to execute it to not only visualize the movement but also move the arm itself.

Figure 12: Planning tab and goal position visualization in RViz plugin

Other options, such as the planning time or the number of planning attempts, can be tweaked in order to account for complex goals, but for most of the cases in the demonstration, changing these parameters won't be required. Another important parameter is the goal tolerance, which defines how close to the goal position we require the robotic arm to be, in order to consider the position as having been achieved.

Planning random goals might be of some interest, but another level of planning is provided by the RViz plugin. As illustrated in *Figure 13*, the robotic arm visualization has a marker on the end effector. This marker allows us to position the end effector of the arm as well as rotate it on each axis. You can now make use of this marker to position the arm towards more interesting configurations.

Figure 13: Using markers to set the goal position in RViz plugin

Manipulation with MoveIt!

Figure 14: Markers out of bounds in RViz plugin

In many cases, planning by positioning the marker might produce no movement at all and show the robotic arm in the same position, but the marker and the end effector might be in other positions. An example of this behavior can be seen in *Figure 14*, and it usually happens when the desired position is out of the range of motion of the robotic arm (when there are not enough degrees of freedom, too many constraints, and so on). Similarly, when the arm is positioned in a state in which it collides with elements in the scene or with itself, the arm will show the collision zone in red. Finally, *Figure 15* shows the different options provided by the MoveIt! plugin's visualization:

Figure 15: Motion planning plugin options in RViz plugin

As the names suggest, all of these options are meant to provide a way to tweak the visualization as well as add more information to it. Other interesting options that the user might want to modify are **Trajectory Topic**, which, as the name suggests, is the topic on which the visualization trajectory is published, and **Query Start State**, which will also show the state from which the arm is about to execute the plan. In most cases, the start state is usually the current state of the arm, but having a visualization cue can help spot issues in our algorithms.

Integration into Gazebo or a real robotic arm

The MoveIt! integration into Gazebo is a relatively straightforward process, which can be divided into two different steps: first of all, we need to provide all of the sensors required by MoveIt!, such as the RGBD sensor, so that motion planning can take the environment into account, and secondly, we also need to provide a controller as well as the current joint states periodically.

When a sensor is created in Gazebo, it interacts with the system as a normal sensor would by simply producing the required data. This data is then used by MoveIt! in exactly the same way that data produced by a real sensor would in order to generate collision artifacts in the planning scene. The process of making MoveIt! aware of those sensors will be explained later in this chapter.

As regards the manipulator's (arm and gripper) definition, a URDF description is provided using Xacro files as with any robot in ROS. In the case of using MoveIt!, we need to configure the controllers for the manipulator joints as `JointTrajectoryController` because the motion plans provide the output with messages for that type of controller. In the case of the manipulator used in this chapter, we need two controllers of this type: one for the arm and another for the gripper. The controller configuration is organized in the `rosbook_arm_controller_configuration` and `rosbook_arm_controller_configuration_gazebo` packages with the `launch` and `config` YAML files, respectively.

This type of controller is provided by the ROS control. Consequently, we need a `RobotHardware` interface for our arm to actually move in Gazebo or in the real hardware. The implementation is different for Gazebo and the real arm, and here we only provide the first. The `rosbook_arm_hardware_gazebo` package has the C++ implementation of `RobotHardware` for the manipulator used in this chapter. This is done by implementing the interface, so we create a new class that inherits from it. Then, the joints are properly handled, by writing the desired target positions (using position control) and reading the actual ones, along with the effort and velocity for each joint. For the sake of simplicity, we omit the explanation of the details of this implementation, which is not needed to understand MoveIt! However, if the number manipulator is drastically changed, the implementation must be changed although it is generic enough to detect the number of joints automatically from the robot description.

Simple motion planning

The RViz plugin provides a very interesting mechanism to interact with MoveIt! But it could be considered quite limited or even cumbersome due to the lack of automation. In order to fully make use of the capabilities included in MoveIt!, several APIs have been developed, which allow us to perform a range of operations over it, such as motion planning, accessing the model of our robot, and modifying the planning scene.

In the following section, we will cover a few examples on how to perform different sorts of simple motion planning. We will start by planning a single goal, continue with planning a random target, proceed with planning a predefined group state, and finally, explain how to improve the interaction of our snippets with RViz.

In order to simplify the explanations, a set of launch files have been provided to launch everything required. The most important one takes care of launching Gazebo, MoveIt!, and the arm controllers:

```
$ roslaunch rosbook_arm_gazebo rosbook_arm_empty_world.launch
```

Another interesting launch file has been provided by the setup assistant, which launches RViz and the motion planning plugin. This particular one is optional, but it is useful to have, as RViz will be used further in this section:

```
$ roslaunch rosbook_arm_moveit_config moveit_RViz.launch config:=true
```

A number of snippets have also been provided, which cover everything explained in this section. The snippets can be found in the `rosbook_arm_snippets` package. The snippets package doesn't contain anything other than code, and launching the snippets will be done by calling `rosrun` instead of the usual `roslaunch`.

Every snippet of code in this section follows the same pattern, starting with the typical ROS initialization, which won't be covered here. After the initialization, we need to define the planning group on which motion planning is going to be performed. In our case, we only have two planning groups, the arm and the gripper, but in this case, we only care about the arm. This will instantiate a planning group interface, which will take care of the interaction with MoveIt!:

```
moveit::planning_interface::MoveGroup plan_group("arm");
```

After the instantiation of the planning group interface, there is usually some code dedicated to deciding the goal to be planned, which will be specific to each of the types of goals covered in this section. After the goal has been decided, it needs to be conveyed to MoveIt! so that it gets executed. The following snippet of code takes care of creating a plan and using the planning group interface to request MoveIt! to perform motion planning and, if successful, to also execute it:

```
moveit::planning_interface::MoveGroup::Plan goal_plan;
if (plan_group.plan(goal_plan))
{
  ...
  plan_group.move();
}
```

Planning a single goal

To plan a single goal, we literally only need to provide MoveIt! with the goal itself. A goal is expressed by a `Pose` message from the `geometry_msgs` package. We need to specify both the orientation and the pose. For this particular example, this goal was obtained by performing manual planning and checking the state of the arm. In a real situation, goals will probably be set depending on the purpose of the robotic arm:

```
geometry_msgs::Pose goal;
goal.orientation.x = -0.000764819;
goal.orientation.y = 0.0366097;
goal.orientation.z = 0.00918912;
goal.orientation.w = 0.999287;
goal.position.x = 0.775884;
goal.position.y = 0.43172;
goal.position.z = 2.71809;
```

For this particular goal, we can also set the tolerance. We are aware that our PID is not incredibly accurate, which could lead to MoveIt! believing that the goal hasn't been achieved. Changing the goal tolerance makes the system achieve the waypoints with a higher margin of error in order to account for inaccuracies in the control:

```
plan_group.setGoalTolerance(0.2);
```

Finally, we just need to set the planning group target pose, which will then be planned and executed by the snippet of code shown at the beginning of this section:

```
plan_group.setPoseTarget(goal);
```

We can run this snippet of code with the following command; the arm should position itself without any issues:

```
$ rosrun rosbook_arm_snippets move_group_plan_single_target
```

Planning a random target

Planning a random target can be effectively performed in two steps: first of all, we need to create the random target itself and then check its validity. If the validity is confirmed, then we can proceed by requesting the goal as usual; otherwise, we will cancel (although we could retry until we find a valid random target). In order to verify the validity of the target, we need to perform a service call to a service provided by MoveIt! for this specific purpose. As usual, to perform a service call, we need a service client:

```
ros::ServiceClient validity_srv = nh.serviceClient<moveit_
msgs::GetStateValidity>("/check_state_validity");
```

Once the service client is set up, we need to create the random target. To do so, we need to create a robot state object containing the random positions, but to simplify the process, we can start by acquiring the current robot state object:

```
robot_state::RobotState current_state = *plan_group.getCurrentState();
```

We will then set the current robot state object to random positions, but to do so, we need to provide the joint model group for this robot state. The joint model group can be obtained using the already created robot state object as follows:

```
current_state.setToRandomPositions(current_state.
getJointModelGroup("arm"));
```

Up to this point, we have a service client waiting to be used as well as a random robot state object, which we want to validate. We will create a pair of messages: one for the request and another for the response. Fill in the request message with the random robot state using one of the API conversion functions, and request the service call:

```
moveit_msgs::GetStateValidity::Request validity_request;
moveit_msgs::GetStateValidity::Response validity_response;

robot_state::robotStateToRobotStateMsg(current_state, validity_
request.robot_state);
validity_request.group_name = "arm";

validity_srv.call(validity_request, validity_response);
```

Once the service call is complete, we can check the response message. If the state appears to be invalid, we would simply stop running the module; otherwise, we will continue. As explained earlier, at this point, we could retry until we get a valid random state; this can be an easy exercise for the reader:

```
if (!validity_response.valid)
{
  ROS_INFO("Random state is not valid");
  ros::shutdown();
  return 1;
}
```

Finally, we will set the robot state we just created as the goal using the planning group interface, which will then be planned and executed as usual by MoveIt!:

```
plan_group.setJointValueTarget(current_state);
```

We can run this snippet of code with the following command, which should lead to the arm repositioning itself on a random configuration:

```
$ rosrun rosbook_arm_snippets move_group_plan_random_target
```

Planning a predefined group state

As we commented during the configuration generation step, when initially integrating our robotic arm, MoveIt! provides the concept of predefined group states, which can later be used to position the robot with a predefined pose. Accessing predefined group states requires creating a robot state object as a target; in order to do so, the best approach is to start by obtaining the current state of the robotic arm from the planning group interface:

```
robot_state::RobotState current_state = *plan_group.getCurrentState();
```

Once we have obtained the current state, we can modify it by setting it to the predefined group state, with the following call, which takes the model group that needs to be modified and the name of the predefined group state:

```
current_state.setToDefaultValues(current_state.
getJointModelGroup("arm"), "home");
```

Finally, we will use the new robot state of the robotic arm as our new goal and let MoveIt! take care of planning and execution as usual:

```
plan_group.setJointValueTarget(current_state);
```

We can run this snippet of code with the following command, which should lead to the arm repositioning itself to achieve the predefined group state:

```
$ rosrun rosbook_arm_snippets move_group_plan_group_state
```

Displaying the target motion

MoveIt! provides a set of messages that can be used to communicate visualization information, essentially providing it with the planned path in order to get a nice visualization of how the arm is going to move to achieve its goal. As usual, communication is performed through a topic, which needs to be advertised:

```
ros::Publisher display_pub = nh.advertise<moveit_
msgs::DisplayTrajectory>("/move_group/display_planned_path", 1, true);
```

The message we need to publish requires the start state of the trajectory and the trajectory itself. In order to obtain such information, we always need to perform planning using the planning group interface first, and using the created plan, we can proceed to fill in the message:

```
moveit_msgs::DisplayTrajectory display_msg;
display_msg.trajectory_start = goal_plan.start_state_;
display_msg.trajectory.push_back(goal_plan.trajectory_);
display_pub.publish(display_msg);
```

Once the message has been filled in, publishing it to the correct topic will cause the RViz visualization to show the trajectory that the arm is about to perform. It is important to take into account that, when performing a call to plan, it will also show the same type of visualization, so you shouldn't be confused if the trajectory is displayed twice.

Motion planning with collisions

It might be interesting for the reader to know that MoveIt! provides motion planning with collisions out of the box, so in this section we will cover how you can add elements to the planning scene that could potentially collide with our robotic arm. First, we will start by explaining how to add basic objects to the planning scene, which is quite interesting as it allows us to perform planning even if a real object doesn't exist in our scene. For completion, we will also explain how to remove those objects from the scene. Finally, we will explain how to add an RGBD sensor feed, which will produce point clouds based on real-life (or simulated) objects, thus making our motion planning much more interesting and realistic.

Adding objects to the planning scene

To start adding an object, we need to have a planning scene; this is only possible when MoveIt! is running, so the first step is to start Gazebo, MoveIt!, the controllers, and RViz. Since the planning scene only exists in MoveIt!. RViz is required to be able to visualize objects contained in it. In order to launch all of the required modules, we need to run the following commands:

```
$ roslaunch rosbook_arm_gazebo rosbook_arm_empty_world.launch
$ roslaunch rosbook_arm_moveit_config moveit_RViz.launch config:=true
```

The snippet of code then starts by instantiating the planning scene interface object, which can be used to perform actions on the planning scene itself:

```
moveit::planning_interface::PlanningSceneInterface current_scene;
```

The next step is to create the collision object message that we want to send through the planning scene interface. The first thing we need to provide for the collision object is a name, which will uniquely identify this object and will allow us to perform actions on it, such as removing it from the scene once we're done with it:

```
moveit_msgs::CollisionObject box;

box.id = "rosbook_box";
```

The next step is to provide the properties of the object itself. This is done through a solid primitive message, which specifies the type of object we are creating, and depending on the type of object, it also specifies its properties. In our case, we are simply creating a box, which essentially has three dimensions:

```
shape_msgs::SolidPrimitive primitive;
primitive.type = primitive.BOX;
primitive.dimensions.resize(3);
primitive.dimensions[0] = 0.2;
primitive.dimensions[1] = 0.2;
primitive.dimensions[2] = 0.2;
```

To continue, we need to provide the pose of the box in the planning scene. Since we want to produce a possible collision scenario, we have placed the box close to our robotic arm. The pose itself is specified with a pose message from the standard geometry messages package:

```
geometry_msgs::Pose pose;
pose.orientation.w = 1.0;
pose.position.x =  0.7;
pose.position.y = -0.5;
pose.position.z =  1.0;
```

We then add the primitive and the pose to the message and specify that the operation we want to perform is to add it to the planning scene:

```
box.primitives.push_back(primitive);
box.primitive_poses.push_back(pose);
box.operation = box.ADD;
```

Finally, we add the collision object to a vector of collision object messages and call the `addCollisionObjects` method from the planning scene interface. This will take care of sending the required messages through the appropriate topics, in order to ensure that the object is created in the current planning scene:

```
std::vector<moveit_msgs::CollisionObject> collision_objects;
collision_objects.push_back(box);

current_scene.addCollisionObjects(collision_objects);
```

We can test this snippet by running the following command in a terminal, as said earlier. Since the object is added to the planning scene, it is important to have the RViz visualization running; otherwise, the reader won't be able to see the object:

```
$ rosrun rosbook_arm_snippets move_group_add_object
```

The result can be seen in *Figure 16* as a simple, green, squared box in the middle of the way between the arm's goal and the current position of the arm:

Figure 16: Scene collision object in RViz

Removing objects from the planning scene

Removing the added object from the planning scene is a very simple process. Following the same initialization as in the previous example, we only need to create a string vector containing the IDs of the objects we want to remove and call the `removeCollisionObjects` function from the planning scene interface:

```
std::vector<std::string> object_ids;
object_ids.push_back("rosbook_box");
current_scene.removeCollisionObjects(object_ids);
```

We can test this snippet by running the following command, which will remove the object created with the previous snippet from the planning scene:

```
$ rosrun rosbook_arm_snippets move_group_remove_object
```

Alternatively, we can also use the Scene objects tab in the RViz plugin to remove any objects from the scene.

Motion planning with point clouds

Motion planning with point clouds is much simpler than it would appear to be. The main thing to take into account is that we need to provide a point cloud feed as well as tell MoveIt! to take this into account when performing planning. The Gazebo simulation we have set up for this chapter already contains an RGBD sensor, which publishes a point cloud for us. To start with this example, let's launch the following commands:

```
$ roslaunch rosbook_arm_gazebo rosbook_arm_grasping_world.launch
$ roslaunch rosbook_arm_moveit_config moveit_RViz.launch config:=true
```

The user might have noticed that the Gazebo simulation now appears to include several objects in the world. Those objects are scanned by an RGBD sensor, and the resulting point cloud is published to the `/rgbd_camera/depth/points` topic. What we need to do in this case is tell MoveIt! where to get the information from and what the format of that information is. The first file we need to modify is the following one:

```
rosbook_arm_moveit_conifg/config/sensors_rgbd.yaml
```

This file will be used to store the information of the RGBD sensor. In this file, we need to tell MoveIt! which plugin it needs to use to manage the point cloud as well as some other parameters specific to the sensor plugin itself. In this particular case, the plugin to use is **Octomap Updater**, which will generate an octomap with the point cloud provided, downsample it, and publish the resulting cloud. With this first step, we have set up a plugin, which will provide enough information to MoveIt! to plan while taking into account possible collisions with the point cloud:

```
sensors:
 - sensor_plugin: occupancy_map_monitor/PointCloudOctomapUpdater
   point_cloud_topic: /rgbd_camera/depth/points
   max_range: 10
   padding_offset: 0.01
   padding_scale: 1.0
   point_subsample: 1
   filtered_cloud_topic: output_cloud
```

As you might have suspected, the file itself is nothing more than a configuration file. The next step we need to perform is to load this configuration file into the environment so that MoveIt! is aware of the new sensor we have added. In order to do so, we will need to modify the following XML file:

$ rosbook_arm_moveit_conifg/launch/rosbook_arm_moveit_sensor_manager.launch.xml

In this XML file, we can potentially specify a few parameters that will be used by the sensor plugin, such as the cloud resolution and the frame of reference. It is important to take into account that some of these parameters might be redundant and can be omitted. Finally, we need to add a command to load the configuration file into the environment:

```
<launch>
  <rosparam command="load" file="$(find rosbook_arm_moveit_config)/config/sensors_rgbd.yaml" />
</launch>
```

Manipulation with MoveIt!

The result of running the commands specified in the beginning with the new changes we have added can be seen on *Figure 17*. In this particular case, we can see both the Gazebo simulation and the RViz visualization. The RViz simulation contains a point cloud, and we have already performed some manual motion planning, which successfully took the point cloud into account to avoid any collisions:

Figure 17: Gazebo simulation (left), point cloud in RViz (right)

The pick and place task

In this section, we are going to explain how to perform a very common application or task with a manipulator robot. A pick and place task consists of picking up a target object, which includes grasping it, and placing it somewhere else. Here, we assume that the object is initially on top of a supporting surface, which is flat or planar, such as a table, but it is easy to generalize it to more complex environments. As regards the object to grasp, we will consider a cylinder that is approximated by a box because the gripper we are going to use to grasp is very simple; for more complex objects, you will need a better gripper or even a hand.

In the further sections, we will start by describing how to set up the planning scene, which MoveIt! needs in order to identify the objects that are there, apart from the arm itself. These objects are considered during motion planning to avoid obstacles, and they can also be targets for picking up or grasping. In order to simplify the problem, we will omit the perception part, but we will explain how it can be done and integrated. Once the planning scene is defined, we will describe how to perform the pick and place task using the MoveIt! API. Finally, we will explain how to run this task in the demonstration mode, using fake controllers so that we do not need the actual robot (either simulated on Gazebo or a real one). We will also show how you can actually see the motion on the simulated arm in Gazebo while it is interacting with the simulated objects in the environment.

The planning scene

The first thing we have to do is define the objects in the environment since MoveIt! needs this information to make the arm interact without colliding and to reference them to do certain actions. Here, we will consider the scene shown in Figure 18:

Figure 18: Environment with manipulator and objects in Gazebo

This scene has the arm with the gripper and the RGB-D sensor as the robotic manipulator. Then, there is also a table and a can of Coke, which are the flat support surface and the cylindrical object, respectively. You can run this scene in Gazebo with the following command:

```
$ roslaunch rosbook_arm_gazebo rosbook_arm_grasping_world.launch
```

This scene is just a simple example that models a real use case. However, we still have to tell MoveIt! about the planning scene. At this moment, it only knows about the robotic manipulator. We have to tell it about the table and the can of Coke. This can be done either by using 3D perception algorithms, which take the point cloud of the RGB-D sensor, or programmatically, by specifying the pose and shape of the objects with some basic primitives. We will see how we can define the planning scene following the latter approach.

The code to perform the pick and place task is the `pick_and_place.py` Python program located in the scripts folder of the `rosbook_arm_pick_and_place` package. The important part to create the planning scene is in the `__init__` method of the `CokeCanPickAndPlace` class:

```
self._scene = PlanningSceneInterface()
```

In the following sections, we will add the table and the can of Coke to this planning scene.

The target object to grasp

In this case, the target object to grasp is the can of Coke. It is a cylindrical object that we can approximate as a box, which is one of the basic primitives in the MoveIt! planning scene API:

```
# Retrieve params:
self._grasp_object_name = rospy.get_param('~grasp_object_name', 'coke_can')

# Clean the scene:
self._scene.remove_world_object(self._grasp_object_name)

# Add table and Coke can objects to the planning scene:
self._pose_coke_can = self._add_coke_can(self._grasp_object_name)
```

The objects in the planning scene receive a unique identifier, which is a string. In this case, `coke_can` is the identifier for the can of Coke. We remove it from the scene to avoid having duplicate objects, and then we add to the scene. The `_add_coke_can` method does that by defining the pose and shape dimensions:

```
def _add_coke_can(self, name):
    p = PoseStamped()
    p.header.frame_id = self._robot.get_planning_frame()
    p.header.stamp = rospy.Time.now()

    p.pose.position.x = 0.75 - 0.01
    p.pose.position.y = 0.25 - 0.01
    p.pose.position.z = 1.00 + (0.3 + 0.03) / 2.0

    q = quaternion_from_euler(0.0, 0.0, 0.0)
    p.pose.orientation = Quaternion(*q)

    self._scene.add_box(name, p, (0.15, 0.15, 0.3))

    return p.pose
```

The important part here is the `add_box` method that adds a `box` object to the planning scene we created earlier. The box is given a name, its pose, and dimensions, which, in this case, are set to match the ones in the Gazebo world shown earlier, with the table and the can of Coke. We also have to set `frame_id` to the planning frame one and the timestamp to `now`. In order to use the planning frame, we need `RobotCommander`, which is the MoveIt! interface to command the manipulator programmatically:

```
self._robot = RobotCommander()
```

The support surface

We proceed similarly to create the object for the table, which is also approximated by a box. Therefore, we simply remove any previous object and add the table. In this case, the object name is `table`:

```
# Retrieve params:
self._table_object_name = rospy.get_param('~table_object_name',
'table')

# Clean the scene:
self._scene.remove_world_object(self._table_object_name)

# Add table and Coke can objects to the planning scene:
self._pose_table    = self._add_table(self._table_object_name)
```

[399]

The _add_table method adds the table to the planning scene:

```
def _add_table(self, name):
    p = PoseStamped()
    p.header.frame_id = self._robot.get_planning_frame()
    p.header.stamp = rospy.Time.now()

    p.pose.position.x = 1.0
    p.pose.position.y = 0.0
    p.pose.position.z = 1.0

    q = quaternion_from_euler(0.0, 0.0, numpy.deg2rad(90.0))
    p.pose.orientation = Quaternion(*q)

    self._scene.add_box(name, p, (1.5, 0.8, 0.03))

    return p.pose
```

We can visualize the planning scene objects in RViz running the following commands:

```
$ roslaunch rosbook_arm_gazebo rosbook_arm_grasping_world.launch
$ roslaunch rosbook_arm_moveit_config moveit_RViz.launch config:=true
$ roslaunch rosbook_arm_pick_and_place grasp_generator_server.launch
$ rosrun rosbook_arm_pick_and_place pick_and_place.py
```

This actually runs the whole pick and place task, which we will continue to explain later. Right after starting the pick_and_place.py program, you will see the boxes that model the table and the can of Coke in green, matching perfectly with the point cloud seen by the RGB-D sensor, as shown in *Figure 19*:

Figure 19: Point cloud seen by the RGB-D sensor of the environment

Perception

Adding the objects manually to the planning scenes can be avoided by perceiving the supporting surface. In this case, the table can be detected as a horizontal plane on the point cloud. Once the table is recognized, it can be subtracted from the original point cloud to obtain the target object, which can be approximated with a cylinder or a box. We will use the same method to add boxes to the planning scene as before, but in this case, the pose and dimensions (and the classification) of the objects will come from the output of the 3D perception and segmentation algorithm used.

Manipulation with MoveIt!

This sort of perception and segmentation in the point cloud provided by the RGB-D sensor can be easily done using the concepts and algorithms. However, in some cases, the accuracy will not be enough to grasp the object properly. The perception can be helped using fiducial markers placed on the object to grasp, such as ArUco (http://www.uco.es/investiga/grupos/ava/node/26) which has the ROS wrapper which can be found at https://github.com/pal-robotics/aruco_ros.

Here, we set the planning scene manually and leave the perception part to you. As we saw, the target object to grasp and the support surface is defined on the code manually by comparing the correspondence with the point cloud in RViz until we have a good match.

Grasping

Now that we have the target object defined in the scene, we need to generate grasping poses to pick it up. To achieve this aim, we use the grasp generator server from the moveit_simple_grasps package, which can be found at https://github.com/davetcoleman/moveit_simple_grasps.

Although there is a Debian package available in Ubuntu for ROS hydro, it does not support any robot properly. For that reason, we need a patched version until the following pull request is accepted. The patched version can be downloaded from https://github.com/davetcoleman/moveit_simple_grasps/pull/16.

Therefore, we need to run the following commands to add the patched branch to our workspace (inside the src folder of the workspace):

```
$ wstool set moveit_simple_grasps --git git@github.com:efernandez/moveit_simple_grasps.git -v server_params
$ wstool up moveit_simple_grasps
```

We can build this using the following commands:

```
$ cd ..
$ caktin_make
```

Now we can run the grasp generator server as follows (remember to source devel/setup.bash):

```
$ roslaunch rosbook_arm_pick_and_place grasp_generator_server.launch
```

The grasp generator server needs the following grasp data configuration in our case:

```
    base_link: base_link

    gripper:
```

```
    end_effector_name: gripper

    # Default grasp params
    joints: [finger_1_joint, finger_2_joint]

    pregrasp_posture:              [0.0, 0.0]
    pregrasp_time_from_start:      &time_from_start 4.0

    grasp_posture:                 [1.0, 1.0]
    grasp_time_from_start:         *time_from_start

    postplace_time_from_start: *time_from_start

    # Desired pose from end effector to grasp [x, y, z] + [R, P, Y]
    grasp_pose_to_eef:             [0.0, 0.0, 0.0]
    grasp_pose_to_eef_rotation:    [0.0, 0.0, 0.0]

    end_effector_parent_link: tool_link
```

This defines the gripper we are going to use to grasp objects and the pre- and post-grasp postures, basically.

Now we need an action client to query for the grasp poses. This is done inside the pick_and_place.py program, right before we try to pick up the target object. So, we create an action client using the following code:

```
# Create grasp generator 'generate' action client:
self._grasps_ac = SimpleActionClient('/moveit_simple_grasps_server/
generate', GenerateGraspsAction)
if not self._grasps_ac.wait_for_server(rospy.Duration(5.0)):
    rospy.logerr('Grasp generator action client not available!')
    rospy.signal_shutdown('Grasp generator action client not
available!')
    return
```

Inside the _pickup method, we use the following code to obtain the grasp poses:

```
grasps = self._generate_grasps(self._pose_coke_can, width)
```

Here, the width argument specifies the width of the object to grasp. The _generate_grasps method does the following:

```
    def _generate_grasps(self, pose, width):
        # Create goal:
        goal = GenerateGraspsGoal()

        goal.pose  = pose
```

```
        goal.width = width

        # Send goal and wait for result:
        state = self._grasps_ac.send_goal_and_wait(goal)
        if state != GoalStatus.SUCCEEDED:
            rospy.logerr('Grasp goal failed!: %s' % self._grasps_
ac.get_goal_status_text())
            return None

        grasps = self._grasps_ac.get_result().grasps

        # Publish grasps (for debugging/visualization purposes):
        self._publish_grasps(grasps)

        return grasps
```

To summarize, it sends an `actionlib` goal to obtain a set of grasping poses for the target goal pose (usually at the object centroid). In the code provided with the book, there are some options commented upon, but they can be enabled to query only for particular types of grasps, such as some angles or pointing up or down. The output of the function are all the grasping poses that later the pickup action will try. Having multiple grasping poses increases the possibility of a successful grasp.

The grasp poses provided by the grasp generation server are also published as `PoseArray` using the _publish_grasps method for visualization and debugging purposes. We can see them on RViz running the whole pick and place task as before:

```
$ roslaunch rosbook_arm_gazebo rosbook_arm_grasping_world.launch
$ roslaunch rosbook_arm_moveit_config moveit_RViz.launch config:=true
$ roslaunch rosbook_arm_pick_and_place grasp_generator_server.launch
$ rosrun rosbook_arm_pick_and_place pick_and_place.py
```

A few seconds after running the `pick_and_place.py` program, we will see multiple arrows on the target object, which correspond with the grasp pose that will be tried in order to pick it up. This is shown in *Figure 20* as follows:

Figure 20: Visualization of grasping poses

The pickup action

Once we have the grasping poses, we can use the MoveIt! `/pickup` action server to send a goal passing all of them. As before, we will create an action client:

```
# Create move group 'pickup' action client:
self._pickup_ac = SimpleActionClient('/pickup', PickupAction)
if not self._pickup_ac.wait_for_server(rospy.Duration(5.0)):
    rospy.logerr('Pick up action client not available!')
    rospy.signal_shutdown('Pick up action client not available!')
    return
```

Manipulation with MoveIt!

Then, we will try to pick up the can of Coke as many times as needed until we finally do it:

```
# Pick Coke can object:
while not self._pickup(self._arm_group, self._grasp_object_name,
self._grasp_object_width):
    rospy.logwarn('Pick up failed! Retrying ...')
    rospy.sleep(1.0)
```

Inside the _pickup method, we create a pickup goal for MoveIt!, right after generating the grasps poses, as explained earlier:

```
# Create and send Pickup goal:
goal = self._create_pickup_goal(group, target, grasps)

state = self._pickup_ac.send_goal_and_wait(goal)
if state != GoalStatus.SUCCEEDED:
    rospy.logerr('Pick up goal failed!: %s' % self._pickup_ac.get_goal_status_text())
    return None

result = self._pickup_ac.get_result()

# Check for error:
err = result.error_code.val
if err != MoveItErrorCodes.SUCCESS:
    rospy.logwarn('Group %s cannot pick up target %s!: %s' % (group,
target, str(moveit_error_dict[err])))

    return False

return True
```

The goal is sent and the state is used to check whether the robot manipulator picks up the object or not. The pickup goal is created in the _create_pickup_goal method as follows:

```
def _create_pickup_goal(self, group, target, grasps):
  # Create goal:
  goal = PickupGoal()

  goal.group_name = group
```

```
    goal.target_name = target

    goal.possible_grasps.extend(grasps)

    # Configure goal planning options:
    goal.allowed_planning_time = 5.0

    goal.planning_options.planning_scene_diff.is_diff = True
    goal.planning_options.planning_scene_diff.robot_state.is_diff = True
    goal.planning_options.plan_only = False
    goal.planning_options.replan = True
    goal.planning_options.replan_attempts = 10

    return goal
```

The goal needs the planning group (`arm` in this case) and the target name (`coke_can` in this case). Then, all the possible grasps are set, and several planning options, including the planning time allowed, can be increased if needed.

When the target object is successfully picked up, we will see the box corresponding to it attached to the gripper's grasping frame with a purple color, as shown in *Figure 21* (note that it might appear like a ghost gripper misplaced, but that is only a visualization artifact):

Figure 21: Arm picking up an object

The place action

Right after the object has been picked up, the manipulator will proceed with the place action. MoveIt! provides the /place action server, so the first step consists of creating an action client to send a place goal in the desired location, in order to place the object picked up:

```
# Create move group 'place' action client:
self._place_ac = SimpleActionClient('/place', PlaceAction)
if not self._place_ac.wait_for_server(rospy.Duration(5.0)):
    rospy.logerr('Place action client not available!')
    rospy.signal_shutdown('Place action client not available!')
    return
```

Then, we will try to place the object until we finally manage to do it:

```
# Place Coke can object on another place on the support surface
(table):
while not self._place(self._arm_group, self._grasp_object_name, self._pose_place):
    rospy.logwarn('Place failed! Retrying ...')
    rospy.sleep(1.0)
```

The _place method uses the following code:

```
def _place(self, group, target, place):
    # Obtain possible places:
    places = self._generate_places(place)

    # Create and send Place goal:
    goal = self._create_place_goal(group, target, places)

    state = self._place_ac.send_goal_and_wait(goal)
    if state != GoalStatus.SUCCEEDED:
        rospy.logerr('Place goal failed!: ' % self._place_ac.get_goal_status_text())
        return None

    result = self._place_ac.get_result()

    # Check for error:
    err = result.error_code.val
    if err != MoveItErrorCodes.SUCCESS:
```

```
            rospy.logwarn('Group %s cannot place target %s!: %s' % (group,
    target, str(moveit_error_dict[err])))

            return False

        return True
```

The method generates multiple possible places to leave the object, create the place goal, and send it. Then, it checks the result to verify whether the object has been placed or not. To place an object, we can use a single place pose, but it is generally better to provide several options. In this case, we have the `_generate_places` method, which generates places with different angles at the position given. When the places are generated, they are also published as `PoseArray`, so we can see them as shown in *Figure 22* with blue arrows:

Figure 22: Visualization of place poses

Manipulation with MoveIt!

Once the places are obtained, the `_create_place_goal` method creates a place goal as follows:

```
def _create_place_goal(self, group, target, places):
    # Create goal:
    goal = PlaceGoal()

    goal.group_name          = group
    goal.attached_object_name = target

    goal.place_locations.extend(places)

    # Configure goal planning options:
    goal.allowed_planning_time = 5.0

    goal.planning_options.planning_scene_diff.is_diff = True
    goal.planning_options.planning_scene_diff.robot_state.is_diff = True
    goal.planning_options.plan_only = False
    goal.planning_options.replan = True
    goal.planning_options.replan_attempts = 10

    return goal
```

In brief, the place goal has the group (`arm` in this case) and the target object (`coke_can` in this case), which are attached to the gripper and the place or places (poses). Additionally, several planning options are provided, along with the allowed planning time, which can be increased if needed. When the object is placed, we will see the box representing it in green again and on top of the table, and the arm will be up again, as shown in *Figure 23*:

Figure 23: Arm after placing an object

The demo mode

We can do the whole pick and place task without perception in demo mode, that is, without actually actuating on the Gazebo simulation, or the real, robotic arm. In this mode, we will use fake controllers to move the arm once the motion plan has been found by MoveIt! to do the pick and place actions, including grasping the object. The same code can be used directly on the actual controllers.

In order to run pick and place in the demo mode, run the following commands.

```
$ roslaunch rosbook_arm_moveit_config demo.launch
$ roslaunch rosbook_arm_pick_and_place grasp_generator_server.launch
$ rosrun rosbook_arm_pick_and_place pick_and_place.py
```

Manipulation with MoveIt!

The special part is the first launch file, which simply opens RViz and loads fake controllers instead of spawning the robotic manipulator on Gazebo. *Figure 24* shows several snapshots of the arm moving and doing the pick and place after running the preceding commands:

Figure 24: Arm doing pick and place task in the demo mode

Simulation in Gazebo

Using the same code as in demo mode, we can actually move the real controllers, either in simulation (Gazebo) or using the real hardware. The interface is the same, so using a real arm or gazebo is completely equivalent. In these cases, the joints will actually move and the grasping will actually make the gripper come in contact with the grasping object (the can of Coke). This requires a proper definition of the objects and the gripper in Gazebo to work properly.

The commands to run the pick and place in this case (as shown previously) are:

```
$ roslaunch rosbook_arm_gazebo rosbook_arm_grasping_world.launch
$ roslaunch rosbook_arm_moveit_config moveit_RViz.launch config:=true
$ roslaunch rosbook_arm_pick_and_place grasp_generator_server.launch
$ rosrun rosbook_arm_pick_and_place pick_and_place.py
```

It is only the first part to launch files that changes with respect to the demo mode; it replaces `demo.launch` in the demo mode. In this case, we spawn the robotic manipulator in Gazebo with the environment containing the table and the can of Coke as well as the RGB-D camera. Then, the `moveit_RViz.launch` file opens RViz with the MoveIt! plugin, providing the same interface as with `demo.launch`. However, in this case, when the `pick_and_place.py` program is run, the arm in Gazebo is moved.

Summary

In this chapter, we have covered most of the aspects involved in integrating a robotic arm with MoveIt! and Gazebo, which gives us a realistic view of how a robotic arm could be used in a real-life environment. MoveIt! provides us with very simple and concise tools for motion planning on robotic arms using an **Inverse Kinematics (IK)** solver as well as ample documentation in order to facilitate this process, but given the complexity of the architecture, it can only be done properly once all of the different interactions between MoveIt!, the sensors, and the actuators in our robot have been properly understood.

We have glanced through the different high-level elements in the MoveIt! API, which would require an entire book of their own to be covered in detail. In an attempt to avoid the cost of understanding a full API to perform very simple actions, the approach taken in this book has been to limit ourselves to very simple motion planning and interacting with both artificially created objects in the planning scene and RGB-D sensors that generate a point cloud.

Finally, a very detailed explanation has been provided for how to perform an object pick and place task. Although not being the sole purpose of a robotic arm, this is one that you might enjoy experimenting with as it is very common in industrial robots, but using MoveIt! motion planning and 3D perception allows you to do so in complex and dynamic environments. For this particular purpose of the robotic arm, a deeper look at the APIs and enhanced understanding of the MoveIt! architecture was required, giving you much more depth and understanding as to the possibilities of MoveIt!

Index

Symbols

2D nav goal 347
2D pose estimate 345, 346
3D visualization
  about 113
  data visualizing, with rqt_rviz 114-117
  frames 117
  frame transformations, visualizing 118, 119
  topics 117
10 degrees of freedom (DoF)
  about 167
  ADXL345 168
  BMP085 168
  HMC5883L 168
  L3G4200D 168
  library, downloading for accelerometer 169
  programming 169-171
  ROS node, creating 172-174

A

actionlib package 362
actuators
  about 2
  adding, Arduino used 153, 154
Adaptive Monte Carlo Localization
  defining 357-359
  URL 357
Allowed Collision Matrix (ACM) 372
Analog Digital Converter (ADC) 193
Arduino
  example program 154-156
  ultrasound range sensor, using 157-160
  URL 154
  used, for adding actuators 153
  used, for adding sensors 153
Arduino Nano
  programming 169-171
  URL 167
ar_pose wrapper
  URL 214
ARToolkit
  URL 214
ArUco
  URL 402
Augmented Reality (AR) 214

B

back data
  bag file 120
  playing 120
  recording, in bag file with rosbag 121
  saving 120
bag file
  about 120
  data recording, with rosbag 121
  messages, inspecting 123-125
  playing back 122, 123
  topics, inspecting 123-125
bags 34, 38
base controller
  creating 324-330
Bayer pattern 182
BeagleBone Black (BBB)
  about 8
  rosinstall, obtaining for 21
broadcaster
  creating 306

[415]

BSD (Berkeley Software Distribution)
  license 3
Bug Ticket System 41
Build space 26

C

callback function 251
camera
  calibrating 197-200
  connecting 182
  FireWire IEEE1394 cameras 182-187
  input images, visualizing 197
  running 182
  stereo calibration 202-206
  USB cameras 187-189
collision checking 372
conditional messages 90
core dumps
  enabling 86
costmaps
  base local planner configuration 342
  common parameters, configuring 340
  configuring 339
  global_costmap, defining 339-341
  local_costmap, defining 339-341
cv_bridge library
  OpenCV image, using with 195
  ROS image, using with 195

D

debug message level
  configuring, of ROS nodes 88, 89
  modifying, with rqt_console 92-95
  modifying, with rqt_logger_level 92-95
  setting 87, 88
Development (devel) space 26
diffdrive_plugin.cpp file
  URL 326
distance sensors
  example 161-163
  messages, sending 160
downsampling 249-254
dynamic parameters
  about 71
  setting 103-105

Dynamic Reconfigure utility
  about 71
  using 71-76
Dynamixel
  about 149, 150
  commands, receiving 150
  commands, sending 150

E

error handling 105

F

filtered messages 90
filtering 249-254
Flexible Collision Library (FCL)
  package 372
FOURCC format
  URL 193
fovis
  installing 225
  URL 225
  used, with Kinect RGBD camera 225-227
frames
  and topics, relationship between 117
  frame transformations, visualizing 118, 119
Frames Per Second (FPS) 189

G

gamepad
  using 130, 131
Gazebo
  about 288, 289
  MoveIt!, integrating 386
  pick and place task, simulation 412, 413
  URL 288
  used, for creating
    odometry 316-318, 326, 327
gazebo_plugins package
  URL 317
GDB debugger
  ROS nodes, attaching 85
  used, for debugging ROS nodes 83
general purpose input/output
  (GPIO) pins 15

global costmap 352
global plan 353
Global Positioning System (GPS)
　example project 177, 178
　messages, sending 176
　using 174-176
goals
　sending 362-365

H

HC-SR04 157
Hokuyo URG-04lx
　about 136-138
　URL 137
holonomic vehicle 343
homography, of two images
　computing 228

I

images
　publishing, with image transport 195
　visualizing 111-112
inertial measurement unit (IMU)
　about 163
　using 163, 164
　Xsens MTi 163, 164

J

joystick
　joy_node, using 131, 132
　joystick data, used for
　　creating movements 132-135
　using 130, 131

K

Kinect RGBD camera
　fovis, using with 225-227
Kinect sensor
　about 143
　data, sending from sensors 144, 145
　example 146-148
　using 143
kinematics 372

L

Laser Imaging, Detection, and Ranging
　(LIDAR) 337
laser rangefinder
　data, sending 138, 139
　Hokuyo URG-04lx 136-138
　laser data, accessing 140, 141
　laser data, modifying 140, 141
　launch file, creating 142
　using 136, 137
launch file
　about 68, 69
　creating, for navigation stack 343-345
　launching 70, 71
libfovis library
　about 215
　URL 215
libviso2 library
　about 215
　URL 215
listener
　creating 307-309
local costmap 351
local plan 354
logging message
　about 86
　conditional messages 90
　debug message level, configuring 88, 89
　debug message level, setting 87, 88
　displaying 91
　filtered messages 90
　naming 90
　outputting 86, 87
　rqt_console, using 92-95
　rqt_logger_level, using 92-95
Long-Term Support (LTS) 4
low-cost IMU
　10 degrees of freedom (DoF) 167
　about 167
　using 167

M

map
　creating, with ROS 330, 331
　loading, map_server used 333
　saving, map_server used 332

master 33
message level
  DEBUG 88
  ERROR 88
  FATAL 88
  INFO 88
  WARN 88
messages 31-33, 38
message types, PCL
  pcl_msgs::ModelCoefficients 235
  pcl_msgs::PointIndices 235
  pcl_msgs::PolygonMesh 235
  pcl_msgs::Vertices 235
  sensor_msgs::PointCloud2 235
  std_msgs::Header 234
metapackage
  about 24, 29, 30
  creating 43, 44
metapackage manifests 24
MicroStrain 3DM-GX2 IMU
  URL 164
motion planning
  about 370, 387
  constraints 370
  goal, planning 388
  objects, adding to planning scene 392, 393
  objects, removing from planning scene 394
  predefined group state, planning 390
  random target, planning 389, 390
  target motion, displaying 391
  with collisions 391
  with point clouds 394, 395
motion planning adapters
  AddTimeParameterization 371
  FixStartStateBounds 370
  FixStartStateCollision 370
  FixStartStatePathConstraints 371
  FixWorkspaceBounds 370
MoveIt!
  about 367
  architecture 368, 369
  collision checking 372
  integrating, into Gazebo 386
  integrating, with RViz 382-385
  kinematics 372
  motion planning 370, 371
  package generating, with setup assistant 374-381
  planning scene 371, 372
  robotic arm, integrating 372, 373
  URL 367
msg files
  creating 61-68

N

National Maritime Electronics Association (NMEA)
  about 174
  URL 174
navigation stack
  in ROS 304, 305
  launch file, creating for 343-345
nodelets 35, 36
nodes
  about 33-35
  building 59-61
  creating 56-59

O

Object Recognition Kitchen (ORK)
  about 215
  URL 215
obstacles
  avoiding 360, 361
Occupancy Grid Map (OGM) 116, 331
Octomap Updater 395
odometry
  creating 319-323
  creating, Gazebo used 316-318, 326, 327
  information, publishing 314, 315
OMPL
  URL 370
OpenCV
  URL 182
  USB camera driver, writing with 189-194
  using, in ROS 196
OpenCV image
  using, with cv_bridge 195

[418]

P

package
  about 24, 27
  creating 336
  structure 27
package manifests 24
parameters
  listing 96-99
  modifying, with rqt_reconfigure 359, 360
parameters, cameras
  brightness 193
  camera_index 192
  camera_info_url 193
  contrast 193
  exposure 193
  fourcc 193
  fps 192
  frame_height 192
  frame_id 193
  frame_width 192
  gain 193
  hue 193
  saturation 193
Parameter Server
  about 33, 39, 55
  using 56
parameters, rosparam tool
  rosparam delete parameter 40, 55
  rosparam dump file 40, 55
  rosparam get parameter 40, 55
  rosparam list 40, 55
  rosparam load file 40, 55
  rosparam set parameter value 40, 55
particle cloud 349
PCL programs
  defining 236, 237
pick and place task
  about 396
  demo mode 411
  grasping 402-404
  perception 401
  pickup action 405-407
  place action 408-410
  planning scene 397, 398
  simulation, in Gazebo 412, 413
  support surface 399, 400
  target object 398, 399
planner plan 355
planning scene
  about 371, 372
  objects, adding 392, 393
  objects, removing 394
Point Cloud Library (PCL)
  about 231
  algorithms 234
  defining 232
  PCL interface, for ROS 234, 235
  point cloud types 233
  reference link 147
point clouds
  creating 237-240
  loading, to disk 241-244
  motion planning 394, 395
  partitioning 259-263
  saving, to disk 241-244
  visualizing 245-248
points, PCL
  pcl::Normal 233
  pcl::PointNormal 233
  pcl::PointXYZ 233
  pcl::PointXYZI 233
  pcl::PointXYZRGB 233
  pcl::PointXYZRGBA 233
portable gray map format (.pgm format) 332
PR2 (Willow Garage) 271
Printed Circuit Board (PCB) 157
public fields, point cloud
  header 232
  height 232
  is_dense 232
  points 232
  sensor_orientation_ 232
  sensor_origin_ 232
  width 232

R

RAndom SAmple Consensus (RANSAC) 264
Real Time Kinematics (RTK)
  URL 175

REEM robot
　about 81
　URL 81
registration and matching
　　　technique 255-259
Remote Procedure Call (RPC) 39
repositories 40
RGBD camera
　visual odometry, performing with 224
RoboEarth project
　URL 215
Robonaut (NASA) 271
robot configuration
　creating 336-339
robotic arm
　integrating, in MoveIt! 372, 373
Robot Operating System (ROS)
　3D model, of robot 271
　about 1, 181
　defining 231
　history 2, 3
　map, creating with 330, 331
　OpenCV, using 196
　origin 2
　tools 27
　URL, for blog 41
rosbag
　used, for recording data in bag file 121
rosbash package
　roscd command 28
　roscp command 28
　rosd command 28
　rosed command 28
　rosls command 28
ROS Community level
　about 40
　blog 41
　Bug Ticket System 41
　distributions 40
　mailing lists 41
　repositories 40
　ROS Answers 41
　ROS Wiki 40
ROS Computation Graph level
　about 33
　bags 34, 38
　master 33, 39
　messages 33, 38
　nodelets 35, 36
　nodes 33-36
　Parameter Server 39
　services 34, 37
　topics 34-37
ROS distributions 40
ROS Filesystem
　about 24
　messages 25, 31, 32
　metapackage manifests 24
　metapackages 24, 29, 30
　navigating by 41
　package manifests 24
　packages 24, 27
　services 25, 32
　workspace 25-27
ROS Hydro, installing in BeagleBone Black
　　　(BBB)
　about 15
　environment, setting 20
　keys, setting up 19
　local machine, setting up 18
　prerequisites 16-18
　rosdep, initializing for ROS 20
　ROS packages, installing 19
ROS Hydro, installing with repositories
　about 4, 5
　environment, setting up 9
　keys, setting up 7
　rosdep, initializing 8
　ROS, installing 7, 8
　rosinstall, obtaining 10
　source.list file, setting up 6, 7
　Ubuntu repositories, configuring 5, 6
　URL 4
ROS image pipeline
　about 207-210
　used, for stereo cameras 210-213
ROS master 39
rosmsg command-line tool
　rosmsg list parameter 38
　rosmsg md5 parameter 38
　rosmsg package parameter 38
　rosmsg packages parameter 38
　rosmsg show parameter 38
　rosmsg users parameter 38

ROS nodes
    attaching, to GDB debugger 85
    core dumps, enabling 86
    creating, for 10 DOF sensor 172-174
    debugging 83
    debugging, GDB debugger used 83
    debug message level, configuring 88, 89
    diagnostics, visualizing 106, 107
    execution, inspecting 96
    graph, inspecting online
        with rqt_graph 100-102
    listing 96-99
    profiling, with valgrind 85
    working with 45-48
rosnode tool
    rosnode cleanup command 35
    rosnode info NODE command 35
    rosnode kill NODE command 35
    rosnode list command 35
    rosnode machine hostname command 35
    rosnode ping NODE command 35
ROS package
    Augmented Reality 214
    building 44, 45
    creating 43, 44
    perception and object recognition 215
    used, for Computer Vision tasks 214, 215
    visual odometry 215
    Visual Servoing 214
rosparam tool
    parameters 40, 55
rosservice tool
    rosservice args /service parameter 38, 52
    rosservice call /service parameter 38, 52
    rosservice find msg-type parameter 38, 52
    rosservice info /service parameter 38, 52
    rosservice list parameter 38, 52
    rosservice type /service parameter 38, 52
    rosservice uri /service parameter 38, 52
rostopic tool
    rostopic bw /topic parameter 37
    rostopic echo /topic parameter 37
    rostopic find message_type parameter 37
    rostopic hz /topic parameter 37
    rostopic info /topic parameter 37
    rostopic list parameter 37

rostopic pub /topic type args parameter 37
rostopic type /topic parameter 37
ROS wrapper
    URL 402
rqt_console
    used, for modifying debug
        message level 92-95
rqt_graph
    used, for inspecting graph of
        ROS nodes 100-102
rqt_gui plugin
    using 126
rqt_logger_level
    used, for modifying debug
        message level 92-95
rqt_plot
    time series plot, creating 108-111
rqt plugin
    using 126
rqt_reconfigure
    parameters, modifying with 359, 360
rqt_rviz
    used, for visualizing data in
        3D world 114-117
RViz
    MoveIt!, integrating 382-385
rviz, for navigation stack
    2D nav goal 347
    2D pose estimate 345, 346
    current goal 356, 357
    footprint, of robot 350
    global costmap 352
    global plan 353
    local costmap 351
    local plan 354
    particle cloud 349
    planner plan 355
    setting up 345
    static map 348

S

scalar data
    plotting 108
    time series plot, creating
        with rqt_plot 108-111

segmentation
  defining 264-268
sensors
  about 2
  adding, Arduino used 153
  information, publishing 310
  laser node, creating 312-314
  reference link 129
Serial Clock (SCK) 169
Serial Data Line (SDL) 169
services
  about 32-37, 52
  listing 96-99
  using 53-55
servomotors
  Dynamixel 149, 150
  example 151, 152
  using 149, 150
simulations, in ROS
  creating 288
  map, loading in Gazebo 296-298
  map, using in Gazebo 296-298
  robot, moving in Gazebo 298-300
  sensors, adding to Gazebo 293-295
  URDF 3D model, using in Gazebo 289-292
Singular Value Decomposition (SVD) 257
SketchUp 286
skid-steer robot 298
SLAM (Simultaneous Localization And Mapping) 304
Source space 26
srv files
  creating 61-68
Stacks 24
Stanford Artificial Intelligence Laboratory (SAIL) 2
static map 348

T

TCPROS 36
time series plot
  creating, with rqt_plot 108-111
tools, ROS
  catkin_create_pkg 27
  catkin_make 27
  rosdep 28
  rospack 27
  rqt_dep 28
topics
  about 34-37
  and frames, relationship between 117
  interacting with 48-51
  listing 96-99
transformation tree
  observing 310
Transform Frame (tf) tree 82, 305
transforms
  broadcaster, creating 306
  creating 305
  listener, creating 307-309
  transformation tree, observing 310
Turtlesim 27

U

Ubuntu
  installing 11
  repositories, URL 5
  URL 11
UDPROS 36
ultrasound range sensor
  used, with Arduino 157-160
Unified Robot Description Format (URDF) 271
Universal Transverse Mercator (UTM) 176
URDF file
  3D model, viewing on rviz 275, 276
  collision properties 279, 280
  creating 271, 272
  file format, explaining 274, 275
  meshes, loading to models 277, 278
  model, converting to robot 278, 279
  physical properties 279
USB camera driver
  writing, with OpenCV 189-194

V

valgrind
  URL 85
  used, for profiling ROS nodes 85

VirtualBox
  about 11
  downloading 11
  installing 11
  URL, for downloading 11
virtual machine
  creating 12-14
viso2
  URL 220
visual odometry
  about 215
  camera pose calibration 216-220
  performing, with RGBD camera 224
  references 215
  URL 215
  used, with viso2 216
  viso2 online demo, running 220, 221
  viso2, running with low-cost
      stereo camera 223
Visual Servoing Platform (ViSP)
  about 214
  URL 214

W

Wiimote
  URL 164
workspace
  about 25
  Build space 26
  creating 42
  Development (devel) space 26
  Source space 26

X

XML Macros (Xacro)
  about 375
  3D modeling, with SketchUp 286-288
  about 280, 281
  constants, using 281
  macros, using 281, 282
  math, using 281
  robot, moving with code 282-286
XMLRPC 39
Xsens MTi
  about 163
  data, sending 164, 165
  example 165-167

Thank you for buying
Learning ROS for Robotics Programming
Second Edition

About Packt Publishing

Packt, pronounced 'packed', published its first book, *Mastering phpMyAdmin for Effective MySQL Management*, in April 2004, and subsequently continued to specialize in publishing highly focused books on specific technologies and solutions.

Our books and publications share the experiences of your fellow IT professionals in adapting and customizing today's systems, applications, and frameworks. Our solution-based books give you the knowledge and power to customize the software and technologies you're using to get the job done. Packt books are more specific and less general than the IT books you have seen in the past. Our unique business model allows us to bring you more focused information, giving you more of what you need to know, and less of what you don't.

Packt is a modern yet unique publishing company that focuses on producing quality, cutting-edge books for communities of developers, administrators, and newbies alike. For more information, please visit our website at `www.packtpub.com`.

About Packt Open Source

In 2010, Packt launched two new brands, Packt Open Source and Packt Enterprise, in order to continue its focus on specialization. This book is part of the Packt Open Source brand, home to books published on software built around open source licenses, and offering information to anybody from advanced developers to budding web designers. The Open Source brand also runs Packt's Open Source Royalty Scheme, by which Packt gives a royalty to each open source project about whose software a book is sold.

Writing for Packt

We welcome all inquiries from people who are interested in authoring. Book proposals should be sent to `author@packtpub.com`. If your book idea is still at an early stage and you would like to discuss it first before writing a formal book proposal, then please contact us; one of our commissioning editors will get in touch with you.

We're not just looking for published authors; if you have strong technical skills but no writing experience, our experienced editors can help you develop a writing career, or simply get some additional reward for your expertise.

Mastering BeagleBone Robotics

ISBN: 978-1-78398-890-7　　　　Paperback: 234 pages

Master the power of the BeagleBone Black to maximize your robot-building skills and create awesome projects

1. Create complex robots to explore land, sea, and the skies.
2. Control your robots through a wireless interface, or make them autonomous and self-directed.
3. This is a step-by-step guide to advancing your robotics skills through the power of the BeagleBone.

Arduino Robotic Projects

ISBN: 978-1-78398-982-9　　　　Paperback: 240 pages

Build awesome and complex robots with the power of Arduino

1. Develop a series of exciting robots that can sail, go under water, and fly.
2. Simple, easy-to-understand instructions to program Arduino.
3. Effectively control the movements of all types of motors using Arduino.
4. Use sensors, GPS, and a magnetic compass to give your robot direction and make it lifelike.

Please check **www.PacktPub.com** for information on our titles

Robot Framework Test Automation

ISBN: 978-1-78328-303-3 Paperback: 98 pages

Create test suites and automated acceptance tests from scratch

1. Create a Robot Framework test file and a test suite.
2. Identify and differentiate between different test case writing styles.
3. Full of easy- to- follow steps, to get you started with Robot Framework.

Raspberry Pi Robotic Projects

ISBN: 978-1-84969-432-2 Paperback: 278 pages

Create amazing robotic projects on a shoestring budget

1. Make your projects talk and understand speech with Raspberry Pi.
2. Use standard webcam to make your projects see and enhance vision capabilities.
3. Full of simple, easy-to-understand instructions to bring your Raspberry Pi online for developing robotics projects.

Please check **www.PacktPub.com** for information on our titles

Printed in Great Britain
by Amazon.co.uk, Ltd.,
Marston Gate.